D1564692

Black Power Ideologies

Black Power Ideologies

An Essay in African-American Political Thought

JOHN T. McCARTNEY

Temple University Press

Philadelphia

Temple University Press, Philadelphia 19122
Copyright © 1992 by Temple University. All rights reserved
Published 1992
Printed in the United States of America

⊛ The paper used in this publication meets the minimum
requirements of American National Standard for Information
Sciences—Permanence of Paper for Printed Library Materials,
ANSI Z39.48–1984

Library of Congress Cataloging-in-Publication Data

McCartney, John T., 1938–
      Black power ideologies : an essay in African-American political
   thought / John T McCartney.
         p.   cm.
      Includes bibliographical references and index.
      ISBN 0-87722-914-7
      1. Afro-Americans—Politics and government.   2. Black power—
   United States—History.   3. Political science—United States—
   History.   I. Title.
   E185.615.M334   1992
   323.1′196073—dc20   91-21747
                              031208

ISBN 13: 978-1-56639-145-0 (paper : alk. paper)

041414-P

Contents

Contents

Preface

The decade of the 1960s was a period of great unrest in America. During that time the country experienced not only a very costly war in Vietnam but also a series of domestic disturbances (termed "riots" by some and "rebellions" by others), especially in the urban centers and universities. Because many of these events involved African-Americans, and because they came at a time when the call for Black Power was receiving national attention, many black and white Americans erroneously identified the concept of Black Power with violence and lawlessness. As a result, the deeper significance of this movement was missed.

For students of political theory who witnessed these happenings, however, the disorderly atmosphere did not obscure the deeper significance; they knew that societal turmoil and debate frequently represent the birth of new ideas and views about politics and society. An individual living in Europe at the time of the investiture controversy of the eleventh century must also have assessed the times as chaotic, as government and church officials were locked in a vicious and seemingly endless controversy over what constituted "right order" in the world. In the struggle, the populace witnessed not only military confrontations but also the excommunication of kings, the dismissal of popes, the interdiction of kingdoms, and the presentation of bulls and decretals of condemnation by papal legates traveling all over the Christian world. But out of this seeming chaos came theories about the relationship between church and state, the limits of monarchy, and the meaning of social justice. The contest may also have presaged modern-age political propaganda and the development of ideological political thought. As Gerd Tellenbach expresses it; "The Investiture Contest was the first medieval crisis to call forth a considerable propaganda literature, in which the aims of the two parties were reflected. It provided a running commentary on practical politics, and in it the theoretical principles are often formulated more clearly than they are in the actions of the great men of the time."[1]

Similarly, during the English Civil War of the Seventeenth century, Oliver Cromwell and the English Parliament struggled with the monarchy for hegemony in the state, and groups like the "Levelers" and "Diggers" advanced ideas about "universal suffrage and government actually in the hands of the people."[2] In fact, through their pamphleteer, Gerrard Winstanley, the Diggers proposed "a plan for a communist government of England."[3] The social and political turmoil of the seventeenth century also provided the background for the political theory of Hobbes and Locke, the great founders of modern (individualistic) liberalism. And out of the convulsions of the French Revolution developed Jacobin revolutionary thought, the first stirrings of working-class political consciousness, as seen in the agitation and polemics of François (Gracchus) Babeuf, and the beginnings of modern nationalism. Indeed, the political theorist Mulford Sibley argues that the French Revolution "became the great inspiration for other modern attempts to change social structures fundamentally, as with the Western European upheaval of 1848, the Russian social earthquakes of 1905 and 1917, and the Spanish affairs of the 1930's."[4] Finally, many of the early statements of socialism came out of the lesser conflicts associated with Chartism in England and the European uprisings of 1848. Times of social and political turmoil often bring forth creative political theories, and the unrest of the sixties was no different. Many who witnessed advocates of Black Power (and their opponents) as they traveled across the United States debating questions about the nature of power, the meaning of political legitimacy, the definition of popular control, and the role of race in politics were reminded of similar events in the history of political thought.

Although creative political ideas were being propounded by the advocates of Black Power, there was little or no effort to develop the ideas systematically and to put them into a historical context. This is unfortunate for at least three reasons. First, the history of ideas enables us to understand the meaning of terms and how they relate to the "way of life of a given region and time."[5] It also demonstrates how the terms change and suggests which terms or propositions "might have universal applicability."[6] Second, the history of ideas is essential to any sort of understanding and criticism, for it shows how ideas relate to each other. It shows how the experiences of a person's life may account for peculiarities in thought, "just as his thought will assist in explaining his actions."[7] Finally, it makes explicit the questions that a people or race have been perennially concerned with, and it helps us identify possible consequences of proposed lines of action. This book is an effort to examine systematically the ideologies of Black Power and to place them in their proper historical context.[8]

I originally felt that the task would involve developing a general conception of Black Power from the serious versions of the ideology and demonstrating how the movement was a natural response to the various economic, social, and political challenges that blacks have faced in the United States (see Chapters VII to X). However, as the study progressed, it became clear that the Black Power Movement of the 1960s had direct links to a past tradition of Black Nationalism that had many of the same goals and used strikingly similar tactics. It was also apparent that the Black Nationalist antecedents of the Black Power Movement faced opposition similar to the movement's constant competition with black groups that accepted the dominant American creed in its entirety. Thus, to fully understand the Black Power Movement, it is necessary to examine the history of black political thought and to show that the Black Power–versus–Black Mainstream competition of the time was not at all unique in the history of African-Americans in the United States (see Chapters II to VI).[9]

Chapter I describes the many disparities between black and white lives and analyzes a number of theories that have attempted to explain those disparities. In all the chapters, including the historical ones, the various forms of black protest, including the Black Power protests, are treated as attempts to rectify the disparities, often by using strategies and rationalizations based on one or more of the theories. Chapter XI consists of a short critique of Black Power and speculation on the movement's permanent contributions to life in the United States.

There is to date no definitive history of black political thought, so a few comments about the method used here are necessary. While the chapters that deal with the Black Power Movement itself exhaust all available primary sources, the chapters on historical antecedents do not. The literature on black protest before the rise of Black Power is so vast that it was necessary to select from those movements and personages that best reflect the type of protest in question to illustrate the ramifications of the manifestation as a whole. As a result, the reader will find extensive treatment of Frederick Douglass, Booker T. Washington, Marcus Garvey, Martin Luther King, Jr., and the Colonization Movement in the historical chapters. By focusing on one major personage as a spokesperson for an ideology or movement, the discussion takes on more life, and comparison becomes clearer. Therefore, the biographical method is used in the chapters on Black Power as well.

One of the concerns of the African-American scholar when writing an essay of this type is the evolution of terms. Historians Mary Frances Berry and John W. Blasingame point out that African-Americans, because they were separated from their original culture, have always "viewed their generic name as intimately related to their self-esteem and their place in American society."[10] They note that until 1899 the designation *African* and its variants *Afro-American*, *African-American*, and *Africo-American* were the designations most used in describing the American black.[11] However, starting in the 1830s about one-third of black magazines and newspapers used the word *colored* to refer to blacks; this number held until 1950. Although the use of *African* and *Afro-American* declined between 1900 and 1950, 28 percent of black publications continued to use these terms.[12] Between 1872 and 1879 only 17 percent of the publications used the word *Negro*, but its acceptance by blacks became increasingly widespread after the Civil War. Blacks capitalized the word *Negro* to distinguish it from white southern usage, since white southerners capitalized the names of all but the black race. Between 1870 and 1930 *Negro* continued to gain in popularity, especially among black intellectuals and in the black press, and by 1933 the United States Government Printing Office was using the word. Blasingame and Berry conclude that by 1950 *Negro* was the most popular designation.[13]

During the activism of the 1960s, however, the terms *black* and *Afro-American* regained popularity, and "between 1960 and 1973 'black' appeared in 82 percent of the autobiographical works containing a racial designation in the title."[14] In the 1990s *African-American* has been used increasingly.[15] The terms *African-American*, *black*, and *Negro* are used throughout this book as the context dictates.

Acknowledgments

A book that has been in preparation for such a long time is both a social product and an individual one and owes much to many. First I would like to thank both my undergraduate and graduate political theory professors who, themselves fired up by a love for the matters of theory, instilled the same love in me. These fine teachers are diamonds that one does not find enough of in higher education today. The list includes Francis Wilhoit, my undergraduate theory professor at Drake University (Des Moines, Iowa); the late Donald Sutherland of the University of Iowa; and Lane Davis, my brilliant graduate advisor at the University of Iowa. Later on, while a lecturer at Purdue University, I was encouraged to pursue my interest in black political thought by Harry Targ, Michael Stohl, and Myron Hale of the Department of Political Science; my insightful and thoughtful friend Kermit Scott of the Department of Philosophy; and Harold Woodman of the Department of History.

The manuscript would not have been completed without the expert help of Jane Cullen, acquisitions editor at Temple University Press, who not only encouraged me to write but selected an excellent and helpful team of reviewers for the manuscript. Thanks are also due to Charles Ault, managing editor at Temple University Press, and to Joan Vidal for her expert supervision of the manuscript through the various stages of its development. Carole Brown helped improve the manuscript by thoroughly critiquing it for style.

On my return to academia after six years in Bahamian politics, I was urged to complete the manuscript by my colleagues at Lafayette College. These include Ilan Peleg, Charles Dana Professor of Social Science and Chairman of the Department of Government and Law; Larry Beer, Kirby Professor of Civil Rights; and James Lennertz. The manuscript was tirelessly typed and critiqued by Ruth Panovec, our most efficient departmental secretary. She was assisted at various stages by Rose Miller. Thanks are also due to my students, especially my pleasant and conscientious assistant, Christine Mangum, who did so much library work for me. Students Jacqueline Simmonds and Jean-Evangeline Harris also helped to proofread the manuscript.

Finally, I would like to thank both my family, who have always encouraged me to pursue the leading questions at whatever the price, and the African-American people, whose courageous struggle has inspired others to greater heights. Although many have assisted, I take full responsibility for all judgments and any flaws contained in this book.

Black Power Ideologies

I

The Background to Black Power

Imbalances and Injustices Against African-Americans

The Black Power Movement of the 1960s in the United States was seen by most of its advocates as the latest in a series of efforts to correct the injustices that existed in almost every dimension of life between black and white Americans. To understand the Black Power Movement fully and to appreciate its suggestions for solving these injustices, it is necessary to give a brief overview of the injustices and describe the attempts to correct them previous to the Black Power Movement itself.

Swedish sociologist Gunnar Myrdal in his 1940s work *An American Dilemma* carried out a comprehensive study of African-American life in the United States that examined in detail the status of African-Americans in this country up to that time. Among the more revealing of Myrdal's findings were those regarding the African-American's place in the American economic system. Myrdal begins by stating that during the slave years and the period right after the Civil War, African-American artisans monopolized nonagricultural labor in the South, and although "white artisans often vociferously protested against the use of Negroes for skilled work in the crafts," the protests were not very successful.[1] This was true particularly during the slave period because politically powerful whites had an economic interest in sustaining the pool of cheap, skilled African-American labor. However, after the Civil War African-American artisans had few protectors because their ex-masters had become impoverished by the war and their replacements were whites who not only lacked a tradition of "caring for the Negro" but, having risen from the white artisan class

1

themselves, shared its general anti-skilled African-American worker prejudices.[2] Myrdal cites the African-American historian Charles B. Rousseve's findings, which state that as a result of these racist attitudes toward the skilled African-American in the southern urban centers like New Orleans the African-American who before the war "performed all types of labor, skilled and unskilled, found himself gradually eliminated from the various trades."[3] Thus, while the Civil War and Reconstruction may have brought political and legal equality to African-Americans (at least in theory), their economic condition in the industrial sector declined.

In the post-Civil War North, the situation for African-Americans was not much better. In both the skilled and unskilled labor sectors that they had come to dominate, the moves toward their exclusion had started even earlier there than in the South. Myrdal notes that in the North as early as three decades before the Civil War, whites and African-Americans had engaged in race riots stemming from the fierce competition for jobs, a competition that escalated with every new wave of European immigration to the United States. Indeed, Frederick Douglass, the great African-American freedom fighter, was well aware of this competition and the decline of the African-American presence in the labor force. Myrdal writes that he complained of whites becoming house servants, cooks, barbers, and the like, which was not the case before the 1830s. Douglass believed that the trend would continue "until the last [economic] prop is leveled beneath us [African-Americans]."[4] Summarizing the African-American economic condition from the Civil War to 1940, Myrdal concludes, however, that although African-Americans were totally excluded from their traditional places in southern industry, in the North (despite the widespread absence of African-Americans from the manufacturing industries) they were making significant gains, especially in some occupations that were "new or where few if any Negroes were allowed to work before."[5] (By the latter, Myrdal is probably referring to the automobile and aircraft industries.)

The injustices that Myrdal outlines were not restricted to employment, for matters of health revealed comparable disparities. He states that "a study made before the Civil War shows that the incidence of tuberculosis was considerably higher for whites than Negroes."[6] However, after emancipation, the African-American overall rate was higher than that of whites, and though it had decreased somewhat by the 1940s, at the time of Myrdal's writing the difference was still immense. (It should be recalled that tuberculosis was a major cause of death in the 1940s.)

The persistence of the injustices that Myrdal wrote about is evidenced by the disparities between African-American and white lives in the 1960s. Examining the 1968 Report of the National Advisory Commission on Civil Disorders, a commission set up to find the causes for the many urban riots of the middle and late 1960s, the continuing imbalances in almost every dimension of life are clear. (The commission is commonly referred to as the "Kerner Commission" because it was headed by Governor Otto Kerner of Illinois.) Economically, the commission found that African-American incomes were not only less than white incomes but growing at a slower pace, despite the fact that "the Negro upper income group is expanding rapidly and achieving sizeable income gains."[7] The report specifically detailed how the "Negro median family income was only 58% of the white median income in 1966";[8] how the gap between African-American and white median incomes (calculated in 1965 dollars) had increased from $2,174 in 1947 to $3,036 in 1966;[9] how "about two-thirds of the lowest income group—or 20% of all Negroes—are making no significant gains—despite general prosperity";[10] and how 16 percent to 20 percent of all African-Americans were "living in disadvantaged neighborhoods of central cities in the United States."[11]

Regarding crime, the commission stated that African-Americans who live in disadvantaged areas are far more likely to be victims of crimes than whites or African-Americans who live in higher-income areas. In fact, the report noted that for African-Americans in general, "the probability of suffering any index crime except larceny is 78 times higher than for whites."[12] Furthermore, it concluded that the nonwhite woman's chance of being raped was 37 times higher than that of her white counterpart, while "the probability of being robbed is 3.5 times higher—for non-whites in general."[13] Other areas of African-American versus white lives reveal comparable discrepancies. For example, "maternal mortality rates for non-white mothers are four times as high as those for white mothers";[14] infant mortality rates for non-white babies "are 58% higher than among whites for those under one month old, and almost 3 times as high among those from one month to one year";[15] and regarding life expectancy, it "was 6.9 years longer for whites (71.0 years) than for non-whites (64.1 years) in 1965."[16] Finally, the report condemned the American public school system for its failure to provide African-Americans with the high level of verbal and quantitative skills necessary to compete successfully in America. To illustrate, the report cited figures from the Selective Service Mental Test in 1965—a test designed to determine basic skills proficiency—which revealed that 67 percent of the African-American candidates failed the exam as compared to a white failure rate of 19 percent.[17] From these figures, the continuance of the historic imbalances between African-American and white lives into the 1960s is obvious, and the commission concluded that the major cause of the dilemma was white racism.

In commemoration of the twentieth anniversary of the Kerner Commission Report of 1968, a nongovernmental committee called the Commission on the Cities was set up in 1988 to review the status of African-Americans since that time. The commission was headed by ex-senator Fred Harris of Oklahoma, a member of the original Kerner Commission, and Roger Wilkins of the Institute for Policy Studies. The commission found that in the past two decades African-Americans and other minorities have made important legal and political gains but that their economic condition has declined in many instances. They point out that today the chances of a deprived minority urban dweller escaping the cycle of poverty "after some improvement between the late 1960's and mid-1970's—are now well below the levels of twenty years ago."[18] Also, they found that nonwhite poverty has grown between 1969 and 1985 "increasing from 12.7% to 19%" over the sixteen year period.[19] For the same period general unemployment doubled, but the African-American unemployment rate, which in 1968 was 6.7 percent as compared to 3.2 percent for whites, was in 1986 still double the white unemployment rate.[20] Finally, the African-American median income, which was 60 percent of the white median income in 1968, dropped to 57.1 percent of the white median income in 1986.[21] Ominously, the Commission on the Cities noted that the physical separation of the races that the Kerner Commission deplored is more marked today than it was in the 1960s. This is also true of "the level of impoverishment, joblessness, educational inequality, and housing."[22] In short, many of the inequalities that spawned the violent manifestations of the 1960s still exist.[23]

These facts indicate that the injustices against African-Americans in American life are serious, extensive, and long standing. Some of the suggestions and theories advanced to explain the persistence of these imbalances will be described in the next section.

While admitting that the African-American's condition looks stark when compared to that of whites, it would be fallacious to conclude that it is hopeless or has not improved over the years. For example, Benjamin Wattenberg and Richard Scammon demonstrated in a 1960s study that while at the time African-Americans were still not as well off as whites, this should not obscure the fact that during the late

1950s and 1960s African-Americans made some spectacular gains, especially economically. As a result of these gains, the authors insisted that the majority of African-Americans, like the majority of whites, are members of the American middle class and that the constant cries of African-American deprivation were simply appeals used by "white liberals and black leaders, for purposes of political strategy."[24] African-American economists like Herrington Bryce refuted the extent of the gains as listed in the Wattenberg-Scammon study, but even Bryce admits that African-Americans made significant gains during that period. One of the more controversial studies on the question of African-American economic progress in the United States has been carried out by the sociologist William Julius Wilson in his book *The Declining Significance of Race: Blacks and Changing American Institutions.*[25] Wilson argues that racial barriers have declined to such a degree in the United States that the racial inequities that do exist have more to do with economic and class factors than racial factors.[26] Wilson's argument serves as a reminder that when listing the black side of the African-American's condition, one should not ignore the progress that has been made.

Theories About Why Inequality Persists

No attempt will be made here to survey explanations of how the imbalances between whites and African-Americans came about. An effort will be made, however, to summarize some well-known suggestions and theories for why this condition has so long endured in the United States, especially given that its continued existence violates the principles on which the country was founded.

Perhaps the most long standing of the theories is a sociological and institutional one. This type of thinking is best exemplified in a study of slavery by the historian Stanley Elkins. Elkins begins by arguing that the reformers and thinkers concerned with the abolition of slavery in the United States had a bias against building the kind of institutions and promulgating the types of laws that would gradually close the gap between whites and African-Americans. In Elkins's view, they saw the issue solely in moral terms, and the solution to it had to be "untouched by society's organic compromises, uncorrupted even by society itself."[27] In effect, they developed an all-or-nothing approach that succeeded in polarizing opinion rather than providing an environment in which evolutionary but qualitative change could take place. What were the elements in American society that worked against the creation of an evolutionary environment for eradicating slavery? According to Elkins, unlike England and other European countries that had established religious and governmental institutions, centuries-old legal systems, and immemorial customs that tended to mediate and control opinion, the United States ever since the Revolution was a nation that lacked such an "establishment." The lack of an establishment helped produce a generation of Americans around abolition years who had little notion of the concept of power—"its meaning, its responsibilities, its uses,"[28] and because of this a reformist solution to the slavery question became impossible.

Elkins goes on to suggest that an ethic of unopposed capitalism further conspired to perpetuate the imbalances between white and African-Americans. America at the time of slavery was as it is today, a capitalist society in which profit is used as the prime measure of economic progress. Unlike Europe, however, where capitalism operated within traditions that moderated its effects, the United States had few such buffers. Elkins points to the Catholic tradition in the Iberian peninsula that recognized the slave as a moral being and legal personality and to the common-law tradition in England that later was to provide some protection for slaves in the British colonies as examples of buffers between the slave and the worst abuses of profit making. In the United States, starting with "the emergent capitalism of colonial Virginia,"[29] a system of large-scale staple production based on slave labor developed "that had no traditional institutions, with competing claims of their own [that could] interpose at any of a dozen points with sufficient power to retard or modify its progress."[30] Elkins goes on to ask, "What happens when such energy meets no limits?"[31] What happened was that the African-American became just another commodity in the process of production and as a result was dehumanized to a degree unparalleled in any other system of Western exploitation except the Nazi concentration camps. Elkins sums it all up by saying, "The only mass experience that Western people had within recorded history comparable in any way with slavery was undergone in the nether world of Nazism. The concentration camp was not only a perverted slave system; it was also—what is less obvious but even more to the point—a perverted patriarchy."[32]

There are those who disagree with but who do not conclusively disprove Elkins's thesis. The historian Philip D. Curtin argues that statistics show that slaves in the United States multiplied more rapidly than any other slaves transported to the New World from Africa. Because of this Curtin concludes that it is questionable whether U.S.

slavery was qualitatively more severe than slavery elsewhere in the hemisphere.[33] Similarly, the famous anthropologist Melville Herskovits, arguing from a cultural, and not a statistical perspective, also concludes that because of the large extent and degree of "Africanisms," remnants of the African tradition still important and observable in African-American life, the slave experience could not have been as culturally destructive as studies of the Elkins variety make it out to be.[34] Suffice it to say, whatever the scope and however the severity of slavery in the United States, Elkins and those who accept his point of view argue that because of the experience of slavery and the various legacies stemming from it, the African-American has been at a distinct and continuing disadvantage in American society when compared to his white counterpart.[35]

Another explanation for the continuing imbalances, in some ways closely allied to the sociological one, is historical and political. The theory originated with the Radical Republican Thaddeus Stevens and is restated today in one of the works of the political and social historian Barrington Moore, Jr. In his book *Social Origins of Dictatorship and Democracy* Moore argues that the American Civil War was the last attempt of progressive capitalism to create an America in which a democracy based on free enterprise could replace a reactionary agrarian society based on slavery. At the time of their greatest power, the progressive forces consisted of a combination of workers, industrialists, and railroad interests, and Stevens, the leader of the Radical Republicans, was their spokesman in the post-Civil War Congress. Stevens felt that the outright destruction and total restructuring of the South was the only way to achieve a truly capitalistic and democratic nation, and he insisted that unless this was done, "all our blood and treasure have been spent in vain."[36] In terms of a practical program, Stevens and the Radical Republicans suggested that plantations over two hundred acres should be confiscated and each African-American given forty acres and a mule so that the race could have an economic base from which to compete.[37]

The problem of African-American versus white, according to the early and present-day proponents of this theory, stems from the fact that African-Americans have had no real economic and political base from which to compete in this pluralist society, and unless and until they achieve this power, the imbalances between white and African-American lives will continue. Underlying the entire theory is the assumption that when the African-American obtains such power there will be a simultaneous rise in democracy and decline of racism.

Black Panther co-founder and leader Huey P. Newton expresses some views on the African-American's inferior power position in America that are strongly reminiscent of the views of Thaddeus Stevens and the Radical Republicans. In his essay "Functional Definition of Politics," Newton argues that black people are not free because they have no political or economic power, and that "Black Reconstruction failed because Black People did not have political and military power."[38] Newton goes on to state that without an economic base in America, a race or interest group has no power to effectively influence political outcomes, which is why "when black people send a representative [to government], he is somewhat absurd, because he represents no political power."[39] He compares the hapless African-American political representatives to their white counterparts who, when unable to achieve a meaningful "political consequence," pressure the rest of society, carrying out actions like those of farmers who allow "their crops to rot in the field,"[40] or by other comparable acts of noncooperation with "other sectors of the economy."[41] Newton sees a socialist revolution (Marxist style) as the only way to eradicate racism and its legacies in America, a solution that places him far to the left of democratic capitalists like Thaddeus Stevens and his successors. Their diagnosis of the cause of the problem however, is strikingly similar.

A third explanation of why the imbalances and racial tensions continue to exist turns to psychology, and this type of thinking is well represented in the work of the social psychologist Harry Hoetnik. Hoetnik, in his classic *The Two Variants in Caribbean Race Relations*, argues that when a child is growing up, he or she forms images or impressions of things to which they are similar or dissimilar, compatible or incompatible. Hoetnik calls these perceptions the "psychosomatic norm image." This process is particularly important during adolescence, after which the individual's "character type" is for the most part set. The images formed during this process are determined to a great degree by the norms and properties of the group to which the child belongs. Thus, if a group (or race) is considered inferior within the norms and properties of the child's "native group," the child's psychosomatic norm image reflects this. Using studies done in the United States and Great Britain, Hoetnik illustrates how in terms of compatibility, preferences in marriage, preferences for naturalization, and many similar categories, whites in these countries prefer blacks less than any other race.[42] Such a situation becomes more complicated by the fact that most African-Americans accept the same standards and images as whites, eventuating in a situation where consciously and unconsciously African-Americans tend to downgrade themselves. As African-American poet Larry Neal puts it, "Thus we are constantly forced to see ourselves through white eyes. We are made to evaluate our impulses against his."[43] The African-American psychologists William H. Grier and Price M. Cobbs, in their revealing little book entitled, *Black Rage*, describe in a more systematic fashion than does Neal some of the devastating results that the aspiration to emulate white cultural norms has on the African-American's psyche.[44] The proponents of this view state that until African-Americans develop a psychological confidence in themselves the imbalances will remain.

A fourth way of explaining why the imbalances continue to exist is a racial-determinist one, and it has both African-American and white adherents. The Nation of Islam (Black Muslims) and the Ku Klux Klan exemplify the extremes of the theory, so their respective diagnoses regarding the nature of the African-American versus white dilemma will help highlight the dynamics of the position.

According to Black Muslim theology, the biblical Adam and his wife were the first parents of all people and also the world's first sinners. Because of his sins Adam was driven from the Gardens of Paradise, which were in the Holy Land in the Middle East, and sent into the hills and caves of Europe, where he was fated to live a life of hard and relentless toil. After Adam was expelled from the Garden of Eden (Paradise), God placed at the east end of the garden cherubims (Muslim guards) and a flaming sword, which turned in all directions to keep Adam and his offspring of European devils out of the way of the "Tree of Life," or the Nation of Islam.[45] The theology goes on to say that God sent prophets to try to save the Adamic (white) race even after they were driven from the Garden of Eden, but they displayed their perfidy by persecuting and killing these prophets. (In their leader Elijah Muhammad's words, "The Adamic White race's history is proof that they are the enemies of God and the righteous, for they never did sincerely accept a prophet of God.")[46] The Adamic race is destined to tempt God's true followers—black people—for six thousand years, after which the whites will be destroyed by Allah. In the meantime, the Black Muslims (headed in the 1960s by the Honorable Elijah Muhammad, now headed by Louis Farrakhan) preach that the eventual African-American separation from white society is the only way to eliminate racial friction. Consistent with the latter belief, the Black Muslims advocate that several southern states be turned over to

African-Americans by white society, although they also insist that African-Americans be law-abiding American citizens until that day ar-
rives. Black Muslim theology is examined in more depth in a later
chapter.

The Ku Klux Klan's position is highlighted very vividly in a letter
from its archleader and Imperial Wizard J. B. Stoner to a Black Muslim convention in Chicago in February of 1957. Stoner begins by de-
claring that whites are superior to African-Americans. As evidence he
cites what to him is a fact, that the black race has never built or maintained a civilization of its own. Stoner's anti-integrationist prejudices
are clear. He believes that the inferiority of African-Americans will
only be highlighted by their efforts to integrate into predominantly
white American society, and he soundly condemns such integration.
Stoner declaims in this regard, "You Africans are afraid to do it alone.
You are afraid that you would get lost without the white man to guide
you and help you."[47] Instead of trying to become a part of white society, Stoner suggests that African-Americans migrate to black Africa or
the British West Indies and aid in building civilizations in these areas.
However, Stoner asserts contemptuously that African-Americans will
stay in the United States "because they have no confidence in themselves."[48] If African-Americans remain in the United States, Stoner implies that permanent segregation should be inaugurated and maintained, for the white founders of the United States "never intended for
America to fall into the possession of a dark race."[49] As Stoner sees it,
"Many of the founders of the nation owned blacks, such as Washington, Jefferson and the great Patrick Henry who said 'Give me liberty or
give me death.' "[50]

The views of Stoner and Muhammad are perhaps typical of the
arguments used by racial determinists who see an integrated America
as an impossible dream. However, racial-determinist theories are not
restricted to people with the obvious prejudices of Stoner and
Muhammad. In the 1920s, for example, a great deal of writing that
claimed to be scientific attempted to rate the world's various racial
groups according to their intelligence. Blacks generally rested at the
bottom of the list.[51] Along the same lines, many see the views of intellectuals such as those of the psychologist Arthur Jensen, who implies
in an article in the Harvard Educational Review in 1969 that blacks
may be inferior to whites in some crucial areas of intelligence, as
stemming from the tradition of the 1920s.[52]

The racial-determinist debate continues into the 1990s. Charles
Murray, who worked on deregulation of Federal Programs in the Rea-

gan administration and whose book *Losing Ground*, which argues that social welfare programs do more harm than good, greatly influenced the Reagan administration's urban policies, has embarked on another project. Along with the controversial psychologist Richard Herrnstein he is now trying to discover "whether there are differences in intelligence between blacks and whites that help explain differences in their economic and social standing."[53] And controversy erupted at the City College of New York when philosophy professor Michael Levin stated that "black representation in a field can be expected, absent any discrimination, to decrease as the intellectual demands of the field increase."[54] These white racial determinists are answered by black racial determinists like Professor Leonard Jeffries, Jr., chairman of City College of New York's Department of Black Studies. Jeffries argues that "the skin pigment melanin is the secret ingredient that makes blacks physically and mentally superior to whites."[55]

A fifth and final theory of why the imbalances persist is ideological and is advanced by sociologists Louis L. Knowles and Kenneth Prewitt. In the opinion of these authors, since their arrival in North America some form of white supremacist ideology motivated the English immigrants.[56] Knowles and Prewitt suggest that this ideology went through a number of different phases and still exists to some extent today.

In its first phase, as seen in the statements of the early colonists, was the belief that one of the colonists' major missions was to Christianize and civilize the heathen. Because the Indians lacked knowledge of the white man's god they were considered inferior to the white. The authors suggest that the enslavement of African-Americans in the United States "and its accompanying justifications would seem to have been products of the same [racial-supremacist] mentality."[57] Defining *institutional racism* as a system in which the institutions and rules of society are based on the values of a dominant racial group and the society's goods and services are distributed according to those values, the authors conclude that continuing discrimination against African-Americans has been one of the "most powerful expressions of institutional racism in the society"[58] and the most devastating legacy of the supremacist ethos.

A nineteenth-century offshoot of this white-supremacist ideology, also used to justify discrimination and oppression, was the social Darwinist theory. The premise behind social Darwinism is that just as in the evolutionary process of nature "the stronger" species triumph over "the inferior" species, in relations between classes, nations, and races the stronger races dominate the weaker.[59] Social Darwinism provided nineteenth-century racial supremacists with "a full-blown ideology to explain the treatment of the inferior race"[60] and is yet another example of the deadly fusion of pseudoscience and racism.

Social Darwinism was reinforced by two more-widely accepted supremacist beliefs in the nineteenth-century, Manifest Destiny and the White Man's Burden. Manifest Destiny was the idea that white Americans were destined not only to control and civilize the North American continent, but, "in many versions of the theory, a much greater share of the earth's surface."[61] (In fact, "many churchmen supported the idea that such expansion was the will of God.")[62] The belief in Manifest Destiny was used not only to justify imperialism against Cuba, Hawaii, and the Philippines, but was also used as a rationale for domestic racism. Social theorist Ronald Segal, whom the authors cite approvingly on the subject of Manifest Destiny, describes the domestic implications of the ideology: "What was sauce [Manifest Destiny] for the Philippines, for Hawaii and Cuba, was sauce [Manifest Destiny] for the Southern Negro. If the stronger and cleverer race is free to impose its will upon 'new-caught sullen peoples' on the other side of the globe, why not in South Carolina and Mississippi? asked *The Atlantic Monthly*."[63] To Segal, this nineteenth-century *Atlantic Monthly* editorial sums up succinctly the rationale for applying the Manifest Destiny ideology to domestic affairs.

Manifest Destiny was thus like social Darwinism, another version of white-supremacist ideology.

Closely related to Manifest Destiny was the belief in the White Man's Burden. Initially used in a poem by Rudyard Kipling, by 1899 it was a popular ideology in the United States. The White Man's Burden most often meant that "the White race, particularly Anglo-Saxons of Britain and America, should accept the (Christian) responsibility for helping the poor colored masses to find a better way of life,"[64] a "responsibility" that served as a rationale for slavery and the later subjugation of the African continent. Knowles and Prewitt insist that the coupling of the Manifest Destiny and White Man's Burden rationalizations has contributed much "to stimulate the modern day myth that colored peoples are generally incapable of self-government"[65] and still fuels racism and its legacies in the United States.

In summary, most advocates of Black Power, whatever their differences, generally agree on two things. First, African-Americans have the right to determine their own destinies. Second, African-Americans have a cultural tradition that is worthy of respect in its own right.

Knowles and Prewitt not only acknowledge the validity of these views, but they see them as healthy reactions to the ideology of white supremacy, especially as articulated in the Manifest Destiny and White Man's Burden theories.

The Context of Black Protest

The description of the imbalances between African-Americans and whites and the suggestions regarding why they persist lead to two conclusions. First, it is apparent that the injustices are long standing and go far back into American history. It thus becomes very clear that consideration of the problem in a historical or time dimension is necessary to fully understand it. Second, the injustices have persisted despite the fact that America has the material and other resources to correct them. In effect, the problem is also one of policy, which leads us to ask the question, Why has America not made it its policy to correct the injustices?

In an attempt to answer the latter question five theories about causes were described. These include the sociological and institutional (Elkins), the historical and political (Moore), the psychological (Hoetnik), the racial determinist (Stoner and Muhammad), and finally, the ideological (Knowles and Prewitt). This seems to suggest that the reason for the failure of policy may be multicausal, with the various causes reinforcing one another. As an example of this multicausality and reinforcement, one sees in Prewitt and Knowles the logic that the ideology of white racial superiority present from the beginning in the white man's dealings with nonwhites has created a psychology of racism that has continued to taint white and nonwhite dealings. Thus, as long as the ideology and psychology exist, human relationships and the society's institutional arrangements will remain racially biased.

The persistence of the injustices and the many suggested causes raises the question of where to begin in dealing with the complex of racial problems. Is racial separatism the answer, as Stoner and Muhammad believe? Is institutional restructuring the answer, as the Radical Republicans and Huey Newton affirm? In effect, we are asking if one key policy can be adopted and by following it through solve the problem. Harold Cruse, for example, believes that if American cultural institutions and modes, especially the communications media, can be altered to fit the facts of what America really is, "a European–African–Indian racial amalgam—an imperfect and incompletely realized amalgam,"[66] the other dimensions of life will be altered also.

In fact, as the historical record will make clear, African-American thought and action has never limited itself to any one line. As the problem it has faced has proven to be both persistent and multi-faceted, so the history of African-American thought has been one of enduring and imaginative efforts to explore many variations on several broad strategies for gaining justice. In the forthcoming chapters an effort will be made to describe that record.

II

Black Nationalist Thought in the Eighteenth and Nineteenth Centuries

The first movement that had as its purpose the eradication of injustices toward African-Americans was a movement that in contemporary language would be classified as Black Nationalist and Separatist. This was the Colonization Movement. In this chapter the Colonization Movement, or Pan-Negro Nationalist Movement, as the historian Hollis Lynch terms it, will be considered from the following perspectives. First, a profile of the movement will be presented, which will include a survey of its origins, its subsequent development, and its successes and failures. Second, the movement's ideology will be described. Third, a brief review of some of the tactics used in the attempts to realize the colonization dream will be listed. Finally, speculation regarding the impact of the Pan-Negro Nationalists on later expressions of Black Nationalism will be made.

The Colonization Movement: A Profile

Ever since significant numbers of African-Americans began populating the United States, some whites and African-Americans have supported colonization, or repatriating African-Americans to a homeland of their own outside the United States. As the African-American historian John Hope Franklin writes, "As early as 1714, a 'native American' believed to be a resident of New Jersey, had proposed sending Negroes back to Africa. The idea did not die."[1]

The black supporters of colonization (whom I shall call Pan-Negro Nationalists) supported the idea because it offered a chance to build a separate black nation. They felt that African-Americans in the United States already constituted a nation within a nation, and since the

15

dominant racial group was white, it would be impossible for the African-American minority to realize its highest ambitions here. It was because of this belief that African-Americans like Paul Cuffee (b. 1759), Bishop James T. Holly (active between the 1850s and 1870s), Martin Delany (active in the mid-nineteenth century), Daniel Coker (active in the early nineteenth century), John Russwurm (d. 1851), Edward Blyden (b. 1832), Alexander Crummell (b. 1811), and finally Bishop Henry M. Turner (1834–1915) supported colonization. Delany sums up the major theme in the Pan-Negro Nationalist credo when he says that "every people should be the originators of their own schemes, and creators of the events that lead to their destiny."[2] Delany continues that since African-Americans are a minority in the United States, where "many and almost insurmountable obstacles present themselves,"[3] a separate black nation is necessary in the march to self-determination. Because of the Pan-Negro Nationalists' efforts to achieve this goal, colonization can be considered the first organized expression of Black Nationalism in the United States.

Some of the Pan-Negro Nationalists did not insist that Africa be the homeland for repatriated blacks from the United States; Delany originally suggested sites in Central and Latin America before deciding on Africa. In a similar vein, Bishop James T. Holly (the first black Anglican bishop) pushed for African-American migration to Canada, Liberia, and the West Indies before "he settled on Haiti, eventually making it his home."[4]

Many whites supported colonization because they felt that African-Americans were inferior and their presence here was a drawback to the development of white American institutions and culture. (This reasoning is a variation of the racial-determinist theory described in Chapter I.) Others, like the Quakers, supported it because they felt that African-Americans had a right to their own homeland, and as such emigration was a humanitarian gesture. Still others, like Thomas Jefferson and later Abraham Lincoln, supported it because they felt that to have a domocracy within which slavery existed was a contradiction, one with the potential to destroy the republic.[5] These examples illustrate the variety of groups and interests from the Pan-Negro Nationalists to white racists that supported the Colonization Movement.

Colonization gained its greatest impetus after Paul Cuffee, a free black, settled thirty African-Americans in Sierra Leone in 1815 at his own expense. Cuffee was born in New England in 1759, became a sailor on a whaling vessel in 1775, and in 1776 was captured and detained by the British in New York. During the revolutionary war Cuffey and his brother "refused to pay taxes in Massachusetts on the grounds that they were denied the franchise."[6] Franklin notes that soon after the Cuffees' protest, "Massachusetts passed a law allowing free Negroes liable to taxation all the privileges belonging to other citizens."[7] In 1780 Cuffee began to build ships of his own and by 1806 owned several ships and considerable property.[8] After joining the Society of Friends, Cuffee became interested in the plight of his fellow African-Americans, became outspoken in his opposition to racism, and was soon convinced that he could contribute best to alleviating their condition by supporting colonization. In 1811 he made his first voyage to Sierra Leone in West Africa to test the feasibility of his dream, but the war with the British prevented any further action on his part until 1815.

In 1816 the white-sponsored American Colonization Society (ACS) was formed with the avowed purpose of finding a home in Africa for freed slaves. (Among the founders of the society when it was organized in the U.S. House of Representatives in 1816 was "a descendant of George Washington and Francis Scott Key, the author of the U.S. National Anthem.")[9] Subsequently, the society sent out agents to raise funds and to interest free African-Americans into emigrating to Liberia, a West African colony that it started in 1822. (Liberia became independent in 1848, and its capital, Monrovia, was named after President Monroe of the United States.) At first, thousands of dollars flowed into the society for the purchase and charter of ships to transport African-Americans to Africa, and noteworthy Americans like Henry Clay, Judge Bushrod Washington, and Senator John Randolph were members of the society. As Immanuel Geiss notes, these distinguished Americans "gave the organization an almost official character."[10]

The society's first ten years were its best, for according to Franklin, by 1830, 1,420 blacks had been sent back to Africa, including some who were freed expressly for that purpose. Franklin also writes that "by 1832 a dozen state legislatures had given approval to the society,"[11] and the idea of African-American emigration had become a respected one nationally. By 1832, however, the Abolitionists had begun to question the morality of the scheme, the society was under widespread suspicion regarding its motives and the settlement in Liberia was mismanaged. As a result, because of rising abolitionist sentiment in the decade before the Civil War the society fell into desuetude. Despite this decline in importance and its internal transformations, the ACS lasted until 1910.

Although the ACS declined in the mid-1800s, the emigration movement as a whole did not die, nor was there a lack of African-Americans and whites who felt that African-Americans would never achieve parity within the American system. Around 1900 one finds Bishop Turner, one of the last of the Pan-Negro Nationalist stalwarts, still strongly supporting emigration, because as he put it, "Hell is an improvement over the United States where the Negro is involved."[12] A significant amount of mass interest in colonization also continued. The historian Edwin Redkey notes that as late as the 1880s and 1890s "letters of urging and application overwhelmed the emigration companies, the ACS, and Turner himself, who since 1893, had served as Liberian consul to the southern states."[13] If we use Bishop Turner's death in 1915 as the end of the traditional Pan-Negro Nationalist Movement, significant interest in emigration continued until the second decade of the twentieth century.

One important expression of colonization that is well worth mentioning as an illustration of the continuing interest in emigration is the Chief Sam Movement. Between 1897 and 1914 significant sentiment for emigration developed among Oklahoma's African-American population, mainly because of the worsening economic conditions there. The sentiment resulted in an effort by Ashanti Chief Alfred C. Sam to settle disaffected African-Americans on the Gold Coast (now Ghana) in West Africa, which was then a colony of Britain. In 1914, a ship called the *Liberia*, purchased by the group, left Galveston, Texas, for the Gold Coast, with sixty African-Americans aboard who were to be the pioneers of the settlement, but the expedition failed. It failed for three major reasons. First, many of the colonists died either on the way or shortly after their arrival. Second, the colonists who survived lacked the provisions to sustain themselves until they could become economically independent. Third, the British made extralegal complications for the voyagers, many "enacted while the 'Liberia' was still at sea."[14] Despite its failure, however, the effort illustrates the continuing African-American emigrationist sentiment.

A different opinion on the outcome of the movement is expressed by the black historian Robert A. Hill. Hill relates that some of the African-Americans who settled in Ghana introduced new technical skills in gin making and tobacco cultivation and made innovations in transportation techniques. Hill notes that Chief Sam is also considered a hero by some Ghanian nationalists.[15]

At the death of Bishop Turner in 1915, the Colonization Movement lost its last great spokesman who had direct links with the past emigrationist tradition. In this regard, Redkey is correct when he says that although "virtually rejected or ignored by Negro historians, Turner's African dream was the link between the pre-Civil War Colonization Movement and the later Chief Sam and Marcus Garvey Back to Africa Movements."[16] Redkey is also correct when he says that "Turner and his followers manifested a nationalism that has always been an option for free Negroes,"[17] an option that shows that if human beings cannot find dignity in one setting, they will seek to achieve it in another.

Reactions to and Criticisms of Colonization

Almost from its inception colonization encountered the opposition and often the outright hostility of many African-Americans and whites. The remarks of the Reverend Peter Williams of New York in 1829 are representative of those African-Americans who felt that they were no longer Africans but were natives of the United States whose "fathers suffered and bled for [American] independence."[18] Williams argued that it was contradictory to urge that African-Americans go back to Africa to improve their "character and condition" when Africa itself was industrially and educationally backward when compared to the United States. As Williams expressed it, "What hinders our [African-Americans] improving here, where schools and colleges abound, where the gospel is preached at every corner, and where the arts and sciences are merging fast to perfection? Nothing but prejudice."[19] Finally, Williams insisted that African-Americans "are natives of this country [the United States and] we ask only to be treated as well as foreigners."[20] Opposition to the emigration movement was expressed by organized African-American organizations and the protests of the Annual Convention of Free Colored People, which was held in 1830 in Philadelphia and other northern cities until the Civil War, is typical of such views. This convention "emphatically [protested] any appropriation by Congress on behalf of this [the Colonization] Movement."[21] Finally, the great African-American Abolitionist Frederick Douglass throughout his career not only opposed state appropriations for colonization schemes, saying, "We ask that no appropriations whatever, state or national, be granted to the Colonization scheme,"[22] but he called colonization "the twin sister of slavery"[23] and castigated it because, in his view, it strengthened beliefs about African-American inferiority.

Many whites also opposed colonization. One of the white critics was Albion W. Tourgee, who in 1893 headed the National Citizens Rights Association and who at the time "was perhaps the strongest white advocate of civil rights for blacks."[24] In 1893 in Cincinnati, Ohio, Bishop Turner called a conference to which he invited all groups and individuals interested in African-American emigration from the United States. On the second day of the conference, after a speech by Bishop Turner in which he made an eloquent appeal for emigration, Tourgee spoke. In an evocation as eloquent as that of Turner, he admitted the failings of America regarding African-Americans but insisted that they should stay in the United States because "the American public still had a vital sense of justice."[25] Tourgee felt that an aroused white "sense of outrage and oppression"[26] and an increasingly influential world opinion would lead to a more just America for African-Americans. As Redkey sums up the convention's proceedings, "The delegates polarized around Turner and Tourgee."[27]

The Pan-Negro Nationalists were quick to respond to integrationist views like those of Douglass and Tourgee. Bishop Turner, in words somewhat reminiscent of the Reverend Jesse Jackson's today, stated that every human being must have the feeling in a society or culture that they can be somebody. ("Underlying all school culture must exist the consciousness that I am somebody.")[28] Turner felt that since this spirit of fulfillment could never be attained by African-Americans as a minority in the United States, Congress should with "millions of dollars help the blacks to establish their own nation."[29] Along the same lines, in direct response to Douglass's criticisms, the Reverend Henry Highland Garnet, president of the African Civilization Society, questioned Douglass's motives. Garnet retorted that he lacked sympathy for Negro leaders like Douglass "who opposed free emigration to Africa simply because slave holders promoted it."[30] Furthermore, Garnet characterized Douglass and his associates as "human beings who oppose everything that they do not originate."[31] In short, the tensions between the two schools of thought on a personal and on an ideological level are clear.

It is interesting to note the attitude of the Pan-Negro Nationalists to the Civil War, the most forceful attempt in American history to integrate African-Americans into U.S. society, because it presages the skepticism of their twentieth century successors toward contemporary integrationist efforts. Separatists like Blyden and Crummell welcomed the Civil War because in Blyden's view it was the "purifier of a demoralised American conscience"[32] and no doubt a means to bring slavery to an end. Crummell viewed it positively because "he saw the decline of Anglo-American civilization in the moral and political convulsion within the United States."[33] However, Blyden was of the opinion that despite the war, African-Americans would never receive equal rights in the United States and that they were "deceiving themselves"[34] if they thought otherwise. The Pan-Negro Nationalists also had a neutral view toward the Civil War because they felt that not the United States but Africa was the land in which the African-American future lay. As Crummell related, God "has destined a great future for the Negro race"[35] on the African continent, for in Africa "a civilization of a new type more noble and generous . . . than has ever existed is on the eve of starting a new life."[36] Obviously, Crummell's view of where the African-American's future lay is unambiguous.

In summary, enough has been said to draw the following conclusions. First, the Pan-Negro Nationalists were in constant conflict and competition with their integrationist opponents both black and white. Second, the emigration movement at certain points in American history has had legitimacy in the minds of distinguished Americans. Finally, emigrationist sentiment in black America has always had a constituency of some size.

The Ideology of the Colonization Movement

Neither the ideology nor the tactics of the Pan-Negro Nationalists can be understood unless we reemphasize and expand on three premises that underlay the Colonization Movement. First, the Pan-Negro Nationalists insisted that as long as African-Americans remain a minority in the United States they will never attain equality. Blyden, perhaps the most famous Pan-Negro Nationalist because of his work in both America and Liberia, depicts the integrationist dream of African-Americans as an understandable one, but goes on to debunk it as "a faith against reason [and] against experience, which consists in believing or pretending to believe very important propositions upon very slender proof, and maintaining opinions without any proper grounds."[37] Blyden's views in this regard are typical. Second, the Pan-Negro Nationalists believed that even if black-white parity could be achieved in the United States, such parity is far less desirable than

African-American self-determination in a black nation. (We may note
that after 1856 most references to a homeland are to Africa.) Once
again Blyden sums up this feeling best, for after noting the eagerness
with which Europeans were "hastening to explore and take away its
[Africa's] riches" he asked somewhat rhetorically, "ought not Africans
in the Western hemisphere . . . turn their regards thither also?"[38] A
third premise that underlay colonization was the belief that only in a
separate nation could African-Americans achieve spiritual regeneration as a racial group. As Delany expresses it, African-Americans had
been in a predominantly white America so long that they had lost
their original ethical ideals and had replaced these ideals, for the most
part, with white America's vices rather than its virtues.[39] Delany insists that African-Americans "as the Poles in Russia, the Hungarians
in Austria"[40] were a nation within a nation and in the same way as
these minorities saw a separate nation as a spiritual necessity, African-Americans felt likewise.

An examination of the Pan-Negro Nationalist literature reveals that
in the case for African-American emigration five justifications that
were variations on the premises just treated were most often used.
These were Christian Nationalism and trade, the mission of civilization, Africa as a land of riches, the black need of a homeland for racial
regeneration, and economic depression in the United States. When
reviewing each of the justifications the writings of Alexander Crummell, Martin Delany, Edward Blyden, and Bishop Henry M. Turner,
the most eloquent articulators of the Pan-Negro Nationalist case, will
be used as references.

Christian Nationalism and Trade

An explicit assumption for most political writers of the nineteenth
century was that nations are natural entities and the natural form of
human organization, and this assumption was clearly shared by the
Pan-Negro Nationalists. The literature reveals that the Pan-Negro Nationalists were in fundamental agreement that blacks had a Christian
right to their own nation and that African-Americans, as a key segment of blacks in the diaspora, had a duty to lead in the attempt to
realize this goal. Crummell taught that Africans outside Africa had a
"natural call" to come and "participate in the opening of the treasures,
of the land of their fathers."[41] He added that although these treasures
were God's gift to the Negro race, "yet that race reaps but the most
partial measure."[42] Blyden articulates the Christian justification for a
black nation even more eloquently than does Crummell. Blyden com-

pares African-Americans to the Jews of the Old Testament who were imprisoned in Egypt. In Blyden's view, just as Canaan was the land in which the Jews were destined by the Divine to make their home, Africa was the home for the black man. Blyden continually cites as the model for the African-American's return to Africa a passage from Deuteronomy that urges the Jewish people to "possess" Canaan. The passage reads in full; "Behold, the Lord thy God hath set the land before thee: go up and possess it, as the Lord God of thy fathers hath said unto thee; fear not, neither be discouraged."[43] Blyden's belief that African-Americans were comparable to the Jews of the Old Testament is also manifested in his reply to those black critics who opposed a return to Africa because they had heard that the continent possessed an inhospitable climate that may kill them. Blyden scoffs at these critics because, as pointed out earlier, he notes that despite the difficulties whites were already exploring Africa and he goes on to scold diaspora Africans for being influenced by false propaganda about Africa just as "another people [the Jews] . . . who, like ourselves, were suffering from the effects of protracted thralldom, when on the borders of the land to which God was leading them."[44] Other Pan-Negro Nationalists are just as insistent as Blyden that blacks have a Christian right to their own nation. Alexander Crummell complains that the person "must be demented who cannot see God's providence in colonization,"[45] and he insists that Africans in the diaspora have a duty "to care for the heathen in general, and for our heathen [African] kin in particular."[46] Similarly, Martin Delany argues that God had enabled the black man to be adaptable to every soil, and it is now up to blacks "to make ourselves the 'lords of terrestrial creation.' "[47] However, Africa, with its "inexhaustible resources," is the continent set aside for black greatness, so "let us go and possess it."[48]

It is interesting that although most Pan-Negro Nationalists saw the slave experience as a most degrading one for African-Americans, Bishop Turner did not. Turner believed that although God did not endorse it, the slave experience was positive in that it taught African-Americans the rudiments of civilization and exposed them to Christianity. While admitting that African-Americans had been exploited by whites, Turner saw this as a part of historical necessity, the whites only failing because they should "have educated us, taught us to read at least, and seen that Africa was well supplied with missionaries."[49] To Turner, God intended for Africa to be the land of redemption, and the redemption would be actualized by former slaves. It is because of his belief in this historical necessity that Turner cautioned that anyone who opposed the return of a sufficient number of ex-slaves to develop Africa, was "fighting the God of the universe, face to face."[50]

Lynch states that the justifications for a return to Africa based on Christian Nationalism are usually combined with arguments about the great need for commerce there. To illustrate, we find Crummell explaining that economic self-interest is as good a motive for going back to Africa as any other. In Crummell's words: "In fine, I address myself to all that class of sentiments in the human heart which creates a thirst for wealth, position, honor and power."[51] Crummell believed that migrants with economic motives would "advance the material growth of Africa,"[52] for if the continent was to develop it needed migrants not only with religious impulses but those with "skill, enterprise, energy [and] worldly talent to raise her."[53] The economic rationale for migration could not be stated more plainly. The literature reveals that Martin Delany and Edward Blyden echo the same sentiments in this regard as does Crummell.

The Mission of Civilization

The second argument used by the Pan-Negro Nationalists to justify migration to Africa is based on the belief that blacks had a mission to civilize Africa. It was the duty of diaspora blacks to carry out this civilizing mission because they had been converted to Christianity, which most of the Pan-Negro Nationalists accepted as the legitimate religion, and they had been brought up in Western civilization, which the Pan-Negro Nationalists viewed as the legitimate civilization for all people. (Critics today would call this view culturally imperialist!) In this regard, Alexander Crummell states that the Western trained black must bring to Africa "light, knowledge, blessedness, inspiring hope, holy faith, and abiding glory."[54] Delany, continuing in the same vein, states that "religion had done its work in Africa" and it was now necessary for Western blacks to bring along with religion "the improved art of civilized life."[55] Blyden insists that Africa would give to the world a new civilization "whenever the millions of men [Africans] at present uncultivated shall enjoy the advantages of civilization"[56] brought to them by Western blacks. Blyden adds that if African-Americans "through unbelief or indolence" fail to rise to the challenge, "others will be brought in to do it, and to take possession of the country."[57] Finally, Bishop Turner suggests that a black diaspora vanguard "of a half-million civilized Christian people"[58] should descend on Africa and create a state where blacks could have their own "high officials, dignitaries, artisans, etc."[59] Turner "dreamed" of the power and influence "that would accrue to the whole race from such a seat of power and influence."[60] It is thus very clear that in the minds of the Pan-Negro Nationalists, the mission of civilization was a strong reason for a black return to Africa.

It was mentioned in passing that the argument of the mission of civilization used by the Pan-Negro Nationalists to justify colonization smacks of "cultural imperialism," and at least one Pan-Negro Nationalist, Blyden, modified some of his earlier views about the relevance of Christian methods to Africa.[61]

Kola Adelaja, in an excellent essay on the religious and political thought of Edward Blyden, states that eventually Blyden revolted against the supremacist attitudes of Western Christians toward the Africans, especially as seen in the behavior of the traders and missionaries.[62] Nevertheless, he remained an ordained Christian minister. Comparing Blyden to Luther, Adelaja explains that it was not Christian doctrine that Blyden revolted against but "the involvement of the church with the secular kingdoms of the world—in this case, the budding imperialist activities [in Africa]."[63] As far as Blyden was concerned, the Europeans had exploited the African for so long that they found "it difficult to shake off the notion of his absolute and permanent inferiority."[64] This contrasted with the attitudes of Islamic religionists and traders toward the Africans, who inspired the Africans psychologically, gave them confidence, and showed a tolerance for their indigenous institutions. As Blyden saw it, in Africa, Islam "strengthened and hastened certain tendencies to independence and self-reliance already at work" and amalgamated its own forms with African ones.[65] Blyden's arguments show that at least one important Pan-Negro Nationalist had great respect for the indigenous African culture and was quite conscious of the need to avoid cultural imperialism.

Africa as a Land of Riches

The next justification for emigration that emerges from the literature is that blacks should return to Africa because it is a land of great riches. The Pan-Negro Nationalists say that if these riches are developed, the ensuing wealth could lay the foundation for a black civilization capable of competing with any in the world. Alexander Crummell declares that Africa's population is less skilled than that of India, but Africa has a resource base that "more than rivals the most productive lands on the globe."[66] Martin Delany supports this favorable view of Africa's potential when he says that if land, population, and natural

resources are the foundations of national wealth, "Africa comprises
these to an almost unlimited extent."[67] Finally, on Bishop Turner's
visit to Africa in 1891, he traveled around the country "reporting the
great promise of coffee plantations, coal and iron deposits, and the
general potential for economic growth."[68] It is clear that in the view of
the Pan-Negro Nationalists, blacks of the diaspora should migrate to
Africa to develop the untapped resources there.

Africa as a Land for Black Regeneration

The fourth justification for emigration stems from the Pan-Negro
Nationalists' belief that because of its large population, mineral wealth,
and general potential, Africa is the continent where all blacks must
regenerate themselves as a people. Lynch is insightful when he notes
that the white colonialists who subjugated Africa after the Congress of
Berlin in 1883 also preached that they were regenerating Africa and
also claimed to be bringing Christianity and civilization. However,
while the whites saw the Africans remaining as wards of the West into
the foreseeable future, the Pan-Negro Nationalists wanted to release
the creative potential of the African masses. Lynch is thus correct when
he argues that African regeneration Pan-Negro Nationalist style consisted of "a frontal assault on notions of white supremacy."[69]

To Martin Delany, it was a biblical promise that Africa would be
regenerated, and he was excited to be a participant in "the grandest
prospect for the regeneration of a people that was ever presented in
the history of the world."[70] In Messianic terms, Delany assures us that
when the Psalmist says that "princes shall come out of Egypt; Ethiopia
shall soon stretch out her hands unto God" (Ps. 68:31),[71] the verse is
referring to the coming age of African regeneration. Delany was not
the only Pan-Negro Nationalist to speak of African regeneration in
Messianic terms; Blyden does the same. He states that blacks will not
respect themselves or "receive the respect of other races" until they
establish a strong African nation in which they can fulfill themselves.
At the same time, he assures blacks that they should not despair of the
attainment of their goal despite the obstacles that have been put in
their way. Such despair was unnecessary because "God tells us
[blacks] by his providence that he has set the land [Africa] before us,
and bids us go and possess it."[72] Finally, Bishop Turner tirelessly repeats the same theme of Africa as the land of black regeneration, for
he prophesies that if the black man is ever to achieve regeneration, he
will never achieve it "by trying to be white or snubbing his native
country, Africa."[73] As is apparent from these examples, the theme of

Africa as the land of black regeneration is a constant and powerful one in Pan-Negro Nationalist literature.

Economic Depression Within the United States

The fifth reason for the rise of emigrationist sentiment, particularly after the Civil War, stems from African-American economic deprivation, especially during depressions in the United States. Edwin Redkey tells how in normal times the African-American economic condition in the South was perilous after the Civil War, because chattel slavery had been replaced there by the sharecropping system, in which the sharecroppers paid almost half their annual crop for the use of the land and used the proceeds from the remaining portion to eke out a bare subsistence.[74] The sharecropping system was sometimes replaced by the crop-lien system, in which the "farmer mortgaged his crop or crop share against the food supplies for that year."[75] The crop-lien system victimized small southern farmers of all races, but particularly African-Americans, and during times of economic recession the situation became worse. It should be noted that well into the 1890s "many farmers could no longer make a living from cotton,"[76] and Redkey states that because of the decline of the cotton economy, many African-Americans desired to emigrate. Even more revealing, Redkey's research shows that the inquiries "at the American Colonization Society offices rose as cotton prices fell."[77] The African-Americans of Arkansas, Mississippi, and Alabama were especially hard hit by these economic conditions, "and Mississippi and Alabama blacks complained of virtual slavery to the landowner and storekeeper."[78] The most obvious area for African-Americans to migrate to were the northern and western parts of the United States. But in the North, the southern "black cotton farmers had little hope of gaining land or jobs," while in the west, land was available but "the black was an outcast."[79]

In the attempts to alleviate their condition African-Americans founded "several all black towns across the South, and in 1890 a black leader attempted to create an all black state in what is now Western Oklahoma."[80] However, these efforts usually failed because antiblack prejudice assured white domination of the land. Thus rebuffed in the United States, African-Americans made numerous attempts in the latter decades of the nineteenth century to migrate from America, most often to Africa. The Chief Sam Movement is an example of these efforts. Later in the history of black political thought, the powerful Marcus Garvey (Black Nationalist) Movement of the 1920s also flourished during a period of economic hard times for African-Americans. This observation leads one to wonder whether there is a correlation between economic depressions and the popularity of Black Nationalist thought in the United States.

The Tactics of the Pan-Negro Nationalists

The Pan-Negro Nationalists used a variety of tactics to gain support for their programs. One of the most common was to lobby for the support of individual whites or white-dominated groups that were pro-emigrationist in outlook. The oldest and most venerable of these was the ACS. Professor Edwin Redkey writes that until 1892 the society either provided or helped pay for the transportation of African-Americans to Africa, but after that date "the task of providing new homes and transportation fell on the blacks themselves."[81] By 1890 the ACS had settled over fifteen thousand African-Americans in Liberia, most of them before 1872. After 1892, the society deemphasized the emigration of unskilled African-Americans to Liberia and tried to uplift the level of education in Liberia itself so that more skilled African-Americans would emigrate there. At the same time, it rededicated itself to educating the American public about the viability of emigration as an option for African-Americans. Many African-Americans were suspicious of the motives of the ACS, however, and in his later years even Paul Cuffee cautioned against "too eager an acceptance of its scheme."[82] However, most of the Pan-Negro Nationalists, including skeptics of the ACS like Paul Cuffee and John Russwurm, continued to support it, because, they felt in Hollis Lynch's opinion, that "whatever the motives of the Society's leaders and supporters, the Society was creating a Negro state in Africa."[83]

The ACS was not the only white-dominated organization concerned with colonization. Some white-led commercial companies that felt that profit could be made in African-American emigration became involved also. Two examples are Martin Paulsen's Congo Company and the International Migration Society. In 1886, Paulsen, after learning that a long-neglected federal law of 1862 had stated that "one fourth of all the proceeds from the sale of abandoned lands in Southern states must revert to the federal government and be used in aiding black emigration from the USA,"[84] jumped at the chance to make some money out of the rising emigration sentiment and formed the Congo Company. However, Paulsen soon learned that a new congressional appropriation act would have to be passed "before the money could

be transferred."[85] Feeling that such action was unlikely, he lost interest in the project and turned the company over to its African-American stockholders. An African-American, the Reverend Benjamin Gas-
ton, who had migrated to Liberia from the United States, next headed
the company, but the scheme eventually failed. Similarly, in 1894
four white men from Birmingham, Alabama, were impressed by
Bishop Turner's glowing rhetoric about the "gain from American-Afri-
can commerce"[86] and decided to enter the business. They devised a
plan whereby for a total charge of forty dollars paid in dollar-a-month
installments, an African-American could buy passage to Africa. After
many privations, on March 19, 1895, their company, called the International Migration Society, succeeded in purchasing a vessel and
sending 220 African-Americans to Liberia on it. However, the company failed to get widespread support in both Liberia and the United
States and eventually folded.

Some white-dominated organizations outside the United States
were also concerned with African-American emigration to Africa and
were willing to support it. In 1802 Cuffee obtained the support of the
African Institution, described by Lynch as a British humanitarian organization largely made up of "former directors of the Sierra Leone
Company," a company that was influential in the affairs of this British
colony set up in West Africa in 1788 to receive freed slaves from English territories.[87] Lynch also tells how on May 18, 1866, Pan-Negro
Nationalists Robert Campbell and Martin Delany were invited to the
home of Dr. Thomas Hodgkin to meet some distinguished English
"noblemen and gentlemen interested in Africa's regeneration."[88] The
result was the formation of the African Aid Society, which was osten-
sibly organized "to assist by 'loans or otherwise,' the emigration of
Negroes from North America to Africa."[89] Lynch adds that the ever-
independent Delany agreed to cooperate with them only when it was
made clear that the relationship would be run on a "strictly business"
basis, and that "Negroes must have control over their affairs."[90]

However, African-Americans did not depend exclusively on
whites to initiate emigration schemes, because they often took the
lead themselves. In 1893, the Reverand Daniel Johnson of San An-
tonio, Texas, very impressed by Bishop Turner's suggestion that if an
entrepreneur would buy "cheap, second-hand British ships" and use
them for African-American emigration to Africa, "southern blacks
would buy the stocks,"[91] formed the Afro-American Steamship and
Mercantile Company. In pursuit of his goal, Johnson organized clubs
all over the United States where shares could be purchased, and he

traveled widely himself to foster the sales. Unfortunately, 1893 was a year of recession in the U.S. economy, and although many African-Americans initially "subscribed for the $10 share, they could not keep up the dollar-a-month payments."[92] Eventually, due to lack of funds and organizational experience, Johnson's effort failed. In 1901 Francis H. Warren, who later became a member of the Colored National Emigration Association (CNEA), subsequently the organ for his activities in Africa, devised a scheme to set up a colony that could experiment with U.S. economist Henry George's "single tax" in a part of Africa "300 miles southeast of Liberia and north of the Congo."[93] For his scheme, Warren tried to recruit the kind of immigrants who could finance their own transportation to Liberia and support themselves for a year. The CNEA collapsed in 1903 for lack of popular support. After 1903, Warren gained new allies for his emigration scheme in Boston publisher Charles Alexander and one Warren Walker. Although the plan was publicized adequately between 1903 and 1907, it failed to gain popular support in the United States. This failure, coupled with the Liberian government's inability to support new immigrants, led to the Warren plan's final demise. Finally, in 1900 Bishop Turner had his Colored Emigration Association (CEA) attempt to buy a ship for transporting migrants to Africa, but lack of sufficient funds led to the organization's collapse in 1906.[94] At the same time, it should be noted that as in any other business activity there were fraudulent schemes. For example, J.P.F. Lightfoot, an African-American preacher, was lynched in Arkansas "when his victims discovered that his $3 tickets to Africa were worthless."[95] Such frauds, preying on the dreams of the African-American for a new homeland, were common in the 1890s.

In summary, the supporters of colonization used a variety of tactics in their attempts to achieve their African dream, and their motives were similarly mixed. The historical record shows that while a few of the schemes had limited success, the majority of them failed because of lack of money, unpopularity, deficient skills, or a combination of all these. However, even the failures are instructive, for they document the African-Americans' continuing resistance to a status quo that too often denied them their dignity as human beings.

Pan-Negro Nationalism and Beyond

Theodore Vincent, in his excellent study on the Garvey Movement entitled *Black Power and the Garvey Movement*, credits that movement with being the source of all the major themes of modern Black

Nationalism. These themes range from an early call for Black Power to the call for the independence of Africa to the call for black cultural dignity. Vincent suggests that "the Black Panther Party's call for a U.N. plebiscite is reminiscent of Garvey's petitions to the old League of Nations, and the Black Power conferences of the 1960s resemble the UNIA [Universal Negro Improvement Association] conventions in their attempts to bring together all proponents of Black Nationalism and Black Power."[96] Without deemphasizing the uniqueness of many of the contributions of the Garvey Movement, Vincent's assessment of Garveyism's novelty is exaggerated. As the foregoing treatment of Pan-Negro Nationalism has demonstrated, many of the Black Nationalist themes that Vincent sees as originating in the Garvey Movement of the 1920s can be traced back to Black Nationalist expressions in the eighteenth and nineteenth centuries, and even before. Redkey is correct when he says that although most slaves were illiterate and thus could not write of their yearning for Africa, some slaves had been educated in the Muslim tradition, and several of them left autobiographies in Arabic in which they "considered Africa [their] true home and a promised land of freedom from slavery."[97] Thus, the theme of Africa as a land of black regeneration has a long history and was as strong in Pan-Negro Nationalism as it was in Garveyism. It is clear then that the roots of the Black Power Movement go far back in American history, and many of its ideas and tactics that seemed novel in the 1960s were already presaged in the Pan-Negro Nationalist Movement.

The Pan-Negro Nationalist Movement, the Garvey Movement, and the Black Power Movement, have another common characteristic: They were all opposed by and in competition with integrationist ideologies. In the next chapter the Abolitionist Movement—the major competitor to Pan-Negro Nationalism—will be profiled.

III

The Abolitionist Movement

The historical record shows that from the beginning of the African-American presence in the United States, African-Americans and whites were calling for their integration into American society. This chapter will deal with the pre–Civil War movement centered on this theme, the Abolitionist Movement. In order to put the Abolitionist Movement in its proper context, the following format will be followed. First, a profile of the movement describing the major permutations and changes that it underwent will be given. Second, the Abolitionist ideology will be discussed. Third, a description of the life and thought of Frederick Douglass, perhaps the most effective of the Abolitionists, will be highlighted to give a feel for the human dynamics of the Abolitionist Movement. Fourth, some comments will be made on the tactics of the Abolitionists.

Early Abolitionism, 1645 to 1807

The historian William Foster documents that from the early years of America's settlement there were voices calling for the abolition of slavery. Examples of such pleas are those of Richard Saltonstall of Massachusetts in 1645, the Germantown Quakers in 1688, and Dr. Benjamin Rush, the famous surgeon, who in 1773 "published an address in Philadelphia against slavery."[1] Many political leaders also objected to slavery, including Alexander Hamilton who was Secretary of the New York Abolition Society, and Benjamin Franklin. (Foster notes that the great French revolutionary in America, Lafayette, asked that Hamilton "propose his name for membership" in the society also.)[2] However, the American Revolution was the greatest catalyst for Aboli-

32

tionist sentiment in the early years, and Foster notes that by 1792 antislavery societies of some sort existed "in practically all the states from New England to Georgia."[3] Foster goes on to say that so swift and widespread was the growth of antislavery sentiment that an Abolitionist convention was held in Philadelphia in 1794 that condemned slavery and "proposed the holding of annual conventions."[4] Subsequently, many African-Americans also became involved in the movement.

In spite of the liberal ideology of the American Revolution, the attitude of American society as a whole was ambiguous toward the African-American, both free and slave. For example, although slavery as an institution was legitimized in the American Constitution, within twenty years of the Revolution all the original states had "either restricted or abolished" slavery, and "in 1803, 1816 and 1818, Ohio, Indiana and Illinois came into the Union as free states."[5] Another sign of increasing Abolitionist sentiment was the large number of individual manumissions that occurred between the end of the American Revolution and 1800. However, concomitant with the rise of the sentiment to free African-Americans especially in the North, there was simultaneously an attempt to "strip free Negroes of the right to vote in many states,"[6] for example, Ohio in 1803, Indiana in 1816, Michigan in 1837, and Iowa in 1846. Foster points out that by the end of the Civil War, "free Negroes were barred from voting in almost every state of the Union."[7] The ambiguous view of American society toward African-American freedom is thus obvious.

Despite the move toward African-American disfranchisement, antislavery sentiment was still gaining nationwide. Why was this so? Foster cites four reasons for this paradox, reasons with which African-American historian John Hope Franklin concurs. To begin with, the climate of the North and Northwest was unsuitable for a plantation system, as the "chief world market crops of the slavery period"[8] did not flourish or even grow in the North. Second, northern farmers opposed the plantation system because it threatened the welfare of free labor with cheap slave labor. Third, antislavery sentiment had been growing in the North since the Revolutionary War because of the widespread belief that slavery was dying. Fourth, "Northern white mechanics, fearing the slave mechanics as competitors, were inclined to support the abolition of slavery in their own states."[9] By 1800, antislavery sentiment in the North was so strong and individual manumission so widespread that at the "American Convention of Abolition Societies, held in 1804, delegates complained of flagging interest in their work."[10] Similarly, in 1809 the antislavery Pennsylvania Society, "after 25 years of existence made a similar complaint."[11] Clearly the end of slavery seemed imminent.

Although it was in the northern states that abolitionist sentiment was strongest, between the end of the American Revolution and 1807 when the British and Americans abolished the slave trade, anti-slave-trade sentiment was increasing in the South. The historian Eugene D. Genovese notes that one by one all the southern states had closed the trade by 1808, and South Carolina alone reopened it before the closure date because "a promising new staple, upland cotton, was offering fresh opportunities" to exploit slave labor.[12] Genovese suggests several reasons for the new sentiment. First, the moral pressure that was brought to bear on the slave trade made slavery increasingly unpopular even in the South. Second, the successful Haitian Revolution of 1790 to 1803 frightened the southern planters because it showed them the "explosive potential" in situations where there were "heavy ratios of blacks to whites and of African-born to American-born slaves." However, the most important reason was that the decline in the tobacco economy "simultaneously caused a loss of interest in slave imports and a rising interest in slave exports to the Deep South."[13] Thus, ironically, the abolition of the slave trade economically benefited planters in slave-selling states, who could now obtain higher prices for their slaves."

Finally, in the decades immediately following the Revolution, the Protestant churches became somewhat less militant in their support of slavery. For example, although they did not cease segregated seating arrangements and officeholding, the Methodists in 1784, the Baptists in 1789, and the Presbyterians in 1793 all declared their opposition to the slave trade.[14] It should be noted that this liberalism did not convince African-Americans of the morality of these churches, for they formed their own denominations once it was clear that segregation would continue in the houses of the Lord despite the declarations.

When in 1807 both the British and American governments outlawed the slave trade, the first phase in the Abolitionist Movement came to an end. Foster succinctly sums up the decline in Abolitionism when he writes, "After the passage of the American anti-slave trading laws of 1808, abolitionist organizations in the country slumped. The national conventions ceased, meetings were no longer, or rarely held, and most of the societies died out. The first anti-slavery movement in the United States was no more. This decline was mainly due to widespread illusions that the slave trade would halt and would finish off the whole system."[15] It should be noted that the statistical historians of slavery Robert William Fogel and Stanley L. Engerman dispute the view that slavery was dying in the United States between the end of the American Revolution and 1810. Instead, they assert that there were "as many Africans brought into the United States during the thirty years from 1780-1810 as during the previous hundred and sixty years of the U.S. involvement in the slave trade."[16]

Abolitionism from 1807 to 1870

Social philosophers are divided on the question of whether technological change also brings progressive advances in human society, as the evidence is contradictory. In the case of American slavery technological advance helped resurrect the system, and it is interesting to see how this took place. One of the reasons why slavery took on a new life in the early nineteenth century was the invention of the cotton gin by Eli Whitney. For generations no device in cotton technology could separate the seed from the cotton fiber. In 1793 "a Yankee mechanic, Eli Whitney, who was in Georgia at that time seeking a job as a school teacher"[17] took ten days to invent such a device. After the invention of the cotton gin, "a slave could clean 150 pounds of cotton a day instead of one pound, and when steam was applied to the mechanism, he could clean 1,000 pounds."[18] With the appearance of the gin the cotton industry took on new life, and by 1859 cotton had become the most important agricultural crop in the United States.[19] Naturally, with the rise of the cotton industry there was a new demand for slaves.

It was during the resurgence of the slave economy that the American Colonization Society (ACS) was formed, and because it initially garnered strong support from many distinguished Americans, including Abolitionists liké Benjamin Lundy, the Tappan brothers, Gerrit Smith, and even the great Abolitionist William Lloyd Garrison, free African-Americans became alarmed.[20] (Foster notes that Garrison later strongly opposed colonization, as is evidenced in his famous pamphlet of 1832, *Thoughts on African Colonization*.)[21] As was pointed out in the last chapter, integrationist African-Americans responded to the colonization threat by founding the black convention tradition, which lasted until the Civil War.[22] At these conventions African-Americans usually went on record as opposing colonization and condemning segregationist laws and other discriminatory practices. They also demanded more jobs and vocational schools. The black conventions also cooperated very closely with the Anti-slavery Society, which will be described presently. It was after attending one of the black conventions in Philadelphia in 1831 that Garrison changed his attitude toward the ACS.

The second phase of the Abolitionist Movement was more national in scope than the first, and it was better organized. It took on concrete form with the publication in 1831 of William Lloyd Garrison's anti-slavery weekly, the *Liberator*, which was followed by the establishment of the New England Anti-slavery Society in Boston in 1832 and the American Anti-slavery Society (AAS) in Adelphia Hall, Philadelphia, on December 4, 1833. Garrison's *Liberator* was the most powerful of approximately fifty newspapers of the time that supported Abolitionism, and the appearance of this anti-slavery press along with the establishment of the antislavery societies gave great impetus to the Black Convention Movement.[23] All the Abolitionists supported the Civil War, although Garrison because of his early stress on moral suasion rather than force as the sole antislavery tactic did not support the call for war until the Civil War's eve in 1861. At the end of 1865, Garrison discontinued *The Liberator* after thirty-five years of "uninterrupted publication and struggle,"[24] a cessation that caused a split between Garrison and Wendell Phillips regarding whether the AAS should be dissolved. In the dispute, Abolitionists like Frederick Douglass, Wendell Phillips, and Robert Purvis opposed dissolution, while Garrison supported it. Garrison resigned after losing the vote, and the society continued under Phillips's leadership until April 19, 1870, when it was dissolved. The society was dissolved because the Abolitionists felt that once the African-American had achieved legal and political rights, the cause of freedom would be assured. But how little did they reckon with the prejudices of men, which as we shall see in the post-Civil War period, were to make such a mockery of African-American freedom.

The Ideology of the Abolitionist Movement

Since Garrison's American Anti-slavery Society was one of the principal voices of Abolitionism, a fairly accurate picture of the ideology that motivated the movement can be garnered from looking at the philosophy of the AAS itself. The AAS stated categorically that slavery was antithetical to every value that the United States stood for and subversive of every democratic institution in this country. In the society's own words, "Slavery is contrary to the principles of natural justice, of our republican form of government, and of the Christian reli-

gion, and is destructive of the prosperity of the country, while it en-
dangers the peace, union and liberties of the state."[25] The society
called for "the 'immediate abandonment' of slavery,"[26] and demanded
that "all persons of color, who possess the qualifications which are
demanded of others, ought to be admitted forthwith to the enjoyment
of the same privileges."[27] The Messianic zeal with which the Pan-Negro Nationalists insisted on separate black development was touched
on in the last chapter; now with the Abolitionists we see an equally
fanatical assertion that the American system can be made to work for
all people. It was this clarity of purpose, coupled with its unambiguous stand against both emigration and compensation to slave
owners for freed slaves, that contributed to the society's success.[28]

In contrast to their clarity of philosophy and goals, the Abolitionists were terribly unclear about the means by which their aims were to
be achieved. For example, the AAS spoke about the need to use political action to attain its goals, but its members were confused about
what "political action" actually entailed. To some, it meant agitation
in the press, speech making, and a general emphasis on nonviolent
tactics to morally dissuade individuals from supporting slavery. To
others, particularly when a civil war that would involve the slave
question seemed inevitable, it meant active participation in the political process and even the sanctioning of violence. Eventually, the AAS
split over the issue.[29]

Considerable confusion among AAS members was later caused by
another feature of the society's philosophy, its stand on the doctrine
of states' rights. Believing that the federal government was the result
of an iniquitous pact that guaranteed slavery, the society insisted that
individual states were the best vehicles for abolishing slavery, especially because the federal government had only "restricted powers."[30]
As a result of its states' rights doctrine and nonviolent philosophy, the
AAS condemned armed insurrection on the part of slaves in its early
years and stated in its constitution that it would never "countenance
the oppressed in vindicating their rights by resorting to physical
force."[31] The states' rights emphasis had some paradoxical results. Because of it giants in the antislavery fight like William Lloyd Garrison
insisted strongly that only "the sword of the spirit"[32] should be used
in the struggle, and he in all good conscience condemned heroic
but militant landmarks in the fight for an equalitarian America, like
"Walker's appeal, Nat Turner's insurrection and John Brown's revolt."[33]
Abolitionists like Smith, the Tappan brothers, and, later, Douglass did
not share Garrison's apolitical views, however. In their opinion, the

Abolitionists needed to make alliances with other mass antislavery forces and to engage in political action. They split with Garrison's AAS in 1840 and formed the American and Foreign Anti-slavery Society.

Historian James M. McPherson points out that around 1860 there were roughly four groups of loosely organized Abolitionist factions in the North. The Garrisonians, centered around Garrison and Phillips, constituted the most cohesive and active of the groups and had the ablest speakers.[34] The more amorphous group of anti-Garrisonians, who had supported the Free Soil Party and kept the Anti-slavery Liberty Party alive during the 1850s, turned the Liberty party into the Radical Abolitionist Party of 1860 and eventually supported the Republican Party during the Civil War.[35] Closely allied with the Radical Abolitionists in 1860 was the Church Anti-slavery Society, the successor of Lewis Tappan's American and Foreign Anti-slavery Society that dissolved in the 1850s, and the American Missionary Society (AMS) organized by Tappan, George Whipple, and Simeon S. Joceyln in 1846. McPherson notes that the AMS was formally nonsectarian, "but in reality it was dominated by the Congregationalists."[36] This group was even more amorphous than the Radical Abolitionists in that it consisted of individuals who belonged to no specific Abolitionist group but who unwaveringly supported the abolition of slavery. McPherson notes that "most of the western political abolitionists had pursued this course and almost completely submerged their abolitionist principles in the weaker anti-slavery principles of the Republican Party."[37] McPherson notes that even in this setting "they remained militant and uncompromising in their basic abolitionist beliefs."[38] Finally, there were abolitionists like George L. Stearns, Gerrit Smith, and Thomas Wentworth Higginson, who supported John Brown.[39] McPherson observes that the crisis of the Civil War led the various factions to overlook "most of their old academic disputes and caused them to close ranks, at least for a time, in the struggle for the freedom and equality of the Negro."[40]

Frederick Douglass: A Profile

A key Abolitionist figure whose life and thought illustrate very well why Abolitionism had to become political to succeed in its goals is Frederick Douglass. Douglass (1817-1895) was born a slave in Maryland, but he escaped in 1838 and went to New York. Three years later at an Abolitionist meeting he made a speech on the evils of slavery that impressed his listeners, among whom was William Lloyd Garrison. Subsequently, Douglass was asked to join Garrison's organization as a speaker, and for the next two decades he remained active in this role.

Douglass was more than an Abolitionist. He supported the cause of women's rights, pleaded for practical training of the African-American long before Booker T. Washington did, and also supported the Temperance Movement. Douglass was also multifaceted in his skills. In addition to being a brilliant orator he was extremely capable in a number of other fields. He was a fine writer and in 1847, despite Garrison's skepticism regarding its success, published his own Abolitionist newspaper, the *North Star*. (Garrison is reported to have said to Douglass that "the land is filled with wrecks of such experiments.")[41] Douglass saw the publication of this paper, whose name was changed to *Frederick Douglass' Paper* in 1851, as evidence that African-Americans could also plead their own antislavery case, and he insisted that despite needing white Abolitionist support, "the man who has suffered the wrong is the man to demand redress."[42] Later, Douglass published a magazine called *Douglass' Monthly Magazine* and wrote a novel called *The Heroic Slave*, "a fictional narrative based on the 1841 mutiny on board the slave ship 'Creole.' "[43] Douglass also wrote two autobiographies, *The Narrative of the Life of Frederick Douglass* (1845) and *My Bondage and My Freedom* (1855). His autobiography in its final version, which combines these autobiographies, was released in 1892 as *The Life and Times of Frederick Douglass* and has become one of the classics of American literature.[44] It is apparent that in Frederick Douglass we are dealing with an African-American leader of exceptional ability and skills.

Douglass's notoriety was not limited to the literary and oratorical fields, for politically he was also nationally known. In his autobiography, Douglass tells of attending the inauguration of President Lincoln in March 1865 where, in Douglass's words, Lincoln went out of the way to ask his impression of the inaugural speech. Douglass notes that when he protested that his opinions were not worth much, the president assured him that "there is no man in this country whose opinion I value more than yours."[45] During the Civil War, Douglass argued strenuously that African-American soldiers had not only the right to fight in the war but they should receive equal pay and benefits and also be eligible for commissions. After the fighting ended, he continued his struggle for equal rights for African-Americans, and in 1889 served in his last governmental post as minister and consul-general to Haiti.

It is a tragic reflection on American intellectual life that despite his status in his own time, Douglass was neglected by the American historical establishment until comparatively recently. William Foster notes that some comprehensive histories of the United States, that of James Forde Rhodes for one, barely mention Douglass. Otherwise excellent economic and intellectual histories of the United States like those of Charles A. and Mary R. Beard and Vernon Parrington ignore him completely.[46] When W.E.B. Du Bois in his classic *Black Reconstruction* indicts American historians at the time of the book's writing (1935) for distorting or ignoring the African-American's contributions to American society, this is the kind of neglect to which he is referring.[47]

Some critics argue that Douglass became a reactionary in the post–Civil War era, an argument based on Douglass's continued support of the Republican Party after it became obvious that the party was treating the question of African-American rights with benign neglect. Frank S. Greenwood argues that after the Civil War Douglass "allied himself with the Republican Party and became the first showcase token Negro."[48] However, despite the extremity of his judgment on Douglass, even Greenwood concedes that "in many respects he outdistanced such great white abolitionists as William Lloyd Garrison and Wendell Phillips."[49] In fact, Greenwood concludes that regardless of his liabilities, Douglass's contributions to the antislavery cause made him "easily the greatest figure in the entire abolitionist movement; including Blacks and Whites."[50]

The Political Thought of Frederick Douglass

Historians of the African-American experience generally delimit three major strategies by which African-Americans have attempted to gain equal rights in the twentieth century. These are the Politics of Accommodation, most often associated with Booker T. Washington; the Legalist Approach, most often associated with the National Association for the Advancement of Colored People (NAACP); and the Moralist Approach, most often associated with Dr. Martin Luther King, Jr. We will treat these approaches in more detail later, but it is necessary to succinctly summarize them at this time to fully appreciate the scope and depth of Frederick Douglass's political thought.

The Politics of Accommodation was based on the view that the African-American living in Booker T. Washington's time should adapt himself to the United States as it was, a post-Reconstruction America that constricted the life of the African-American especially in the South, with racist laws and segregationist practices. Within this racist environment, Washington urged that African-Americans should struggle to create an economic base from which they could slowly ascend to embrace broader economic and political rights. More specifically, Accommodation as Washington conceived it involved the African-American garnering with the help of sympathetic whites the technical and business skills necessary to compete successfully in the United States, and from this initial step proceeding to agitate for the more abstract political and civil rights. From 1895 to 1915, largely because of Washington's influence and use of his power, this was the dominant ideology of struggle in the African-American community.

The Legalist Approach was directly opposed to that of Washington. It maintained that African-Americans are legally citizens of the United States, and as such they are entitled to all the rights and privileges due such citizens. Because of this, in all cases where suffrage, equal economic opportunity, unbiased courts, and the like, were denied them, they have a right and duty to protest. The legitimate method of agitation was through the institutions and by the use of the techniques guaranteed in the U.S. Constitution, and the courts and voting booths were particularly crucial in this regard. From 1909 to 1954, Legalism replaced Accommodation as the dominant method of protest in the African-American community. As stated earlier, the NAACP was the major organ that pushed this point of view.

Finally, after 1954, with the massive attempts at national integration of schools stemming from the prointegrationist *Brown vs. Board of Education* decision of that year eliciting so much resistance, the Moralist Approach gained ascendancy as the most influential philosophy of protest in the African-American community. Usually Dr. Martin Luther King, Jr., is considered the major representative of Moralism. The Moralist point of view was premised on the belief that the problem of black versus white is not simply a legal problem, that is, a problem of how to apply the laws equally to blacks and whites, but more fundamentally a moral problem. Stated as simply as possible, this problem asks, In its treatment of African-Americans, can American society justify its continual transgression of the values on which it was founded? The answer as far as many African-Americans and whites were concerned was no, and they were prepared to confront

America's injustices directly, to highlight the contradiction between ideals and practice.[51]

In the introductory chapter it was stated that black political thought and practice has been generated from a variety of ideologies and strategies. Douglass's life and thought illustrate the truth of this observation. The record shows that Douglass not only combined elements of Moralism, Legalism, and Accommodationism in his theory and practice, but it may even be argued that he used them in a more creative fashion than any of the other leaders covered in this book. Evidence for this claim is considered in the following discussion.

Moralism

A close reading of his autobiography reveals that Douglass believed that the universe was a moral one that functioned according to the Christian God's laws and moral imperatives. As a result of their God-given consciences, all human beings could recognize these imperatives, and it was by adhering to them that a universal humanity could and would in Douglass's view be realized. Douglass very directly expresses his belief in a moral universe when he objects to a reactionary Supreme Court decision of 1882 that declared unconstitutional the Civil Rights Law of 1875. Douglass views the decision as but a temporary setback to the African-American cause and says with a faith that only the true believer can muster, "The lesson of all ages upon this point is, that a wrong done to one man is a wrong done to all men. It may not be felt at the moment, and the evil may be long delayed but so sure there is a God of the Universe, so sure will harvest come of evil."[52]

Given this pronouncement, Douglass's strong faith in a moral universe needs little further elaboration. Waldo E. Martin, Jr., in his book The Mind of Frederick Douglass argues that it was "Douglass's belief in a moral universe and moral progress [that] buttressed his philosophy of social reform especially its characteristic optimism." It also made him confidont in his faith that despite setbacks "men are growing better in the march of time and events."[53] Martin suggests that the general spirit of the nineteenth-century American social reform combined "a deep secular millenialism" stemming from both the rationalism of the Enlightenment and the sensibility of nineteenth-century romanticism, with the religious evangelicalism of Evangelical Protestantism of the time. He concludes that the values of "basic human goodness, progress, human perfectibility and [a belief in] the millenium" that resulted from this amalgam are exemplified in Douglass's philosophy of social reform.[54]

Douglass often used his personal experiences to demonstrate the existence of a moral universe in the Christian sense. For example, he compared his empty spiritual life before his conversion to Christianity (he became a Christian as a slave) with the spiritually invigorated Frederick Douglass who emerged after his call. Although still a slave, he insisted that his conversion gave him a new source of strength with which to face the cruelties of slavery. At one point this strength resulted in Douglass's refusal to accept the unjust punishment decreed to him by his master by physically resisting it. As Douglass's logic would explain the resistance, the master was a child of God and so was Frederick Douglass, thus it was immoral for one child of God regardless of what human law dictates to inflict unjust suffering on another. After this act of resistance his master never tried to physically punish him again. Douglass notes how as a Christian "he saw the world in a new light, and my great concern was to have everybody converted."[55]

Stemming from his resistance to his master, the belief that there should be active resistance to oppression by the use of violence if necessary was to remain with Douglass throughout his life. In fact, he was in the forefront of those who argued that a civil war that resulted in freedom for the slaves was a just war, as mentioned earlier, the issue that caused the split in the Abolitionist Movement. As an example of his continuing belief in active and even physical resistance to evil, Douglass tells of speaking at an Abolitionist rally in Salem, Ohio, in 1847, where he expressed the view that only bloodshed could destroy slavery. At that point, he says that he was sharply interrupted by a fellow Abolitionist, the African-American hero Sojourner Truth, who asked, "'Frederick, is God dead?' 'No,' I answered, 'because God is not dead, slavery can only end in blood.' "[56] Douglass goes on to note that because Sojourner Truth was a member of "the Garrison school of non-resistants [she] was shocked at the sanguinary doctrine, but she too became an advocate of the sword when the war for the maintenance of the union was declared."[57]

Unlike King, who later accepted most of Douglass's moral maxims except his theory of force, Douglass insisted that it was only through the threat of force that human beings could assure their dignity. Recalling that the fight with his master brought his self-respect back to him and gave him "a renewed determination to be free,"[58] Douglass concluded that "a man without force is without the essential dignity of humanity. Human nature is so constituted that it cannot honor a helpless man, though it can pity him, and even this it cannot do if signs of power do not arise."[59] It would be erroneous to deduce that Douglass was an "apostle of violence," for when Captain John Brown told Douglass that only violence could solve the slavery question, Douglass at one point suggested that Brown attempt to convert the slaveholders. In fact, because there were also some strong Accommodationist and Legalist strains in his thought, Douglass always felt that the use of violence was a last resort.

It is noteworthy that the split between the Garrisonians and non-Garrisonians regarding the use of violence, states' rights, and even the question of separate African-American antislavery organizations, which Garrison opposed, split the African-American Abolitionists also. In 1836 the Black Convention Movement split with the pro-Garrison faction, calling itself the American Moral Reform Society. Thus, pro-Garrison African-Americans like William Nell, James G. Barbadoes, and William P. Powell upheld the Garrison line in the African-American community, while they were opposed by a faction led by Samuel E. Cornish, Christopher Bush, and Charles Ray.[60] The dispute started before Douglass escaped from slavery in 1838, and at first he was a Garrisonian. Later Douglass opposed Garrison's apolitical form of struggle and split with him. However, despite their differences, "Douglass always remained a warm friend of the old white battler for Negro Emancipation."[61]

His belief in a moral universe and his conclusion that all human beings were equal as a result, led Douglass to champion the rights of women, especially their right to vote. Douglass felt, however, that American racism was a more immediate and pressing problem than sexism, and he was critical of feminists of the Elizabeth Cady Stanton school who disagreed with his ranking. For example, Stanton and her followers insisted that the Fifteenth Amendment, which gave the vote to African-American males, should have been followed by a sixteenth amendment to give the vote to women. As she remarked in rather racist fashion, "We [women] are moral, virtuous and intelligent, and in all respects quite equal to the proud white man himself and yet by your laws we are classed with idiots, lunatics and Negroes."[62] On the other hand, Douglass felt that there was a fundamental distinction between sexism and racism. To Douglass, racism represented "conscious as well as unconscious efforts to dehumanize black people," while sexism was "a less dehumanizing form of conscious and unconscious oppression."[63] Once African-American male suffrage was attained, "Douglass unequivocally embraced woman suffrage as the next step in the struggle for universal suffrage."[64] Most black feminists criticized the failure to give women the vote, "but supported the [Fifteenth]

Amendment as an important advance in the recognition of black rights." Nonetheless, Sojourner Truth "asserted that the battle against sexism was equally as important [as racism] and necessitated at least equal commitment." The battle between the Douglass and Stanton factions ended in 1876 when they "agreed upon a truce and united to work together for woman suffrage."[65]

Finally, Douglass's belief in a moral universe is illustrated by his stand on the ethnological controversies of the time. As Waldo Martin, Jr., notes, prior to the publication of Charles Darwin's *Origin of Species* (1859), ethnologists devoted much time and effort trying to prove whether there had been one human creation (monogenesis) or several human creations (polygenesis). Indeed, even after Darwin the debate continued because "some ethnologists, for instance, thought Darwinism quite consistent with polygenism."[66] Many of the polygenesists used the theory to prove that blacks were an "inferior and brutish human species." Douglass reacts angrily to these views, insisting that "the Negro . . . shared with all mankind the exact physical, mental, behavioral and ethical makeup." Douglass goes on to say that the Negro's human properties of speech and reason "plant between him and brute creation, a distinction as eternal as it is palpable."[67] Douglass concludes, "God had 'endowed' mankind with organizations capable of countless variations in form, feature and color."[68] In summary, Douglass's moralism was the basic building block not only for his political philosophy, but for his ethics, his conception of women's rights, and his ethnological stands.

Legalism

The Legalist strains in Douglass's thought stem from his almost divine belief in the American creed and its promise, and examples of this deep faith abound in his writings. On January 1, 1863, when the Emancipation Proclamation was declared, Douglass criticized it as being "marked by discrimination and reservation" and noted that it was not a decree that gave liberty to all America's inhabitants.[69] ("Discrimination and reservation" refers to the realization by the Abolitionists and other antislavery forces that the proclamation did not specifically free the slaves in the border states or the parts of Virginia and Louisiana occupied by federal troops.)[70] Yet despite his reservations, Douglass states that the proclamation gave freedom to the Negro and legitimacy to the Republic, and he correctly predicted that "it gave a new direction to the Councils of the Cabinet, and to the conduct of national arms."[71]

An even better example of Douglass's Legalism occurs in a speech
he gave in 1880 to a meeting of West Indian blacks celebrating the
anniversary of their emancipation from slavery. (The British freed
their West Indian slaves on August 1, 1834, and the French in 1848.)[72]
In comparing status of the African-American and West Indian blacks,
Douglass states that the African-American is as legally free as the West
Indian, because the U.S. Constitution guarantees African-Americans
"all the rights and liberties granted to any other variety of the human
family residing in the U.S."[73] However, despite their legal equality,
Douglass points out that the southern states made a mockery of the
Constitution in the eyes of African-Americans, as they are denied the
right to vote, excluded from the right of free association, and more
unfortunate, "the old master class is today triumphant, and the newly
enfranchised class in a condition but little above that in which they
were found before the Rebellion."[74] However, this grave situation does
not evoke from Douglass either a militant protest or call for a solution
outside of the American system; in fact, he goes on to say that taking
all things into consideration, African-Americans had no reason to despair. Douglass felt that a better day was coming and that African-
Americans "by pretence, industry and economy may hasten that better
day."[75] Douglass next makes an implied criticism of the Pan-Negro Nationalists by admonishing his audience that "I will not listen myself,
and I would not have you listen to that nonsense, that no people can
succeed in life among a people by whom they have been despised and
oppressed."[76] Even in the darkest times, Douglass's faith in America
and his belief that African-Americans could succeed in it prevailed.

Douglass's Legalism is also evidenced in his hostile reaction to the
Supreme Court decision of 1883, mentioned previously. Douglass condemns the reactionary decision and hopes for the day when the Supreme Court will make decisions that reflect humane rather than anti-
Negro interests. ("Oh, for a Supreme Court in the United States which
will be as true to the claims of humanity as the Supreme Court formerly was to the demands of slavery.")[77] Yet, he tempers this condemnation with an extremely Legalistic view that urges obedience even to
bad laws. According to Douglass, "Among the great evils which now
stalk abroad in our land, the one I think, which most threatens to
undermine and destroy the foundations of our free institutions in this
country is the great and apparently increasing want of respect enter-
tained for those to whom are committed the responsibility and duty of
administering our government."[78]

Douglass's words have been cited in full because they illustrate not only the Legalist but also the conservative streak in this Abolitionist who had so often supported the theory of force. Douglass's conservatism becomes even clearer when he goes on to counsel embittered blacks in words similar to those the conservative leader of the NAACP, Roy Wilkins, advised the Black Powerites of the 1960s, that whatever "the incidental mistakes or misconduct of rulers, government is better than anarchy, and patient reform is better than violent revolution."[79] In summary, strong Legalist and even conservative features are apparent in the political thought of Frederick Douglass, and Waldo Martin is correct when he concludes that Douglass saw even separate black communities and organizations as "temporary expedients: a black means toward a humanist, yet culturally Anglo-American, end."[80]

Accommodationism

If one means by *accommodation* an attempt to arrive at a noncontroversial modus vivendi with the status quo and the fostering of an educational system that promotes it, there is a strong element of Accommodationism in Douglass's thought. In a letter to Harriet Beecher Stowe in 1843 in answer to her request about how she could best help with the education of African-Americans, Douglass replied that due to the low status of African-Americans, especially economically, she should not encourage the building of high schools or colleges but schools of agriculture and mechanical arts. In words that Booker T. Washington was later to echo, Douglass stated that high schools and colleges should come at "a point of progress that we [blacks] as a people have not yet attained."[81] He continued, saying that since African-Americans have been accustomed "to the rougher and harder modes of living," they should not expect to reach the higher callings of "ministers, lawyers, doctors, editors, merchants, etc.," until they have successfully mastered "the immediate gradation of agriculture and mechanic arts."[82] (Ironically, Douglass's own career is a refutation of the educational mode that he is prescribing here for the black masses.)

Douglass's essentially American middle-class outlook also led him to teach, like Washington, that African-Americans could create the economic base necessary for their continued advancement in the United States only if they exercised the middle-class values of sobriety, prudence, saving, and so on. It is because of this outlook that Douglass embraced the Temperance Movement, for not only would black sobriety help eradicate the traditional stereotype of blacks as drunks, but temperance was a "means . . . toward helping to break their [the African-Americans'] physical chains and letting them go free."[83]

It is true that Douglass did tell Stowe that more and more white colleges were opening their doors to African-Americans, so the building of black colleges would be unnecessary duplication. However, Douglass argued that even when African-Americans have gone to these colleges, they have received a classical education that "educated them above living conditions."[84] But, Douglass opposed a higher educational focus for African-Americans mainly because he believed it would aid the Colonization Movement, as after receiving higher education men like, "the Russwurms, the Garnetts, the Wards, the Crummells, and others, all men of superior ability"[85] refused to countenance America's racial prejudice and became advocates of emigration. As Douglass summarized the feeling, "It would seem that education and emigration go together with us, for as soon as a man rises amongst us, capable, by his genius and learning, to do us a great service, just so soon he finds that he can serve himself better by going elsewhere."[86] Historians of the African-American experience generally assume that most African-Americans wanted to fulfill themselves within the American system, and this may be so; but it is apparent that Douglass never underestimated the attraction of the emigrationist ideology especially for educated African-Americans and regarded its challenge as an important and continuing one.

Exactly what was Douglass's view of Africa and its relationship to the African-American? Unlike the racists of the time, Douglass felt that African culture, especially its Egyptian variation, which he believed "had been essentially Negroid,"[87] had a history of past glory. It is because of this past that Douglass, like the Pan-Negro Nationalists, hoped for the future regeneration of Africa. However, despite his historical and anthropological interest in Africa, Douglass's feelings about it and its people coincided with the mostly negative views of the continent that were held by the Europeans of the time and by many African-Americans who were influenced by them. In Douglass's statements about Africa, he refers to it as "dark," "savage," and "uncivilized," and he wonders "why anyone would leave this land [United States] of progress and enlightenment and seek a home amid the death-dealing malaria of a barbarous continent."[88] Similarly, while opposing European colonialism in Africa, Douglass rationalized the European presence there by insisting that it was an "ultimately beneficial manifestation of human progress."[89] Throughout his life, Douglass preached that the destiny of African-Americans lay not in Africa but in the amalgamated or "composite" American nationality into which they would one day be "blended." Thus, America and not Africa was their home.[90]

Martin suggests that because Douglass was a mulatto, he "lacked the fierce race pride associated with Delany, Blyden and Alexander Crummell, fullblooded black leaders and intellectuals." This assessment of Douglass is echoed by one of Douglass's critics of the time, Rev. Benjamin Tucker Tanner, editor of the African Methodist Episcopal Church's *Christian Recorder*, who in 1870 accused Douglass of being "ashamed of his color" and of having a "preference for light-skinned blacks like himself."[91] (Douglass's second marriage to Helen Pitts, a white woman, in 1884 resurrected this latter controversy.)[92] However, Douglass continually condemned such intraracial divisiveness and stressed that skin color "was incidental to human identity and only a secondary element of racial identity."[93] Douglass's Accommodationism was thus based on the faith that the African-American would be assimilated successfully into the American system one day. Indeed, Douglass declared that "a blow struck successfully for the Negro in America, is a blow struck for the Negro in Africa."[94]

The Tactics of the Abolitionists

The ideological splits that bedeviled the Abolitionist Movement have already been described, but in spite of these stresses the Abolitionists were able to attack slavery on every level. In spite of the splits and financial difficulties, Abolitionist organizations were usually racially integrated. For example, Frederick Douglass began his career as a speaker in Garrison's American Anti-slavery Society, and six African-Americans served on the board of managers of the society.[95] An integrated civil rights movement that made few distinctions on the basis of skin color was a powerful symbol in the racist amosphere of the time. This does not mean that the race relations were ideal; at times even Douglass felt that the white Abolitionists were paternalistic toward African-Americans, and he was hurt when Garrison tried to discourage him from starting his own newspaper. Douglass was also disappointed when in a speech in 1848 at Fanuel Hall in Boston, in which he welcomed the overthrow of the autocratic Bourbon dynasty of Louis Phillipe in France, the audience cheered. But when he stated that he wanted to see a successful slave uprising against southern tyranny comparable to "what the Republicans of France achieved against the Royalists of France,"[96] the audience was silent. The selective use of outrage was not lost on Douglass. Despite these tensions, however, the interracialism of the Abolitionist Movement was sustained and served as a guide to what was possible in the United States as a whole.[97]

In addition to means such as public lectures, petitions to the legislatures, and alliances with political parties, the Abolitionists also made an impression by publishing books and novels critical of the slavery system. Hinton Helper, in his masterpiece *The Impending Crisis: How to Meet It* demonstrated the economic inefficiency of the slave system. Similarly, Harriet Beecher Stowe's novel *Uncle Tom's Cabin* destroyed the myth of the humanitarian nature of slavery. (As mentioned, in the early 1850s Douglass also published a novel, *The Heroic Slave*, based on the 1851 mutiny on the slave ship *Creole*.) This antislavery literature both popular and scholarly went a long way toward influencing public opinion against slavery. In this case the pen helped to pave the way for the sword that was to be wielded against the peculiar institution later on.

Undoubtedly, the antislavery activity that is most illustrative of the moral commitment of the Abolitionists was their operation of the Underground Railroad, which funneled escaped slaves from the South to the North. Aiding escaped slaves was in flagrant violation of the fugitive slave laws, the last of which was passed in 1850, giving slave owners the right to pursue their escaped slaves, that is, their property, into the northern states and return them to the South. Historians Franklin and Foster note that an underground railroad of some sort had existed since the seventeenth century. Franklin writes that George Washington complained in 1786 "of a slave escaping from Alexandria to Philadelphia, whom a society of Quakers, formed for such purposes attempted to liberate."[98] By 1831, just when the AAS was about to be formed, the "underground" escapes escalated, and the Abolitionists and especially their Quaker supporters felt it their moral obligation to participate in it. The Underground Railroad became so effective that "between 1830 and 1860 at least 60,000 slaves made their way to freedom."[99] In this regard it should be noted that largely because of her work in the Underground Railroad the African-American Harriet Tubman was called "the greatest heroine of her age."[100]

The Abolitionists were bitterly opposed by proslavery elements both North and South, including many northern merchants and lawyers, and like all fighters for freedom they paid a heavy personal price. Although they had a significant amount of public support, suffering was often their lot, as "mobbing, tar and feathering, houseburning, rotten egging, beating and even lynching"[101] were inflicted on them both in the North and the South. Negative reaction to the Abolitionists took on especially virulent form in the South. There vigilante committees beat, lynched, and brutalized many Abolitionists. At the same time, successful attempts were made to stop the flow of Abolitionist literature through the mails, and slaveholders in the various state legislatures attempted to deny Abolitionists the right of petition. Despite the obstacles, the cause of Abolitionism grew, and the AAS alone had expanded to 250,000 members when the split took place in 1840.

The fate of the Abolitionist John Brown, who attempted to start an antislavery war by carring out a raid on the federal arsenal at Harpers Ferry, Virginia, on October 16, 1859, profiles in microcosm the fate of the Abolitionist movement as a whole. John Brown's raid failed, and in addition to being hanged for his efforts, he was considered a terrorist by some, a fanatic by others, and slightly demented by still others. Less than two years later, however, when Union armies responded to the South's attack on Fort Sumter on April 12, 1861, they went into the field singing "John Brown's Body," a popular song that originated out of this Abolitionist's struggle. Such singing not only vindicated the life of John Brown; it vindicated the struggle of the Abolitionists for an America that lived up to the ideals of its constitution.[102]

Abolitionism and Beyond

McPherson argues that although most historians date the end of Abolitionism with Garrison's dissolution of the American Antislavery Society and cessation of the publication of his *Liberator* in 1865, Abolitionists continued to struggle for black equality during the Reconstruction period, and in reality "showed a greater concern for the plight of the Negro after 1865 than anyone else."[103] However, even McPherson concedes that the main activist force during Reconstruction was the Republican Party, and he implies that perhaps the Abolitionists' greatest utility within this context was to serve as the "conscience of the Radical Republicans."[104]

Reconstruction is generally defined as the eleven-year period beginning with the end of the Civil War and ending with the Hayes–Tilden election controversy of 1876, a controversy that was settled by allowing the Republican Hayes to take office in exchange for

the removal of federal troops from the South. These troops represented the last instrument that the federal government possessed to
enforce African-American rights in the region. Reconstruction started
out very well for African-Americans as largely through the efforts of
the Radical Republicans a series of progressive laws was passed. The
Thirteenth Amendment of December 18, 1865, outlawed all forms of
servitude in the United States, the Fourteenth Amendment of June 26,
1868, established a color-blind citizenship criterion in the United
States, and the Fifteenth Amendment of March 30, 1870, gave African-
American males the right to vote.[105] In addition, African-Americans
became wage workers; started to elect political officeholders; com-
menced the building of economic, civil, and educational institutions;
and launched careers as independent farmers. Franklin captures the
positive side of Reconstruction perfectly when he writes that "Reconstruction laid the foundation for more democratic living by sweeping
away all qualifications for voting and holding office, and by establishing a system of universal public education."[106]

Starting on April 14, 1865, when Andrew Johnson replaced the
assassinated Lincoln as president, a conservative reaction toward civil
rights developed all over the United States and especially in the
South. Johnson was sympathetic to this reaction, and he tried to sabo-
tage every piece of progressive legislation on behalf of the ex-slaves.
After 1876, when federal troops were withdrawn from the South, not
even a token effort was made by the national government to extin-
guish the terror and fraud that the southern racists were employing to
drive African-Americans into second-class citizenship. Eventually
they succeeded in their efforts to snuff out African-American political
and other activities. By 1886 African-Americans had been driven from
the public arena in the South, and except for a brief period of black–
white cooperation during the Populist period in the late 1880s and
early 1890s, from a citizenship standpoint they became invisible men
and women. The great African-American sociologist W.E.B. Du Bois
brilliantly sums up the African American dilemma at this time when
he describes the economic pressure that was used to depoliticize the
southern black. According to Du Bois, "The decisive influence was
the systematic and overwhelming economic pressure. Negroes who
wanted to work must not dabble in politics. Negroes who wanted to
increase their income must not agitate the Negro problem. Positions of
influence were only open to those Negroes who were certified 'safe
and sane' and their careers were closely scrutinized and passed upon.
From 1880 onward, in order to earn a living, the American Negro was

forced to give up his political power."[107] Give up political power is exactly what the Negro did, for the last African-American member of Congress in the nineteenth century was George H. White of North Carolina, who served from 1896 to 1901. The drought of nationally elected African-American officials lasted until 1928, when as a result of the turn-of-the-century northern black migration, the black Republican Oscar De Priest was elected to Congress.[108] Du Bois's moving portrait describes the context out of which the next major strategy developed to correct the imbalances between African-Americans and whites in the United States. The strategy was the Politics of Accommodation and the architect was Booker T. Washington.

IV

The Politics of Accommodation

By the 1880s most African-Americans, the majority of whom lived in the South, had for all practical purposes been driven out of political life. Into this cheerless black world stepped an optimistic ex-slave named Booker T. Washington (1856–1915), whose message of hope called the "Politics of Accommodation" would capture the imagination of both blacks and whites for nearly thirty years.

The power of Washington's Accommodationist ideology within the black community, especially between 1895 and 1915, can be illustrated in many ways. Martin Duberman, in his book *Paul Robeson*, a well-written but controversial biography of the famous African-American artist and civil rights activist Paul Robeson (1898-1976), writes that the undergraduate class of 1919 at Rutgers University, of which Robeson was a member, "prophesied" in its yearbook that because of his academic, athletic, and artistic skills "Paul, by 1940, would be governor of New Jersey, would have 'dimmed the fame of Booker T. Washington' and would be the leader of the colored race in America."[1] The citation illustrates well the conclusion that Booker T. Washington set the standards by which black leadership was measured not only during his own time but for a considerable period afterward. The assessment is confirmed when Duberman speaks of the reactions of Robeson's friends to his decision in 1924 to pursue an artistic career over one in law. (Robeson graduated from Columbia University Law School in 1923.) As Robeson himself commented according to Duberman, his "many friends, convinced he should be the next Booker T. Washington, had continued mildly to rebuke him for deserting the law."[2]

54

In Washington's time his reputation was even more legendary and Washington mentions that after his famous Atlanta Exposition address of 1895, his supporters suggested that he "take the place of 'leader of the Negro people,' left vacant by Frederick Douglass's death."[3] Douglass had died in 1895.

Booker T. Washington: A Profile

It is said that an individual's background often helps to structure his or her political and social philosophy, and this saying is most true of Booker T. Washington (1856-1915). The son of a black slave and a white man, Washington was born a slave in Franklin County, Virginia, probably in 1856, "in a typical log cabin, about fourteen feet square." He lived in this cabin with a brother, a sister, and his mother until after the Civil War when they were freed. To the statistical historians who tend to play down the harshness of slavery, Washington's personal description of his early life is testament to their folly, for as he reminisces, his life began "in the midst of the most miserable, desolate and discouraging surroundings."[4] Washington describes his early life as desolate not because his master was particularly cruel (he was not), but because slavery deprived the slave of all rights and feelings. However, Washington teaches that despite their enslavement blacks were faithful to their masters during the war, and many were reluctant to leave them in its aftermath. Later on, Washington insisted that notwithstanding the subsequent post–Civil War acrimony between the races, he "had long since ceased to cherish any spirit of bitterness against the southern white people on account of the enslavement of my race."[5]

As a youth, Washington describes how he worked in a salt mine and a coal mine while simultaneously struggling to learn how to read and write. Despite the tough conditions, however, he managed to sustain a love for learning that led him regardless of the lack of funds and the privations to enroll successfully in what was then a technical college, the Hampton Institute, in August 1872. August Meier writes how "Yankee Puritan, industrious Hampton" and the already hard-working Washington "clicked from the first," and Washington himself tells how he learned the virtues of "thrift, economy and push" in the Christian environment of Hampton.[6] Through hard work, scrimping at meals, the philanthropy of whites, and other means, he eventually graduated from Hampton in 1875. He attributes much of his success there to General Armstrong, the president of the institution. Armstrong, in Washington's view, was not only a model administrator and educator, but he was also typical of the "white men and women who went into the negro schools at the close of the war by the hundreds to assist in lifting up my race."[7]

After his graduation, Washington briefly considered the ministry, law, and politics as careers, but after a two-year teaching stint at Hampton starting in 1879, he decided that he could best serve in an educational capacity. The opportunity to do so came when in return for the vote in an 1880 election in Macon County, Alabama, a former Confederate, Colonel W. F. Foster (a Democrat), promised to establish a school for blacks if they supported him in the elections. Foster was elected, and as a result, $2,000 was appropriated by the legislature to pay a teacher to start the college. Lewis Adams, the black Republican who delivered the African-American vote, wrote to Hampton asking for a teacher to establish the school. Washington was recommended, and he took the job.[8] From 1881 to 1895, Washington struggled to establish Tuskegee and make it a success, and so successful was he that by the turn of the century he was the most powerful African-American in the United States.

Washington's political philosophy of Accommodation and his concept of industrial training at Tuskegee became so famous that he was a political confidant of Presidents Roosevelt and Taft, the darling of philanthropists like Andrew Carnegie, and the patronage dispenser for both the rich and politically powerful in the black community. So internationally renowned was he that on his first trip to Europe in 1899 he met royalty, including Queen Victoria, Prince Henry of Prussia, and the King and Queen of Denmark.[9] At the same time, despite this fame, Washington's philosophy of Accommodation declined in popularity during his last years, and soon after his death the Tuskegee political machine through which he had wielded so much power, especially over the African-American community, collapsed.[10]

Washington wrote several books, including *The Future of the American Negro* (1899), *The Story of My Life* (1900), *Up from Slavery* (1901), *The Story of the Negro* (1909), and *My Larger Education* (1911). His autobiography, *Up from Slavery*, became a world classic in the early years of the twentieth century, and Louis Harlan states that it was translated into at least fifteen languages, including Chinese, Japanese, Zulu, and Hindi.[11]

Booker T. Washington's Philosophy of Education

Washington's political philosophy, as well as his political and philanthropic activities, were based on his educational philosophy. James D. Anderson, in his book *The Education of Blacks in the South*, argues that Washington adhered to the "Hampton Model of Normal School Industrial Education," especially as it was practiced in the years 1868 to 1915. (Anderson calls the model's educational theory "the Hampton-Tuskegee philosophy.")[12] Anderson argues that while the general aim of African-American education after the Civil War was "to develop a social and educational ideology singularly appropriate to their [the ex-slaves'] defense of emancipation and one that challenged the power of the planter regime," Armstrong developed a pedagogy that was designed to have blacks accept without challenge the "traditional inequities of wealth and power."[13] Anderson notes that, paradoxically, although Hampton was later identified as a model for the teaching of mechanical and agricultural skills and the work discipline to blacks, until close to the end of the nineteenth century it mainly produced black teachers. Indeed, he relates that Hampton did not give its first trade school certificate until 1895, long after Armstrong's version of industrial training for blacks was praised by educators and politicians North and South as the way to "assist in bringing racial peace, political stability and material prosperity to the American South."[14] Schools other than Hampton required that the students carry out manual labor, other schools also saw such labor as a means of encouraging thrift, hard work, and other such values among the students and as a help to the college financially. Among these schools were respected institutions like Mt. Holyoke Seminary for Women, Welleseley College, and Oberlin College. At Hampton, unlike the others, manual labor "formed the core of the teacher training program,"[15] for it was seen there not as an adjunct to academic training, but as the major means to demonstrate to black teachers the relevance of the "ethic of toil" for "the children of the South's distinctive black laboring class," whom they would teach.[16] Ironically, the full-fledged manual training program was established in 1879 "when Armstrong created the night school with Booker T. Washington as principal."[17]

The record shows that despite their propaganda about the relevance of industrial education, both Hampton and Tuskegee failed miserably in their supposed mission to produce skilled blacks. In 1903 Daniel C. Smith, Tuskegee's auditor, found after an investigation of the 1,550 students' skill levels that "only fifteen boys could lay a brick," and only a dozen could do "a fair job as joiners."[18] Similarly, Hampton's students complained about the lack of skill training there. William W. Adams, who entered the school in 1878 to become a printer, was dismayed that "no one could teach him the printing trade." He left the school and charged that it was "greatly overrated."[19] There are numerous cases like those of Adams, and, indeed, the charges against Hampton persisted until 1929, when the Hampton students revolted and when both Tuskegee and Hampton were compelled "to become standard institutions of higher learning"[20] because of both student demands and changing requirements.

At the same time, Anderson maintains that the major aim of the Hampton model was not educational but ideological and political, and in this regard it was very successful, especially in the hands of Washington, who transformed the educational philosophy into a world outlook that captured the imaginations of both blacks and whites.[21] Ideologically, Armstrong viewed industrial education both as a means of inducing blacks into accepting "a subordinate role in the emergent new South"[22] and as a way of keeping blacks, whom Armstrong saw as "not capable of self-government," out of politics. Armstrong, who advertised himself as the "friend of the Negro," urged blacks to "let politics alone," charged that black votes enabled "some of the worst men" to become involved in American politics, and insisted that black voters had created situations "no white race on this earth ought to endure or will endure."[23] This is the very General Samuel Chapman Armstrong who was both the tutor and idol of Booker T. Washington!

The lessons of industrial education and political acquiescence that were taught at Hampton by Armstrong made a strong impression on Washington very early in his career. In 1877 Washington was involved in what turned out to be a successful campaign to move the capital of West Virginia from Wheeling to Charlestown. (It was moved in 1885.)[24] Washington was so effective as a campaigner that it was suggested that he become a politician. Washington refused a political career, however, saying that the first priority for blacks "was to get a foundation in education, industry and property."[25] At this time Washington observed that a large number of blacks were receiving the kind of education that would enable them to become "great lawyers, or Congressmen, and many of the women wanted to be music teachers." However, he stressed that even then, he had the "fixed idea" that a prior training was necessary to "prepare the way for successful lawyers, Congressmen and music teachers."[26] This prior training was industrial education. Finally, as early as 1877 Washington was convinced that blacks should use their skills in the rural South where most blacks lived, because it is in the country where all successful nations "have gotten their start."[27] This rural orientation was to remain with Washington throughout his life, and that is why Louis Harlan concludes that despite his worldwide fame, Washington remained "a Southern based political boss of a people still overwhelmingly Southern and rural."[28]

The job at Tuskegee gave Washington the chance to put theory into practice, and his belief in industrial training as a priority for the masses of blacks was confirmed on his arrival. Here he saw poor blacks wishing to live like middle- and upper-class Americans but lacking the elementary habits of thrift, prudence, and industry that in his view were essential to attaining such a level. He tells of going to dinner at the home of a black family but finding only one fork for five people. In the corner of the same house was a sixty-dollar organ being paid for in one-dollar installments. "One fork, and a sixty dollar organ"[29] seemed a tragic misplacement of priorities to Washington, and he felt that it was this mentality that hampered black progress. Washington also tells of staying at Tuskegee during the Christmas holidays. Instead of putting the holidays to spiritual and personal use, the black populace there used them for drinking whiskey, rough dancing, and engaging in squabbles. To Washington, such revelry not only hurt blacks financially but encouraged the kind of behavioral patterns that destroyed industry.[30] Washington was determined to combat this backwardness through industrial education, and Tuskegee was his tool.

Washington admitted that there were many people of the time who doubted that the African-American could "hew his own path" unless he was guided by others, a view with which he strongly disagreed. (Here Washington is apparently referring to the White Man's Burden thesis.) But Washington cautioned that the issue would not be settled by arguments regardless of their complexity, but by "self-sacrifice, by foresight, by honesty and industry, we must re-enforce arguments with results."[31] Washington concludes a 1903 essay, in which his views are compared for the first time to those of W.E.B. Du Bois, by listing what he saw as acceptable results. As he sees it:

One farm bought, one house built, one home sweetly and intelligently kept, one man who is the largest taxpayer or has the largest bank account, one school or church maintained, one factory running successfully, one truck

garden profitably cultivated, one patient cured by a negro doctor, one sermon well preached, one office well filled, one life cleanly lived—these will
tell more in our favour than all the abstract eloquence that can be sum-
moned to plead our cause.[32]

Given Washington's view of acceptable results, the challenge to blacks
is obvious.

Louis Harlan writes that Washington might have been deferential
"to those whose money or favor he sought" and a "suave interracial
diplomat," but he ran Tuskegee like his own plantation. Indeed, Harlan suggests that in administrative philosophy, Washington was the
African-American counterpart of the "planters and business tycoons
for whom he always reserved the highest public flattery." Harlan concedes that, perhaps, firm examples of discipline were needed to correct "the slovenliness [among the ex-slaves] that was a heritage from
slavery and poverty," but despite the nobility of Washington's effort,
he was an extremist in these matters even given the post-Reconstruction setting.[33] He was obsessive in detail, found fault with everything
from the kitchen to the laundry, delegated authority reluctantly, and
was fanatical about the proper decorum of both faculty and students.
But it was not simply Washington's personal style that was stiff. Harlan concludes that the strong hierarchical structure at Tuskegee can be
traced to Washington's outlook, which like Armstrong's was based on
a faith "not in equality and democracy but in leadership and discipline."[34]

The Social and Political Thought of
Booker T. Washington

Despite his persistent emphasis on industrial training[35] and his
downgrading of both the liberal arts and political activism,[36] Washington could not have succeeded to the extent he did unless he was also
an astute politician.[37] Like his educational philosophy, his social and
political thought has social Darwinist roots, the best illustration of
which is seen in his theory of the "American Crucible."[38] As Washington saw it, in America the degree of rights and privileges one acquires,
including political rights, depends not on race but on the degree to
which one successfully performs in the Crucible of the American Experience. Washington gives no summary definition of this term, but in
an 1896 speech at Harvard University he describes its operations in
the following way: "In the economy of God, there is but one standard
by which an individual can succeed—there is but one for a race. This

country demands that every race shall measure itself by the American standard. By it a race must rise or fall, succeed or fail, and in the last analysis mere sentiment counts for little."[39] How should blacks succeed in the American Crucible according to Washington? To succeed, blacks must exercise patience, thrift, hard work, and economy and "disregard the superficial for the real, the appearance for the substance, to be great and yet small, learned and yet simple, high and yet the servant of all."[40] He continues, saying that blacks must exercise these virtues to a higher degree than whites if the race is to advance as a whole.

Meier notes correctly that the African-American variant of social Darwinism that Washington accepted reversed the popular interpretation of the dogma rationalizing black inferiority and instead asserted the opposite. The African-American social Darwinists depicted chattel slavery not as a sign of black inferiority but as a "test of nature" that blacks had survived well.[41] This ability to survive in spite of the most oppressive conditions meant that the race's future in America, where conditions were still harsh but less discriminatory, was secure. As a result, the African-American social Darwinists were optimistic about the African-American's future prospects here. The acceptance of the black variant of social Darwinism accounts for Washington's optimism.

In his political theory, Washington saw three entities as critical in deciding how the Crucible operated—the federal government, the state governments, and the rich—and he speaks at length on how they have related to black people and how blacks should relate to them. Washington praises the federal government for abolishing slavery but at the same time criticizes it for its failure "to make some provision for the education of our people in addition to what the states might do, so that the people would be better prepared for the duties of citizenship." He also laments that northerners during Reconstruction preyed on blacks by using them in their effort to "punish the southern whitemen," and he insists that Reconstruction's politics distracted blacks "from the more fundamental matters of perfecting themselves in the industries at their doors and securing property."[42] W.E.B. Du Bois, in his classic *Black Reconstruction*, demonstrates that blacks on the whole performed creditably in the Reconstruction legislatures and criticizes most standard interpretations of American history for pushing a contrary view. On the other hand, Washington seems to accept the contrary view, for while admitting that there were some excellent black Reconstruction politicians, he spends far more time severely criticizing the many black officeholders "who in some cases could not read or write, and whose morals were as weak as their education."[43]

Washington's deprecation of blacks and their condition, especially before white audiences, seems to have been one of his standard tactics. Indeed, Louis Harlan is correct when he says that Washington's constant repetition of "stock-in-trade" stories like, "There seems to be a sort of sympathy between the Negro and a mule," served to "reinforce the white man's stereotyped view of the Negro."[44] At the same time, it must be conceded that at other times Washington spoke and wrote of the African-American in a noble way. In his *Story of the Negro*, he writes eloquently of the excellence of the Negro race, an excellence that was symbolized in the worth of his "good and gentle and loving mother."[45] He even insists in this book that the study of both African-American and African history be mandatory for both blacks and whites.

Despite his criticisms of the federal government's Reconstruction policies, Washington appreciated its importance in setting the parameters of national policy, and he realized that to advance, black people needed access to it. Consistent with this view, Washington succeeded in creating a black presence on the federal level by developing a very close relationship with Presidents Cleveland, McKinley, Roosevelt, and Taft. August Meier argues that Washington, despite his nonpolitical public stance, was involved in "patronage distribution" under both Roosevelt and Taft and got "out the negro vote for Republicans at national elections." Meier goes on to say that Roosevelt consulted Washington "almost as soon as he [Roosevelt] took office," and Roosevelt later claimed that "Washington had approved his policy of appointing fewer but better qualified negroes."[46]

Oddly enough, despite his political success at the federal level, like William Lloyd Garrison, Washington felt that ultimately state governments would go beyond the federal government in meeting the political needs of black people. Washington produces very little evidence to support this assertion, but he makes it clear in his autobiography that he feels that the end of the political inequalities between blacks and whites will come when each state applies the franchise laws equally to both. Washington concludes by insisting that any other solution "will be unjust to the Negro, unjust to the white-man, and unfair to the rest of the states in the union."[47]

The federal and state governments both have a role to play in assuring that the "rules of the game" are equally applied in the American Crucible, but in Washington's view the people who truly make the system work are the rich Americans. In *The Republic*, the philosopher Plato argues that virtue will be achieved in the state only when an elite class of specially trained guardians rule. Socrates (through whom Plato speaks) teaches that the guardians "will be the best of all citizens."[48] When one reads Washington's opinions regarding the rich, it is clear that he views them as "guardians" of the American Crucible, for in his mind they possess all the virtues that the other classes must emulate to succeed. What are the exemplary virtues that the rich possess and that are lacking or deficient in others? First, Washington notes that the rich are charitable, and he lambasts the critics who dispute their claims in this regard, saying that "if wealthy people were to part all at once with any large proportion of their wealth," it would disorganize and cripple great business enterprises.[49] Second, Washington felt that what made the rich succeed was that they believed that they were instruments of divine will, and that tampering with their stewardship of the American economy could only end in regression and suffering. Washington's relationship with John D. Rockefeller vividly illustrates this. He says, "The more I come into contact with wealthy people, the more I believe that they are going in the direction of looking upon their money simply as an instrument which God has placed in their hands for doing good with. I never go to the office of Mr. John D. Rockefeller, who more than once has been generous to Tuskegee, without being reminded of this."[50] Third, Washington argued that the rich were successful guardians because they had mastered the virtues of patience, self-control, politeness, and the like, characteristics that always impressed him when he came "into contact with wealthy and noted men."[51] Finally, Washington was convinced that no one could become a guardian in the American Crucible unless he or she engaged in the pursuit of wealth as if it were a religion, and in his famous Atlanta Exposition address of 1895, he constantly adumbrates this theme.[52] In summary, self-control, patience, politeness, and the loss of self in a great cause, these are the necessary virtues for success in America, and Washington saw them best manifested in the rich and least manifested in black society of the time.

Soon after the Altanta Exposition address, in which he repeats more forcefully than at any previous time the view that blacks should accommodate themselves to the status quo and that the future of the black race was in the South, opposition began to develop to Washington's views, opposition that became more effective and vocal as time progressed. However, before considering this, some comments should be made on Washington's tactics, which many insist included the unfair stifling of the critics of the Tuskegee political machine.

The Tactics of Booker T. Washington

Historians of African-American thought argue that Washington was publically apolitical but privately sought to rectify many of the political and civic wrongs that he was either ambiguous about or silent on in public. Meier demonstrates that his nonpolitical stance to the contrary, Washington "was deeply involved in efforts to prevent disfranchisement and other forms of discrimination."[53] Meier documents how Washington privately "lobbied against the Hardwick disfranchisement bill in Georgia in 1899," although his public ambiguity on the subject of equality of the vote "permitted southern whites to think that he accepted disfranchisement."[54] Similarly, he was involved behind the scenes in trying to prevent a disfranchisement law from being passed in Maryland and fought railroad segregation and lack of black representation on juries.[55] Meier insists that despite his accommodating tone, "Washington was surreptitiously engaged in undermining the American race system by a direct attack upon disfranchisement and segregation, and in spite of his strictures against [black] political activity he was a powerful politician in his own right."[56]

In the previous section, we discussed Washington's strong links to Presidents Roosevelt, Taft, Cleveland, and McKinley, and we examined his ties to the rich. It should be noted that appropriations made by philanthropists and philanthropic organizations like Andrew Carnegie, Julius Rosenwald, and the Jeanes funds were greatly influenced by Washington's suggestions, and it is believed that "negro schools that received Carnegie libraries received them at Washington's suggestion, and even applied for them upon his advice."[57] As a result of his connections and popularity with whites, Washington wielded a great deal of influence in the black community, influence that was felt in areas besides just "philanthropy and political appointments."[58] For example, he had considerable control over the Negro press and the Negro churches, and he also controlled the Afro-American Council, the most powerful black civil rights organization between 1902 and 1904.[59] At the height of his power, Washington exercised an almost authoritarian control over blacks' dealings with white society, a power that eventually alienated many blacks, including W.E.B. Du Bois, from his program.[60]

Washington had great influence on black development not only inside the United States but outside and especially in Africa. Indeed, many of the white colonialists in Africa requested and received Washington's advice on their own racial problems. Lord Grey of the British South Africa Company, which controlled Rhodesia; E. B. Sargent, the South African Commissioner of Education; and the Germans in Togo, all asked for Washington's advice regarding the blacks in their colonies. The Germans requested and succeeded in persuading Washington to send African-Americans trained at Tuskegee to aid in building the cotton industry in Togo. Washington also urged South African blacks to adopt "the same accommodation, economic and cultural subordination, and incentives to individual self-help that characterized his racial philosophy in the United States."[61]

Despite Washington's accommodating attitude toward colonialism, many black Africans avidly sought his aid and advice. In 1908, prominent Liberians asked Washington to intercede with President Roosevelt for a loan that was finally approved by the Senate in 1912. Rev. John L. Dube, the famous Zulu educator who subsequently became president of the South African National Congress and who was later dubbed "the Booker T. Washington of South Africa" for his Accommodationist philosophy of education, also visited Tuskegee and was deeply influenced by Washington. Finally, Washington helped sponsor the International Conference on the Negro in 1912, and although more whites (mostly Christian missionaries) attended than blacks, a significant number of blacks, including Bishop Henry M. Turner attended. (Plans for a second conference were interrupted by Washington's death.) In 1900 while in London, Washington also met with Henry Sylvester Williams of Trinidad and the other organizers of the First Pan-African Conference that was held there that year. This conference brought together blacks from all over the world to discuss their common fate. It was the first of five conferences, and W.E.B. Du Bois attended it.[62] Regardless of his activity on behalf of foreign blacks, Washington was not a Black Nationalist in the mode of Bishop Turner. In fact, although he was receptive to plans for "American negro enterprise and ethnocentric philanthropy in Africa," he totally rejected the concept of emigration for African-Americans. Harlan is close to the truth when he concludes that internationally Washington believed in the concept of the White Man's Burden and as a result was cool to a militant Black Nationalism, exactly the kind of black nationalism that would be needed to end the colonial system.

The attacks on Washington grew increasingly intense after 1900, and the opposition took on firm organizational form with the formation of the strongly political and integrationist National Association for the Advancement of Colored People (NAACP), in 1910. The formation of the NAACP signified that Washington was rapidly losing his hold over the fortunes of blacks in America, and indeed "by the time he died Washington had lost much of his power."[63] However, to understand this fall requires a brief examination of the ideology of his critics.

Opposition to Booker T. Washington

Washington's opponents were mostly the educated elite of African-American society, especially in the North, and a minority of southerners who could not accept the Politics of Accommodation. The northern opposition spanned a broad spectrum of the professions, including educators, doctors, and journalists, but most of its members were distinguished lawyers and northern ministers of upper-class denominations. Typical of the ministers was Francis J. Grimke, who, for many years, pastored Washington's fashionable Fifteenth Street Presbyterian. At first Grimke followed the Tuskegee line but as early as 1900 began to oppose it after he realized it justified the disfranchisement of most blacks because they could not meet certain property and other qualifications. Grimke depicted the supporters of this practice as "traitors" to the Negro race and "insisted that negroes should never cease to agitate until their manhood and citizenship were recognized." Later, Grimke became president of the Washington branch of the NAACP and by 1903 denounced the notion that "if Negroes acquired property everything would be all right."[64]

Another northern critic who vehemently opposed the accommodating ideology of Washington and also attacked paternalists toward the Negro, like Presidents Roosevelt, Taft, Wilson, "and anyone else," was Harvard-educated William Monroe Trotter. Trotter founded the black newsweekly the *Boston Guardian* in 1901, and he used its pages to call for full civil rights for the African-American and to castigate the Tuskegee machine. As George W. Forbes, the coeditor of Trotter's newspaper, expressed the anti-Tuskegee sentiment, "It would be a blessing for the race if the Tuskegee school should burn down, etc."[65] The Trotterites challenged the Tuskegee line in the press, confronted Washington at meetings of his Afro-American Council, and in 1902 nearly started a riot when they disrupted a meeting of the Boston branch of his National Business League as Washington attempted to speak.[66] For his role in the disruption, Trotter was jailed for thirty days for disturbing the peace.[67] Trotter continued to criticize Washington, and in 1905 along with W.E.B. Du Bois was instrumental in founding the pro–civil rights and anti-Washington Niagara Movement, the first effort to give the anti-Tuskegee line an organized national voice. Eventually, most of the supporters of the Niagara Movement, including Du Bois, became members of the NAACP when it was founded in 1910. After the NAACP's founding, the opposition to Washington's line intensified.

The sociologist John Dollard, in his book *Caste and Class in a Southern Town*, suggests that the struggle between Washington and his critics was at base a conflict between the more militant northern black and the less strident southern black.[68] Dollard's view is an oversimplification of this complex issue, however. For example, President John Hope of Atlanta Baptist College, the son of a well-to-do white man of Augusta, Georgia, and an 1894 graduate of Brown University, was a southern black critic of Washington. Indeed, Meier writes that six months after Washington's Atlanta Exposition address, Hope urged blacks to be "dissatisfied," to refuse to accept an accommodating status in society, and to "agitate for complete equality, even social equality."[69] On the other hand, Dollard is correct when he suggests that Washington's strongest support was in the South, support that was centered among groups like businessmen of all sectors who depended on the Negro market; southern ministers; southern educators, especially graduates of Tuskegee; and black newspaper editors. Typical of these educators are William Hooper Councill (d. 1909) of the State Normal and Industrial School at Huntsville, Alabama. Councill had been an editor and minor politician during Reconstruction and was appointed to head the school in 1876. In his public statements he was perhaps more accommodating than Washington, for he praised the virtues of domestic work and advised of the need for blacks to start from the bottom to reach the top. He even suggested that discrimination actually helped the Negro by forcing him to support Negro business. At the same time, continuing a pattern that we saw in Washington himself, many blacks like ex-Texan Populist John B. Rayner openly supported the Accommodationist line but privately condemned the system. Meier reveals that Rayner privately wrote that "God did not intend for one part of humanity to feel superior to another part, complained of the limitations upon negro aspirations and of deprivation of rights and called the southern whites the most unreasonable of men."[70]

One of the major ways by which the Tuskegee machine dominated the African-American community was through its control of the press, and it is believed that two important black papers, The Age and The Colored American Magazine, were "for a time, partly owned by Washington."[71] Although the black press generally supported the Washington line, not all editors were submissive to it. Thomas Fortune of The Age began his journalistic career as a militant but in the 1890s became a friend of Washington and a proponent of the Tuskegee approach. However, after President Roosevelt discharged three black regiments on charges of rioting in Brownsville, Texas, in 1905—charges that were later proven false—Fortune, unlike Washington, openly criticized the decision. As Meier relates, Fortune "declined to preach the gospel of goodwill or to refrain from saying anything that would irritate the situation, since this could be done only by submission to prejudice, discrimination and mob rule."[72] It is apparent that some of the strongest supporters of the Politics of Accommodation gave it only qualified support, a kind of support that would sometimes turn into outright opposition when the situation warranted it.

The most pernicious method by which Washington controlled the African-American community was by the illegitimate, deceitful, and spiteful use of his political power, of which press control was but a facet. Harlan tells how Washington paid spies to infiltrate his opponents' gatherings, including the Niagara Movement,[73] controlled black fraternal organizations,[74] prevented opponents from obtaining employment, and even engaged in exposés of his critics. For example, Washington had pro-Tuskegee reporters depict innocent interracial meetings of Mary White Ovington's Cosmopolitan Society of America (Ovington was a wealthy white supporter of the NAACP) in 1908 and 1911 as interracial trysts. This yellow journalism so embarrassed Ovington that as late as her 1947 memoirs she was blaming the bad publicity on the "connivance of a few clubmembers." Little did she realize that it was Washington who had orchestrated the affair.[75] One of the best examples of Washington's spitefulness is his treatment of the outspoken Atlanta journalist J. Max Barber, who had attended the meeting at Niagara. Washington had initially supported Barber's Voice of the Negro, but when he realized that Barber would criticize anyone, including himself, Washington turned against him. Washington became an outright enemy of Barber after Barber secretly sent a telegram to the northern press critical of the local whites and the role of the press during the Atlanta Riot of 1906. Washington's white patrons were upset, and they had Washington put so much pressure on Barber that he fled to Chicago. Barber then tried to restart the *Voice*, but it folded, and he subsequently founded a newspaper called *The Chicago Conservator*. After this effort failed he went to Philadelphia to teach at a manual labor school. However, after a member of the school's board of trustees learned from Washington that Barber was "incompetent," and taught "colored people to hate white people," he was fired.[76] In the end, Barber worked his way through dental school and set up practice in Philadelphia to escape Washington's wrath. In short, the nonpolitical Washington wielded power like a Machiavellian prince, while publically teaching accommodation.

W.E.B. Du Bois's Criticism of Washington

The most articulate critic of the Politics of Accommodation was the famous black sociologist W.E.B. Du Bois (1868–1963). Du Bois was born and reared in Massachusetts, attended Fisk University, and went to Harvard, where in 1895 he received a Ph.D. in sociology. He subsequently studied in Berlin and taught at many universities, including Atlanta University, Wilberforce in Ohio, and the University of Pennsylvania. Du Bois was a prolific writer whose works include *The Philadelphia Negro; Black Reconstruction in America 1860–1880; Dusk of Dawn*, his autobiography; and *The Suppression of the African Slave Trade*, to name a few. From 1910 to 1934 he was editor of the NAACP's monthly publication *The Crisis*. After his retirement as a professor of sociology, he served as NAACP research director from 1944 to 1948 and was fired by the NAACP in 1948 as he became increasingly left wing.[77] As his background shows, Du Bois, by academic training and exposure, possessed all the intellectual and other tools that would allow him to approach African-Americans' problems from a broader perspective than that of Washington, which was why although they both shared many of the same premises at the start, they radically diverged in the end. He makes his most open attack on Washington in the essay "Of Booker T. Washington and Others," in his classic *Souls of Black Folk*. This essay will be used as the context from which to outline his criticisms.

Meier states that until 1900 the ideologies of Du Bois and Washington seemed quite similar, and in fact as late as 1902 the outspoken critic of Washington, William Monroe Trotter, characterized Du Bois as "trying to get into the bandwagon of Tuskegee" and concluded that "he is no longer to be relied upon."[78] According to Meier until 1900, "both [DuBois and Washington] tended to blame Negroes largely for their condition, and both placed more emphasis on self-help and duties than on rights. Both placed economic advancement before universal manhood suffrage, and both were willing to accept franchise restrictions based not on race but on education and/or property qualifications equitably applied."[79]

Du Bois states that by 1900 he was becoming increasingly concerned about Washington less because of ideology than because of his powers of patronage in the black community and his control of the black press.[80] This political and press power combined with the fact that Washington downplayed the open struggle for political and civil rights made the authoritarian Tuskegee machine especially dangerous in Du Bois's opinion.

Du Bois begins his critique by saying that by succeeding in gaining the support of both blacks and whites for the Politics of Accommodation, Washington had accomplished what no other black in American history had done, including Frederick Douglass. Therefore, as a result of his success, Washington was not only a leader of the black race but the white race also. ("Booker T. Washington arose essentially the leader of not one race but two—a compromise between the South, the North and the Negro.")[81] Du Bois goes on to say that the times were propitious for the success of Washington's ideology, because the northern interests that were investing strongly in the southern economy wanted "peaceful cooperation" rather than racial ferment there.[82] Furthermore, Washington had thoroughly mastered the "thought of triumphant commercialism and the ideas of material prosperity" that had become the accepted path of America of the post-Reconstruction period. Du Bois concludes that as a result, it should not be surprising that Washington in his commitment to the "gospel of wealth" saw as "unproductive the picture of a lone black boy poring over a French grammar amid the weeds and dirt of a neglected home."[83] Du Bois notes that the accommodationism in Washington's thought, aptly exhibited in the Atlanta Exposition speech, also enabled him to become the "national compromiser" to whom both white racists and conservatives could point as a model. To the white racists, the speech represented a black "surrender of the demand for civil and political equality"; to the conservatives it was seen as a "working basis for mutual understanding." Du Bois adds, "So both approved it, and today its author is certainly the most distinguished southerner since Jefferson Davis, and the one with the largest personal following."[84]

Next, Du Bois criticizes Washington's Atlanta speech by saying that in the speech Washington was asking blacks to give up three things—political power, insistence on civil rights, and higher education. Du Bois argues that the speech revealed that Washington's ideology had become one of "work and money to such an extent as to overshadow the higher aims of life."[85] Du Bois urges influential blacks like the Grimkes (ministers), Kelly Millers (intellectuals), and Bowens (theologians) to speak out against Washington and insisted that the reconciliations between the North and South should not be marked by the "industrial slavery" and "civil death" of the African-American.[86] Finally, he urges educated African-Americans to lead the fight to obtain those "inalienable rights" that are granted in the Constitution and to persevere in the struggle, although "such opposition involves disagreement with Mr. Booker T. Washington."[87]

Whenever he criticized Washington's educational philosophy, Du Bois attacked most vehemently Washington's belief in the primacy of industrial training. As Du Bois sees it, a child needs two kinds of education, "one dealing with knowledge and character, the other part seeking to give the child the technical education necessary to earn a living under present circumstances."[88] Du Bois agrees that part of this is accomplished by industrial training, but only a part, because the people who teach in these schools must understand modern civilization in order to impart it to the children. This understanding is primarily achieved through a study of the liberal arts, and so to provide industrial training without first providing higher training in the liberal arts "is simply throwing your money to the winds."[89] Du Bois insists that "schoolhouses do not teach themselves—piles of brick and machinery do not send out men,"[90] and he stresses that every race including the Negro race must have a broad training for its top 10 percent or "talented tenth." Finally, Du Bois states that it is from the talented tenth that the "missionaries of culture" will be produced who will carry the "real breath of life into the black community."[91]

It should be noted that Du Bois was by no means the first to challenge Washington's educational views. Anderson relates how all along, a "powerful cadre of missionary educators and black leaders would not accept industrial training as the dominant form of black education." Nevertheless, although it was rejected "by black teachers and the leaders of black schools and colleges," the Hampton–Tuskegee ideal was eagerly embraced by America's political and business elite.[92] This enabled it to overshadow the alternate view. Du Bois's contribution is unique because it made the differing outlooks on black education not only a pedagogical but a political issue.

Paradoxically, Arnold Rampersad, in his book *The Art and Imagination of W.E.B. Du Bois*, contends that by 1933, in the aftermath of the depression and the generally slow progress toward African-American equality, Du Bois moved closer to Washington in strategy. At this time Rampersad depicts Du Bois as advising the African-American to practice a "voluntary self-segregation,"[93] to focus on practical training and economics, and to recognize that because of the lack of a coherent philosophy and modern skills training, both liberal arts schools and vocational schools had failed blacks. During this period Du Bois "called for a united college and vocational system, a new rigor of training and scholarship, greater emphasis on industrial training, and a dedication to ideals of poverty, work, knowledge and sacrifice."[94] Unlike Washington, however, Du Bois did not disapprove of inter-racialism, insisting that voluntary self-segregation not come at the expense of the African-American's "civil, economic, or social rights,"[95] and, indeed, Du Bois saw such self-segregation as a means to enhance rather than take away the African-American's rights. In his African-American civil rights advocacy Du Bois never dismissed any strategy that might be useful, including Accommodation. At the same time, he insisted that if a strategy's core values taught a retreat from equal citizenship for African-Americans, he would reject it and fight it.

The Odyssey of W.E.B. Du Bois

As was stated, Du Bois was instrumental in helping to form the NAACP and became editor of its publication The Crisis, in addition to serving as the organization's research and publicity director. After his debate with Washington, however, Du Bois's ideology continued to undergo changes regarding the status of African-Americans. At one point he saw the white working class as the African-American's biggest enemy, but "by 1904 he had come to believe that economic discrimination was in a large part the cause of the race problem, and to feel sympathetic toward the Socialist Movement."[96] Later, Du Bois viewed both African-Americans and Africans as exploited by capital, "and he predicted that the exploited of all races would unite and overthrow capital, their common oppressor."[97] Finally, Du Bois became disillusioned about the possibilities for solving the race and class question in America, and in 1961 he migrated to Ghana under Kwame Nkrumah. (Ghana was the first black African country to gain independence from the colonial system. It did so in 1957.) Du Bois became a citizen of Ghana in 1961 and died there in 1963.[98] Meier sums up succinctly Du Bois's contributions to the struggle for American racial integration in the following way: "In fact, despite his early tendencies toward an accommodating viewpoint, and despite his strong sense of racial solidarity and integrity, Du Bois expressed more effectively than any of his contemporaries the protest tendency in Negro thought, and the desire for citizenship rights and integration into American society."[99]

V

Marcus Garvey and the Resurgence of Black Nationalism

Racial Equality by Integration: A Survey

After the decline of the Politics of Accommodation, the National Association for the Advancement of Colored People (NAACP), the Urban League, and later the African-American union organization the Brotherhood of Sleeping Car Porters were the major organizations committed to fighting for integration. The interracial NAACP was founded in 1910, after a white socialist, William English Walling, saw a race riot in Springfield, Illinois, in 1908. Most of the members of the Niagara Movement joined the new organization, although William Monroe Trotter declined because he was "suspicious of the motives of white people."[1] The NAACP was made up of a "distinguished gathering of educators, professors, publicists, bishops, judges and social workers," and Moorfield Storey of Boston was elected its first president.[2] The only African-American officer, W.E.B. Du Bois, was given the post of director of publicity and research.[3]

The NAACP's call for full civic, economic, and political rights; equality in transportation; integrated education; a jury of one's peers; and so on, was identical to that of the Niagara Movement, and its commitment to fight directly for these rights was equally firm. At its inception, the NAACP was attacked as "a capricious, irresponsible organization that would draw its main inspiration from the dreamings of the Niagara Movement," and as most of America's leading white philanthropists supported Washington, they denounced it. Some blacks also thought its formation unwise.[4] Until the 1930s, the NAACP's efforts were aimed mainly at educating the American public about the miseries under which many African-Americans lived, and it launched public campaigns against lynchings and voting discrimination and made efforts to mobilize the black vote. The height of success for the NAACP in its early years was reached in 1930 when President Hoover's nominee to the Supreme Court, Judge John H. Parker, was rejected by the Senate because he once opposed Negro suffrage. Other organizations were involved, like the Urban League and the Brotherhood of Sleeping Car Porters, but most of the credit went to the NAACP. This political victory vividly illustrates the distance that African-Americans had traveled from the apolitical days of the Politics of Accommodation.

The Urban League, organized in New York in 1910, was an interracial organization that sought to do by conciliation and persuasion what the NAACP was trying to do more actively. Its emphases from the beginning were mainly in the job-training and social-welfare areas, and they remain the same today. Booker T. Washington supported the Urban League, not only because it included among its founders strong Tuskegee supporters like Ruth Standish Baldwin, the widow of William H. Baldwin, Jr., a Tuskegee trustee and adviser, but because its emphasis on seeking job opportunities and alleviating African-American working conditions reflected his own nonconfrontational public style. As a result, he urged his supporters to join it, and "he also gave friendly advice to its staff officers from time to time."[5] The Brotherhood of Sleeping Car Porters, headed by a former African-American socialist, A. Philip Randolph, was organized in 1925 and became an important political and social pressure group both in labor circles and in the area of civil rights. The brotherhood was instrumental in pressuring President Franklin Roosevelt into signing an executive order in 1941 outlawing discrimination in war industries and the armed services. Of these three groupings, the NAACP became the largest and most famous and eventually became as influential in its own time as Booker T. Washington was in his.

Despite the fact that by the second decade of the twentieth century the NAACP had become very influential, there was a feeling among some African-Americans, especially the migrants from the South who were now flocking to work in northern industries, West Indian immigrants, and ex-servicemen, that the NAACP was oriented toward middle- and upper-class blacks. As the sociologist E. Franklin Frazier characterized it, "The National Association for the Advancement of Colored People, which had fought uncompromisingly for the Negro, had never secured, except locally and occasionally, the support of the masses. It has lacked the dramatic element."⁶ Into this vacuum stepped a Jamaican-born black who was determined to write a different script. This future black hero was Marcus Mosiah Garvey.

Garvey's Early Career

Marcus Garvey (1887–1940) was born in St. Ann's Bay, Jamaica, on August 7, 1887, the son of a stonebreaker. Garvey was born a Methodist, and his early education was at a Methodist school, although he became a Catholic later in his life. Garvey left school at sixteen and after a series of odd jobs became a printer in the firm of P. Austin Benjamin in Kingston, the capital of Jamaica. Garvey was a quick study and soon advanced to the post of foreman of the printing plant. It was during his tenure as foreman that Garvey became aware of the severe economic exploitation of the Jamaican masses by the white oligarchy and of the debilitating color prejudice that prevailed among the nonwhites of Jamaica. Garvey discovered that the Jamaican upper, middle, and lower economic and social classes roughly corresponded to skin color. In this scheme, the ruling minority was usually white, the middle class was most often brown, and the masses on the bottom were mostly black. Unlike in the United States, where racial barriers were not fluid, Garvey noted that a minority of blacks because of business successes, educational or cultural attainments, or a combination of these were accepted into the upper classes. Unfortunately, Garvey noted that most of the successful blacks saw the world "from a white and coloured mind" and failed to help the other, less fortunate, blacks.⁷

In the wake of an earthquake that ravaged Jamaica in 1907, Garvey's printers' union went on strike, and despite his youth, Garvey, became the strike leader. The strike was eventually broken, but Garvey, who had been offered money to defect, never deserted his fellow strikers and refused to return to the job even after most of the others did so. For his militant stand, Garvey was blacklisted by private printers, and he later took a job in the government's printing office. After the strike experience, Garvey felt that positive action had to be taken to raise the consciousness of the Jamaican black masses. To fulfill this need he founded a periodical called *Garvey's Watchman* in 1907. He was inspired to pursue this goal by Dr. Robert Love, a U.S.-educated black from the Bahamas, who was already publishing a nationalist weekly paper there.[8] After this project failed, with Dr. Love's assistance Garvey formed a political group called the National Club around 1908 and subsequently founded another publication called *Our Own*. However, Advised by Dr. Love to seek more experience and in need of money, Garvey left Jamaica in 1910 for Central America.[9]

In his travels to Costa Rica, Panama, Nicaragua, and Honduras, Garvey was shocked by the treatment of the West Indian migrants who worked on the Panama Canal and on the United Fruit Company's plantations, and in 1911 he returned to Jamaica to protest. The British rulers there refused to commit themselves to protect "overseas" Jamaicans, however, and insisted "that if the Jamaicans disliked their treatment abroad they could always return home."[10] Rebuffed in Jamaica, Garvey decided in 1912 to go to England itself to protest.

Garvey stayed in England for two years despite being appalled at the low status of blacks there. He took classes at Birbeck College and used the opportunity to meet "blacks from all over the world." While in England, he also became acquainted with the Egyptian nationalist Duse Mohammed Ali, who in his *African Times and Orient Review* was already preaching Black Nationalism and anticolonialism. (Subsequently, Ali became editor of Garvey's *Negro World* for a period.) Most importantly, in England Garvey read Washington's *Up from Slavery*, which brought to his attention the strictures that the Jim Crow system placed on African-Americans. It was after reading Washington's autobiography that Garvey exclaimed, "Where is the black man's government? Where is his King and Kingdom?"[11] Soon after, Garvey decided to go back to Jamaica and form the Universal Negro Improvement Association (UNIA) to correct the deficiency. He left Southampton, England, on July 15, 1914.

Illustrative of the extreme racism that dominated the world's thinking at the time is the fury with which even Jamaican blacks greeted Garvey's use of the word *Negro* in the name of the organization. However, with the assistance of some friends, including several whites, he started his organization in Kingston on July 20, 1914.[12] Soon afterward, Garvey made plans to visit Booker T. Washington, whose 1912 Conference on the Negro was attended by blacks from many countries and whose proceedings were reported in Mohammed's *African Times and Orient Review*. Washington died before Garvey arrived, but he decided to visit Tuskegee anyway. Garvey arrived in the United States on March 23, 1916, the date that begins the history of the Garvey Movement in this country.

Garvey's Later Career and the Garvey Movement

After visiting Tuskegee, Garvey decided to make a quick tour of thirty-eight American states to get some pointers from various African-American leaders that would be useful in his struggle in Jamaica. Garvey was not impressed with the leaders he encountered, however, feeling they lacked concrete programs and were "opportunists."[13] Eventually, Garvey decided to set up a branch of the UNIA in Harlem and then return to Jamaica. Unfortunately, the Harlem branch was characterized by frequent splits even before Garvey left the country, and the members requested that Garvey take it over to "save them from the politicians."[14] The historian Lawrence W. Levine questions Garvey's claim that he needed the "inducement" of peacemaker to base the UNIA in the United States. Levine suggests that Garvey quickly saw that America's large and diverse black population offered better opportunities than those in Jamaica for a race leader with worldwide ambitions. Levine feels that Garvey admitted as much eight months later, when he stated that "industrially, financially and economically, blacks worldwide must 'defer to the American brother.'"[15] In any case, the Harlem branch, largely due to Garvey's presence, became the center of the movement. From that base the movement spread all over the United States, Central America, and the Caribbean, and by 1919 there were thirty branches.

What were the reasons for the phenomenal growth of the Garvey movement? Professor Theodore Vincent advances four reasons, and most Garvey scholars tend to support his conclusions. First, Vincent notes that World War I, in which blacks saw the Western European nations fighting among themselves and even needing blacks to secure victory, destroyed in their minds the myth of white invincibility, making them more open to a Black Nationalist appeal.[16] Second, Vincent argues that many African-Americans debated whether they should participate in the "white man's war," and he notes that one issue of an African-American newspaper, the *Richmond Planet*, was barred from the U.S. mail for advocating noninvolvement in World War I.[17] Such dissidents Vincent notes were prospective Garveyites. Third, Vincent suggests that returning African-American servicemen who had shed blood for democracy in World War I were not prepared to passively accept American postwar racism. When the racism did not cease (indeed, race riots escalated after World War I) they formed a critical mass for which Garvey's Black Nationalist message struck a responsive chord.[18] Finally, the war stimulated a labor shortage in the

North as millions of men were drafted and German naval activity curtailed mass emigration from Europe. The gap was filled by black migration from the South. These migrants felt rightly or wrongly that the message of the NAACP and Urban League was not targeted at them, and John Hope Franklin is in agreement with Vincent by saying that "it was this feeling, regardless of its justification, that made possible the rise of Marcus Garvey and his Universal Negro Improvement Association."[19]

At the height of the UNIA's popularity, Garvey made a special effort to focus the world's attention on the colonial system that was exploiting Africa. Garvey appealed to the League of Nations asking that this body set up a colony for blacks in Africa, an appeal that was rejected. After this rejection, he opened up unsuccessful negotiations with Liberia for the same purpose. These latter negotiations ended with Garvey criticizing the Liberian government as elitist and class oriented, and having little interest in the masses of black people. Finally, Garvey formed the Universal African Legion to aid in eventually liberating Africa. Regarding propaganda, Garvey's newspaper the *Negro World*, printed in English, Spanish, and French, was so effective that "the Imperial and Colonial Governments immediately passed laws forbidding [its] circulation."[20]

Garvey and the Garveyites also engaged in a variety of other activities. Garvey was instrumental in forming a steamship line called the Black Star Line, and he formed a nurses corps and a flying corps. So successful was he that by 1920 he declared himself Provisional President of the African Empire and claimed to have four million followers.[21] Critics dispute the figures, but even they agree that he had at least half a million followers.[22]

By 1922, however, the critics of Garvey who had opposed his Separatist ideal all along (like the socialists, communists, and NAACP) began to strike a responsive chord with the American public. To begin with, despite Garvey's claims to the contrary, most blacks felt that America was their homeland and were not prepared to leave to go to Africa. This is not to say that Garvey saw the African return as an immediate possibility, but this is how it was interpreted by his critics.[23] Second, Garvey alienated the middle and upper classes of blacks and liberal whites who questioned the practicality and morality of his schemes. Third, as Judith Stein writes, Garvey's prosecution was aided by "a witch's brew of principle and opportunism, righteousness and revenge, [that] rationalized the decisions of the individual blacks within and outside the UNIA to cooperate with the prosecution."[24] It was mostly middle- and upper-class blacks who had varying gripes against Garvey, three of whom (newspaperman and socialist Chandler Owen, newspaperman Robert S. Abbott, and NAACP official William Pickens) wrote a long letter to Attorney General Harry Daugherty on January 1, 1923, "warning of the numerous dangers of Marcus Garvey."[25] Finally, many European allies of the United States, especially those with African colonies, were uneasy about Garvey. In 1925, Garvey, never a sharp businessman, was found guilty of mail fraud and given a five-year term in the Atlanta Penitentiary. After much clamor regarding clemency, in 1927 he was pardoned by President Coolidge and deported to Jamaica, where he continued his struggle and tried unsuccessfully to create a political presence. Efforts to run his movement from Jamaica and London failed, however, and he died in that city in 1940. After Garvey's death, his movement lost its effectiveness, and except for small Garveyite and Islamic sects that survived, the Black Nationalist challenge to integrationist ideology suffered an eclipse that lasted for nearly forty years, until the rise of the Black Power Movement in the 1960s.

The Political Thought of Garvey

Marcus Garvey did not write a formal treatise on political theory as did Plato or Locke or Rousseau or Aristotle. However, political theory is found not only in formal treatises on the subject but in varied sources including religious works, poetry, art, journalism, and speeches of public figures. St. Augustine and St. Thomas Aquinas were primarily theologians, but one can arrive at a fairly consistent picture of their political thought by examining the ideas contained in works like St. Augustine's theological masterpiece *The City of God*, or in *The Summa Theologica* (The sum of theology) of St. Thomas Aquinas. Similarly, when we review the speeches, messages, axioms, and short statements of Marcus Garvey, we find three recurring themes that give us a very good picture of his political ideas. These themes are his view of people, his theory of nationalism, and his theory of state. We shall deal with each of the themes in turn.[26]

Garvey's View of People

Garvey had a very firm and clear view of people. To Garvey, God made all people equal, whether they were black, yellow, red, or white; thus no race should accept inferiority. ("That God we worship and adore has created man in his own image, equal in every respect, wheresoever he may be; let him be red, let him be black; God has created him the equal of his brother.")[27] Garvey argues that all the races in the world, except for the black, accept themselves as equal and approach life in all its dimensions with an equalitarian ethos. As a result of this equalitarian spirit, Garvey insists that these races are daily mastering nature and trying to impose the kind of social and political conditions on the world that will insure their continued equality. Garvey saw it as his "race mission" to instill equalitarianism into the Negro's psyche. As he puts it, "The UNIA desires that the four hundred million members of our race see life as the other races see it." He goes on to remark that the "great white race sees life in an attitude of sovereignty," and so do the other races. This is his vision for the black race also.[28]

Garvey suggests that one of the reasons why blacks may have fallen behind in the equalitarian quest was that they held erroneous conceptions about the proper relationship between the physical and spiritual realms. As Garvey saw it, we must realize that while God is interested in our spiritual being, "man's physical body is for his own protection, is for his own purpose."[29] Thus, it is up to the particular race to master its own fate in the world "and not blame God and Christ for the things that happen to us in the physical." Following this logic, Garvey argues that black people are responsible for their own fates in the physical world and should not "blame the white man for physical conditions for which we ourselves are responsible."[30] To Garvey, in the physical world, "power is the only argument that satisfies man," and he counsels that blacks will never achieve an equalitarian status until they have "power of every kind." It is only when blacks achieve power in areas like "education, science, industry, politics and higher government" that other nations will see them, or, as Garvey goes on to declaim, "if they will not see, then feel."[31]

Because of Garvey's attempt to link the past history and future destiny of blacks to a particular conception of God, some Garvey scholars, including Randall K. Burkett, categorize the Garvey Movement as mainly a religious movement. Burkett sees Garvey struggling with the religious "problem of the day," as he attempts to define God in such a way that God is not responsible for a "suffering world," while insisting that God's purposes are being achieved through that suffering.[32] Efforts to explain the Garvey Movement as mainly a religious rather than a political movement are not persuasive, however. Garvey's emphasis on ceremony, rituals, titles, and the linking of rulership to God is roughly similar to the British Erastian religious tradition with which Garvey, as a British subject, was familiar. Garvey's God seems but the religious counterpart of a Hobbesian secular monarch whose energies are focused on dealing with the "three principal causes of quarrels . . . in man's nature," which are "first, competition; secondly, diffidence; thirdly, glory."[33] In short, the Garvey Movement is eminently political in its thrust.

Next, Garvey warns blacks that they will have to be aware of three factors if his assertions of equality are to be realized. First, they must recognize that freedom for the individual or the group must come through people's own initiative. ("If you want liberty you yourselves must strike the blow.")[34] Second, Garvey tells blacks that they will not win the struggle with their competitors unless they are true to their consciences, a truth of conscience that will allow them to persevere whatever the obstacles. (Conscience in the Garveyan lexicon, is comparable to the "divine spark" of God or to the "daimon" of Socrates.) Using his 1925 detention in the Atlanta Penitentiary as an example, Garvey insists that although the courts had convicted him, his conscience had not. Thus he would continue to fight despite the setback. ("When a man's conscience convicts him there is no appeal. Thank goodness I am not convicted.")[35] Third, Garvey warns that the race will lose out in world competition unless it views the cause of racial upliftment as a righteous cause. It is this righteousness of cause that will allow blacks to triumph over their enemies "because God almighty is our leader and Jesus Christ our standard bearer."[36] Finally, Garvey advises that if blacks practice these maxims, they will conquer their biggest enemies, racial disunity and ill discipline, and maximize their strengths—senses of love, justice, equity, charity, and so on— which no other races possess.[37] To maximize these virtues, however, Garvey, like the Pan-Negro Nationalists, insists that blacks need a nation of their own.

Garvey's Theory of Nationalism

The philosopher Aristotle in his treatise *Politics* states that the polis (Greek city-state) is the ultimate form of human organization, for it is only in the polis that people can fully realize themselves. Like his Pan-Negro Nationalist predecessors, Garvey can be depicted as arguing that nations are similar natural entities and only in their own separate nations can the various races and the individuals who belong to them realize themselves. There are literally hundreds of places in Garvey's writings where he stresses the importance of racial nationalism, but one of the most important examples is in a speech that he gave in

Madison Square Garden in New York in 1924. Welcoming back a UNIA delegation that had been sent to Europe and Africa to negotiate for a black homeland there, Garvey says:

All men should be free—free to work out their own salvation. Free to create their own destinies. Free to nationally build up themselves for the upbringing and rearing of a culture and civilization of their own. Jewish culture is different from Irish culture. Anglo-Saxon culture is unlike Teutonic culture. Asiatic culture differs from European culture, and, in the same way, the world should be liberal enough to allow the Negro latitude to develop a culture of his own.[38]

Garvey goes on to insist that of all the black organizations in the United States, the UNIA was the only one fighting for an independent black nation. The others, like the NAACP, were trying to make blacks integral parts of existing nations. Garvey states, "The difference between the UNIA and the movements of this country, and probably the world, is that the UNIA seeks independence of government, while the other organizations seek to make the Negro a secondary part of existing governments."[39] This difference in philosophy between Garvey and the other civil rights organizations in the United States led to many clashes and eventually contributed to bringing about his expulsion from the United States.

What are some of the advantages that Garvey sees as accruing to blacks in their own nation? First, Garvey insists that as long as blacks are subjects of other nations or minorities in predominantly white countries, like African-Americans in the United States, the race will never realize its highest ambitions. To illustrate, Garvey says that African-Americans may live in the United States "two hundred or 5,000 years," but since they are a minority they "will never get political equality in this country."[40] Second, Garvey preaches that only in their own nations will blacks be able to set priorities based on their own needs and not be forced to adapt to the needs and aspirations of others. Garvey predicted that in another few decades American white society would face an economic crisis, and if whites have "a problem to feed [their] own children," they certainly will allow blacks to "die to give way, and make way for others who are better prepared to live."[41] Finally, Garvey teaches that a return to Africa will enable a true black aristocracy whose honors will be based on merit to emerge. This meritorious aristocracy will be the exact opposite of the "false" aristocracy that in Garvey's eyes "bombastic Negroes" have tried to maintain in the Western world at the expense of the masses.[42] In summary, the rise of a true meritocracy, progress based on a solid foundation, the space in which to actualize their highest ambitions, and a community whose policies will reflect the black self-interest are the benefits that Garvey sees as accruing to blacks from the establishment of a separate nation.

Garvey's Ideal State

It speaks for the profundity of Garvey's thought that unlike most of the Black Nationalists covered in this study, he had a very vivid vision of the kind of ideal society he wanted to build in Africa. To begin with, Garvey states quite clearly that he is an elitist, and he minces no words when he declares that the burden for good government in a black-run Africa will fall on the shoulders of the ruling minority. As Garvey explains the charge, "A greater responsibility [will be placed] upon the shoulders of the elect and force them either to be the criminals, that some of us believe they are, or the good representatives we desire them to be."[43] In Garvey's good society the elite will exercise a kind of enlightened despotism quite reminiscent of that in Plato's *Laws* and *Statesman*, which Garvey may have read during his studies at Birbeck College in London.[44] As an illustration of his elitism, Garvey explains that although the president of the Republic will be elected, his word will be absolute and he will be "thoroughly responsible for himself and the acts of his subordinates."[45] According to Garvey, the president should also have "the absolute authority to appoint all his lieutenants from cabinet ministers, governors of states and territories, administrators and judges to minor officers."[46] The president will also be paid and looked after satisfactorily, so that neither he nor his dependents will go wanting or be tempted by bribes during his administration. After his term of office has been completed, both "he and his family should be permanently provided for," in order to "remove him from the slightest possible material temptations or want."[47] Finally, Garvey insists that all these provisions will also serve to keep the president independent of "friends" and totally dedicated to state service.[48]

While good public service will be amply rewarded and honored in Garvey's ideal state, a poor public service record will be met with severe punishments. A corrupt president should be removed from office, "publically disgraced, and put to death as an outcast and an unworthy representative of the righteous will of the people."[49] And corrupt judges, administrators, and lesser officials will "be taken from the public, disgraced and stoned to death."[50] Garvey also insists that the wives of all officials from the president downward must keep a strict accounting of all domestic outlays, and if they are dishonest, the offending official and his wife "should be publically disgraced and put to death."[51] Finally, in words reminiscent of George Orwell in 1984, Garvey assures the public that if "any child or member of the family" reports dishonest actions before they are found out by the state officials, the person "should be spared the disgrace and publically honored by the populace for performing a duty to the state."[52]

What kind of economic system would Garvey approve for his state? First, Garvey rejects socialism, because he believes that it encourages "the dreamer's vision" that one day the rich will "divide up their worth with the loafer."[53] Second, he criticizes communism, insisting that a high level of capitalist activity is needed to spur economic development. He further criticizes communism, socialism, and trade unionism because in his view, white communists, socialists, and trade unionists are just as racist toward blacks as white capitalists.[54] (Indeed, Garvey advised blacks to be strikebreakers, for strikes were the few occasions when blacks could take the places of whites.)[55] Finally, although Garvey supported capitalism, he envisioned it in a mixed economic framework in which individual investments over one million dollars and corporate investments over five million dollars would be banned. As he says, "Beyond this, all control, use and investment of money, should be the prerogative of the state with the concurrent authority of the people." Garvey felt that a mixed economic system would better curtail economic imperialism "and prevent the ill-will, hatred and conflicts that now exist between races, people and nations."[56]

Garvey believed that it would take about thirty years to realize his dream of an African nation, but in the meantime he urged blacks to work in three ways to prepare for the day. First, they should rely on their own efforts to advance and not "look to whites in a false direction," as the NAACP was teaching blacks to do.[57] Second, until a black nation was achieved, Garvey urged, like the Black Muslims were to do later, that blacks be loyal citizens in the nations or empires in which they were located. ("We can be as loyal American citizens or British subjects as the Irishman or the Jew, and yet fight for the redemption of Africa, a complete emancipation of the race.")[58] Finally, Garvey warned blacks that they should avoid race mixing and integration because integration is a sham and intermarriage goes against "the laws of

nature."[59] In summary, racial separation, racial self-reliance, and a loyalty to their respective nations are the major obligations that blacks
must fulfill during the interregnum.

Garvey's Organization and Tactics

Although volumes have been written about Marcus Garvey, very
little systematic work has been done on how Garvey concretely went
about organizing the UNIA. The scattered references in the vast Garvey literature show that the key institutions in the Garvey network
were what Garveyites termed "Liberty Halls." Liberty Halls were established in every city where there was a chapter of the UNIA, and
they functioned both as social centers and political meeting places.
The social functions held at these halls consisted of religious worship,
concerts, dances, and public meetings. The New York chapter of the
UNIA and its Liberty Halls constituted the strongest division of the
movement, and while Marcus Garvey headed both the division and
the entire organization, there were heads of the various chapters in
each city.

The chapters hosted a variety of activities for their members. For
example, "members could hold rank in the African Legion, a parami-
tary marching society." They could work for the Royal African Motor
Corps, which consisted of a fleet of moving vans in New York, Philadelphia, and Pittsburgh. The drivers of the vans saw themselves as
"preparing to use their trucks in the struggle for African liberation."[60]
Women could serve in the nurses corps, called the Black Cross
Nurses. As Vincent points out, "few were trained nurses but many
were [already] doing the work of nurses [as maids] at servants wages."
By performing in their Black Cross outfits Vincent suggests that they
"pointed the way to a much needed uplift in status and pay for all
engaged in housework and nursing."[61] During 1917, the UNIA began to
rent and buy property "for what would become cooperative grocery
stores, resturants, laundries, garment factories, dross shops, a greeting
card company, and a publishing house." According to Vincent, "Most
of these businesses were part of the Negro Factories Corporation, an
economic cooperative whose directors were elected annually at UNIA
conventions."[62] In 1919 Garvey's shipping line, the Black Star Line,
was formed. Stein notes that despite its centralized organizational
structure on paper, each chapter adapted itself to the "culture of the
surrounding community." While all tried to provide services like
death and sickness benefits, some focused on social entertainment,

others like the New York division focused on elite culture, yet others like the Boston branch pushed education.[63]

At its 1920 convention the UNIA delegates "created an international leadership comprising nearly two dozen titled officers,"[64] and in 1922 the noble order of the Knights of the Nile was created to honor leaders of the race both in and out of the movement. According to Amy Jacques Garvey, at the 1920 convention the delegates created "the top posts of Potentate, Provisional President of Africa, and American Leader, and two leaders for the West Indies—Eastern and Western Caribbean."[65] The potentate, whom some likened to the Pope because he was "the spiritual head of the organization," along with his deputy, was required to have been born in Africa and to reside there.[66] The specific plans that the UNIA had for the potentate were kept secret, but Amy Jacques Garvey says that the potentate had to show the ability, "capacity and courage to serve in Africa under adverse conditions," because to succeed in his task, he had to "create fraternal and secret orders among the tribes as the exigences of a particular area demanded."[67]

The dynamo of the movement was, however, Garvey. Garvey was not only a brilliant speaker and a keen analyst of the psychology of blacks, he was a tireless campaigner and a creative political tactician. Garvey states that at times he would carry out three months of constant campaigning returning to the New York office only for a few days, and then go out again.[68] Despite his political skills, the record suggests that Garvey was not skilled in business operations, and this lack of business acumen eventually led to the charge of mail fraud. Most Garvey experts suggest that although the crime was legally pinned on Garvey, in fact the errors were due to business incompetence rather than dishonesty. For example, Judith Stein insists that in Garvey's case, "the common legacy of fraud was nonexistent."[69]

Garvey's critics both inside and outside of the organization accused him of using bully tactics against them, including force to get his way. The charges became more intense after the Reverend J. W. Eason, who was elected leader of American Negroes at the UNIA Convention of 1920, was assassinated by two Jamaican immigrant supporters of Garvey in New Orleans, Louisiana, in January 1923.[70] The Eason assassination, along with Garvey's meeting with a Ku Klux Klan leader in 1922, forced figures like A. Philip Randolph and Du Bois to oppose him. Garvey's relations with his critics were not eased by the fact that he distrusted most "light-skinned, middle-class Negroes who constituted so many of the leaders in America," comparing them to

the light-skinned middle class in Jamaica, whom Garvey saw as traitors.[71] In short, the UNIA reflected all the strengths and weaknesses of
Marcus Garvey himself, which is why it collapsed when he was ex-
iled.

Minor Expressions of Black Nationalism

The Garvey Movement was the most powerful expression of Black
Nationalism in the United States from the post-World War I period
to Garvey's deportation in 1927, but the movement was not without
Black Nationalist rivals. In fact, the Garvey era in the United States
was an age of ideological debate and ferment in the black world that
did not occur again until the mid-1960s, so it was by no means certain
at the start that Garveyism would overshadow its Black Nationalist
competitors. It is impossible in a few brief pages to cover all these
expressions; instead, an effort will be made to give a representative
sample of them.

First, there was the African Blood Brotherhood (ABB) of Cyril
Briggs, a former journalist. Briggs organized this secret black brotherhood in 1919, and in the spirit of the Pan-Negro Nationalists and his
future rival Marcus Garvey called for a separate black nation either in
the United States or in South America, the Caribbean, or Africa. In
pursuit of this goal, at one point Briggs urged ABB members to infiltrate the Garvey movement and influence its policies, but Garvey
ousted its members.[72] Shunned by the UNIA, Briggs became a communist in 1925, after which the brotherhood declined.[73]

Another early rival of the UNIA was a group called the Star Order
of Ethiopia and Ethiopian Missionaries to Abyssinia, formed by one
Grover Cleveland Redding in Chicago. (The organization also had
branches in Detroit, New York, and Washington, D.C.) Redding advocated a return to Africa and suggested that African-Americans take out
Ethiopian citizenship under a 1904 Ethiopian–American Agreement.[74]
Redding was more militant than Garvey, and he "secretly sought
funds for an 'armed train' to ride into Dixie and herald the battle for
freedom."[75] After Redding and his followers got involved in a flag
burning incident in 1919 in which two policemen were killed, he was
charged with murder and executed in the summer of 1920.

Another rival to the Garvey Movement was the Islamic line of
Black Nationalism started by Timothy Drew, later the Noble Drew Ali,
of North Carolina. Ali started his movement by preaching to small
numbers of Negroes in North Carolina, but it soon expanded to New-

ark, New Jersey, where he founded the first Moorish Science Temple in 1919, and then to Pittsburgh, Detroit, and Chicago. Ali taught that blacks were actually Moors from Morocco, not Africans, who had been kidnapped and placed in America. Ali claimed that he had come to restore blacks to their true identity and asserted that in the same way as John the Baptist was a messenger for Jesus, Marcus Garvey was a messenger for Ali. Ali urged blacks to cast off their Christian names for Islamic ones, adopt the Islamic religion, be nonviolent and law-abiding American citizens, practice separation from whites, and "wait for the inevitable destruction of the white or European rule, of which the sign from heaven would be a star with a crescent moon."[76] Ali's movement grew, but in 1929 in a factional struggle Ali's chief rival was killed. Ali was arrested and charged with the murder, but after he was released, he disappeared.[77] A follower of Ali, Wallace Fard, went on to found the Black Muslims, to be discussed in a later chapter.

Another Black Nationalist strain that appeared around 1915 is the Movement for Black Judaism. There were many expressions of black Judaism in the 1920s. Indeed, Howard Brotz points out that between 1919 and 1931 "there are records of at least eight black Jewish cults that originated in Harlem."[78] The most interesting sect was led by one Arnold Ford. Ford, like Garvey, preached that Africa was the land of redemption for black people, and he was impressed by the Garvey Movement's militancy, its glorification of blackness, and "its eleva-tion of Africa as the source of all civilization." Despite Garvey's re-fusal to "adopt Judaism as the negro's religion," Ford brought his six hundred blacks into the UNIA.[79] By the late 1920s most of the black Jews that Ford had brought into the UNIA had left it, but he remained as musical director of the UNIA until 1926 "and tried to mediate be-tween the factions that year." After 1926, Ford left the United States and "took his family to Ethiopia to practice Judaism among the native black Jews. He corresponded frequently with Garvey, but his main interest was now with his religion."[80] Ford is supposed to have died in Ethiopia and is believed to have become a Muslim in later life. Brotz speculates that at the period when Ford allegedly went to Ethiopia, America was in the depression, and it is unlikely that Ford's group could have found sufficient funds for a significant migration to Africa. Thus, it may be that Ford resettled in Detroit and the "W. Fard, Ford, or Farrard who founded the Islamic cult in that city and Arnold Ford are the same."[81]

Finally, a more direct descendant of the Garvey Movement itself was the Ethiopia Pacific Movement established in Chicago in 1932.

The movement was headed by Mittie Gordon, "a former lady president of the Chicago division [of the UNIA] and a leading figure at the 1929 UNIA convention." Gordon and her followers remained nominal members of the UNIA, and her movement was obviously "a conscious attempt to carry Garveyism forward under a new banner."[82] In the early 1930s, the group supported Senator Bilbo in his call for repatriation of blacks to Africa. Gordon launched a nationwide attempt to get signatures, and within "eight months some 400,000 signatures were obtained." In 1934, three hundred of Gordon's followers assembled a fleet of "dilapidated trucks, and headed for Washington to lobby for the Bilbo proposal." Most of the trucks never made the Chicago city limits, and since Bilbo's proposal was "a demagogic stunt in the first place," the campaign fizzled.[83]

Vincent notes that on two subsequent occasions Gordon was hauled before U.S. authorities. First, in August of 1941 she was accused of counseling blacks to avoid the draft, but "she denied this, asserting that the organization's principal aim was repatriation of all black people." In her defense, Gordon added that distinguished Americans like Thomas Jefferson and Abraham Lincoln had also advocated emigration. Finally, after the Japanese attack on Pearl Harbor, she ran afoul of the authorities once again, this time for advocating the cause of the Japanese and preaching hatred for the whites.[84] In its militancy the Ethiopia Pacific Movement was a direct descendant of the Garvey Movement and depicted itself as such.

After Black Nationalism suffered an eclipse in the early 1930s, center stage in the African-American struggle was occupied for the next thirty-six years by those expressions of protest that sought to solve the racial dilemma within the existing system. In the next chapter, these approaches will be examined and their records assessed.

VI

Martin Luther King and Moralism

After the decline of the Garvey Movement, the National Association for the Advancement of Colored People (NAACP), with its integrationist philosophy, continued to be the major organ of protest within the black community. The period between 1915 and 1955 is generally considered the most influential of the NAACP's years, and its contributions can best be understood by examining the major strategies it used to advance African-American rights during those forty years. Its first strategy, employed between 1915 and 1948, was to increase African-American voting power by using the courts to strike down discriminatory laws preventing African-Americans from exercising the franchise. In fact, in 1939 it established its tax-exempt arm, the NAACP Legal Defense Fund. It won the case Gunn vs. United States (1915), which declared the "grandfather clause" illegal, and it also filed successful suits against the white primary system, winning cases like Nixon vs. Hendon (1927), Nixon vs. Condon (1932), and Smith vs. Allwright (1944). Of the twenty-six cases it argued before the Supreme Court during this period, it won twenty-four of them.[1] As Joanne Grant notes, these legal successes increased the African-American total vote count only by a fraction, but even this small increment allowed African-Americans to affect the balance of political power in most of the midwestern, northeastern, and border states. Grant cites Henry Lee Moon, director of research for the NAACP, who suggests that it was this mostly pro-Roosevelt African-American vote that enabled Democrat Franklin Roosevelt, to triumph over the Republican governor Thomas Dewey in the 1944 presidential election.[2] Taking advantage of the new international focus that typified American foreign policy after World War II, the NAACP in another strategy presented to the newly

91

formed United Nations a document called an "Appeal to the World," protesting the treatment of African-Americans. This signaled that the NAACP realized the potential influence world opinion could bring to bear on the racial problem in the United States.[3] The NAACP continued to pursue a strategy of struggle against racism in public accommodations, a struggle symbolized by the fact that in Washington, D.C., as late as 1951 blacks were "barred from theaters, movie houses, hotels, and 'white' restaurants."[4] By 1945, however, the NAACP came to see segregated schooling as the basis for the continued racism, and from that time to 1954 it focused on making integrated education the law of the land.

The NAACP's fight against educational segregation had started long before the postwar period. A March 15, 1933, desegregation suit filed against the University of North Carolina was lost on a technicality. In 1935 NAACP counsel Thurgood Marshall (a justice of the U.S. Supreme Court until his retirement in July 1991) "persuaded the Maryland Court of Appeals to order the state university to admit [a black student] Donald Murray"; and starting in Maryland in 1936, the NAACP began its long "and generally successful campaign to equalize teachers' salaries."[5] It was not until 1945, however, when NAACP lawyers like Thurgood Marshall and William Hastie decided to frame future petitions against school segregation so that they would "permit a direct attack on segregation if an opportunity presented itself" that the struggle for school desegregation was joined in earnest. School desegregation as the law of the land was achieved in two stages. In a series of cases like *Sweatt vs. Painter* (1950) and *McLaurin vs. Oklahoma State Regents* (1950), the Supreme Court ruled that "white universities must admit negroes to graduate facilities, if a desired course of study was not available in a negro institution."[6] Then, in the monumental *Brown vs. Board of Education* decision of 1954, a case involving black children of elementary school age in Topeka, Kansas, the Court ruled that school segregation constituted "a denial of equal protection of the laws."[7] This 1954 decision finally made integrated education the law throughout the country.

The question that arises out of the NAACP's intense legal activity is, Why was school desegregation given such a high priority? The answer is because a fundamental tenet of American democracy is that an educated populace is the best assurance for the continuation and preservation of the American system. As an example of this belief, Thomas Jefferson "saw education not only as a means whereby democracy could be preserved, but also a means by which each man must be led to his own happiness."[8] Following this tradition, both black and white Americans see education as the way to foster individualism and become a success in society, and the NAACP chose to use the courts to assure African-Americans this basis for realizing the American dream. After the Supreme Court's 1954 ruling in favor of the NAACP's suit, euphoria hit the African-American community. Integrationists felt that the last great roadblock to racial equality in the United States had been surmounted and that a nonracist United States was a distinct possibility in the not-too-distant future. Events were to prove such hopes premature, however, for despite some notable efforts to comply with the law throughout the United States, massive resistance, especially in the South, greeted the Supreme Court's decision. Several southern state legislatures refused to implement the decision, Southern congressmen issued a "manifesto" in 1956 in which they pledged to work to reverse the decision,[9] random violence and threats were used against many parents and students who tried to comply with the law, and numerous countersuits were filed by local school boards against the Supreme Court's order. Everywhere "defiants of the Court fought as they still do, to prevent equal opportunity for education."[10] Finally, the mounting white resistance to the Supreme Court's ruling and the awareness that long years of litigation would still be required to integrate specific schools gradually deflated the African-American optimism that the legal approach would prove sufficient by itself to solve the racial problem. When in Montgomery, Alabama, in 1955 African-Americans succeeded in integrating a segregated bus line by boycotting it for one year, those who were aware of Legalisms' limits now felt they had found the perfect supplement to it—that of nonviolent protest.

The Moralist Approach: A Profile

Most students of African-American history call the style of protest starting with the famous Montgomery bus boycott of November 1955 and ending with the tragic assassination of Dr. Martin Luther King, Jr., in 1968 the "Moralist" style of protest. It was so named because its adherents reasoned that racial discrimination is not only illegal but runs counter to the American social conscience, which is at base humane and equalitarian. It is because of this rationale that pioneers in the Montgomery bus boycott like E. D. Nixon, an African-American railroad porter;[11] Fred Gray, "a young negro lawyer only one year out of law school, who moonlighted on weekends as a preacher";[12] Clifton

Durr, a white Montgomery lawyer and ex-New Dealer who was instrumental in the effort to file the early suits against Montgomery bus
segregation;[13] Rosa Parks, the seamstress whose refusal to obey the segregationist seating arrangement on a Montgomery bus on December 1,
1955, triggered the boycott; and King, then a twenty-six year-old pastor at Dexter Avenue Baptist Church in Montgomery Alabama, all decided to confront directly the practices of racial discrimination.

Starting with the successful bus boycott of 1955, Moralist tactics
consisted mainly of nonviolent protest against job discrimination, the
challenges against racist practices in public accommodations, support
of nonracists in elections, court suits against all varieties of discrimination, and demonstrations against the illegal elimination of African-
Americans from the voting rolls. In effect, the Moralists, unlike the
Legalists, unleashed a multifaceted and frontal assault on racism and
all its practices in the United States. The Moralist Approach even
added some new words, tactics, and phrases to the rhetoric of American and world protest, for the various "sit-ins," "swim-ins," and even
"jail-ins" of the period were later emulated in locales where civil
rights were lacking from Johannesburg, South Africa, to Warsaw, Po-
land, to Manila, the Philippines, and to Santiago, Chile.[14] It should be
noted that college students played a role in these activities; in fact,
two of the major organs of Moralist-type protest were the Student
Non-Violent Coordinating Committee (SNCC) and the Southern Christian Leadership Conference (SCLC) led by Dr. King.[15]

The mood of optimism engendered by the Moralists reached its
height in the famous march on Washington in the summer of 1963,
when thousands of blacks and whites traveled to Washington, reaf-
firming their commitment to work for the eradication of racism from
American life and restating their faith in the American creed. King
summed up the mood best when he said in the keynote address at the
march: "I have a dream that one day the nation will rise up and live
on the true meaning of its creed: 'We hold these truths to be self-
evident: that all men are created equal.'"[16] Their tactics seemed to pay
off during the years from 1954 to 1965. Almost a direct result of the
Moralists' efforts, the Civil Rights Act of 1964 and the Voting Rights
Act of 1965 were passed during the Johnson administration, segregation in public transportation was eliminated, racism in public facilities was banned, and thousands of African-Americans were added to
the voting rolls.

There was another side to the ledger, however. In the South, all the
confrontations and activity brought little immediate political or eco-

nomic change in the daily lives of the people. Indeed, when the activists left and the demonstrations ceased, the local blacks and their supporters, economically poor and lacking political power, were left to face the full fury of the southern white backlash. A good illustration of the malaise is seen in the fate of the Mississippi Freedom Democratic Party (MFDP). The MFDP was a multiracial Democratic Party delegation from Mississippi formed by black and white Mississippians in 1963. Led by Aaron Henry, it was formed in an attempt to replace the traditional racially exclusive Mississippi Democratic Party delegation at the Democratic Party's convention in Atlantic City in 1964. Given the climate of the times, the hope was that the national Democratic leadership would unseat the all-white party regulars. Instead, the convention, "led by Lyndon B. Johnson and Hubert Humphrey arranged a compromise in which the credentials committee seated the regulars, and decided that the two MFDP delegates could be seated as delegates at large."[17] The compromise embittered the black MFDP delegates, and the great Mississippi civil rights activist Fannie Lou Hamer summed up these feelings well when she said, among other things, that blacks would not support the compromise "because we [blacks] do not have anything to compromise for."[18] Experiences like this led to a great deal of frustration in the Civil Rights Movement, and for the first time some Moralists began to doubt if America had the will to truly come to grips with the racial problem.

Meanwhile, in the northern United States, unemployment coupled with black disgust triggered a series of massive urban riots starting in Harlem in 1964, which spread to all major cities in the United States. During the resulting turmoil a more militant African-American leader, Malcolm X, appeared on the scene. Unlike Dr. King, Malcolm X argued that blacks should not put faith in white society's good will but should instead organize political and economic power bases from which they could proceed to demand relevant change. Ominously, Malcolm warned that the preferred changes should come through ballots, but bullets should be used if that failed. As Malcolm X expressed this philosophy, "In Jacksonville, those were teenagers, they were throwing Molotov cocktails. Negroes have never done that before. But it shows you there's a new deal coming in. It'll be Molotov cocktails this month, and grenades next month, and something else next month. It's be ballots, or it'll be bullets.[19]

By 1966, as the war in Vietnam and its costs escalated, much of the euphoria of the early Civil Rights Movement and the concomitant belief in the efficacy of nonviolence dissipated. In the same year Dr.

King, hitherto almost unanimously praised by blacks, was booed in Chicago by a group of young blacks who termed themselves "Black Power" advocates. King had been introduced to the slogan by Stokely Carmichael and others in late 1966 on a march to complete the abortive Mississippi march of the civil rights activist James Meredith. Meredith, the first black to attend the University of Mississippi, was injured in June of 1966 in a shooting by racists as he attempted a solo antiracist protest. Quickly overcoming his skepticism of the term, King realized that the slogan represented genuine disappointment on the part of African-Americans, especially the young, with both the American system and the Moralist Approach. In other words, King eventually conceded that the "Black Power" slogan was a legitimate expression of Black Nationalism and not a new form of black chauvinism. When the young Chicago blacks booed Dr. King, he asked in puzzlement, "Why would they boo one so close to them?"[20] King answers that they had booed him because he and others had been preaching to them for twelve years that in a "not too distant day they would have freedom all, here and now," but that the "dream they had so readily accepted [had turned] into a frustrating nightmare."[21] Two years later, in Memphis, Tennessee, King was fatally shot, after which the Moralist Approach to civil rights, which had held center stage for nearly fourteen years, lost its mass appeal among African-Americans.[22]

King's Background and Intellectual Influences

As the thought of Marcus Garvey, Booker T. Washington, and Frederick Douglass captured the essence of the political theory of the protest movements of their times, so the political ideas of Martin Luther King Jr., capture the essence of theory of Moralism. In fact, the political theorist Sam Cook, in characterizing the years 1954 to 1968 as the beginning of the modern "black revolution,"[23] depicts King, as not only "the principal leader, catalyst, architect and prophet of the black revolution," but the "chief theorist and interpreter of it as well."[24] Cook goes on to compare King's theoretical and practical contributions to the United States of his time to those of George Washington at the birth of the nation, to John C. Calhoun's for the slaveholding South, to Lenin's for the Russian Revolution, and to Gandhi's for Indian independence.[25] To Cook, what makes King's contributions especially notable is that unlike the others he held no public or political offices with "stable and continuing sources of power, influence and privilege. King was a private citizen."[26]

Martin Luther King, Jr. (1929–1968), was born in Atlanta, Georgia, on January 15, 1929. King states that from his childhood his parents had sensitized him to the evils of racism. His mother, herself the daughter of a successful minister and a college graduate, had told him about segregated schools, restaurants, lavatories and had counseled him that such discrimination was "a social condition rather than a natural order."[27] King's father, the son of a sharecropper and a successful Atlanta minister, had begun to strike back at segregation's brutalities and inanities at an early age and even before King was born had refused "to ride the city buses, after witnessing a brutal attack on a load of Negro passengers."[28] Thus, from his early years, questions of morality and "right order" were placed before King.[29] Later in his life, another influence on King was his wife Coretta, whom he married in 1953. Born in rural Alabama to Obadiah Scott, a fairly well off black farmer, she was very conscious of the evils of racism and has in her own right been a continuing proponent of nonviolent protest, especially after Dr. King's death in 1968.[30]

King followed in his father's footsteps, becoming a Baptist minister, and after attending Morehouse College in Atlanta and Crozier Theological Seminary in Chester, Pennsylvania, he received his Ph.D. from Boston University in 1955. In 1954, while writing his dissertation, he became pastor of Dexter Avenue Baptist Church in Montgomery, Alabama. It is at Dexter that King's civil rights activism began.

Unlike most of the other figures covered so far in this survey of African-American political thought, Dr. King is very explicit about the intellectual and other influences that helped to shape his philosophy and way of life. He explains that even before he went to Morehouse in 1944 he had seen how racist practices had impoverished his playmates and how those practices had split the black and white workers in a plant where against his father's wishes he had worked for two summers.[31] Not until 1944, however, after he had read Henry David Thoreau's famous essay "Civil Disobedience" did he begin to think of the moral reasons why one should refuse to cooperate with an evil system. Spurred on by concern about the moral basis of evil, King states that on entering Crozier Seminary in 1948, he began "a serious intellectual quest for a method to eliminate social evil."[32]

King describes how his intellectual quest led him to read the works of Walter C. Rauschenbach and the great philosophers "from Plato and Aristotle down to Rousseau, Hobbes, Bentham, Mill and Locke,"[33] as well as the works of Hegel, Marx, Nietzsche, Mahatma Gandhi, and the theologians Edward S. Brightman, Reinhold Niebuhr, and L. Harold De Wolf. King undertook this very extensive study of the major Western thinkers, not only to discover insights that would shed some light on the question of evil, but to apply those insights to resolving the racial tragedy in the United States. A survey of what King gleaned from the most relevant of these thinkers will be useful in tracing how he formed his theory of nonviolent protest.

While reading Rauschenbach's *Christianity and Social Crisis*, King found that he disagreed with Rauschenbach's optimistic view of human nature and his belief that man could eliminate most human evils by rectifying poor social and economic conditions. This latter position King felt tended to identify "the Kingdom of God with a particular social and economic system," a tendency he urged "should never befall the Church." Despite these shortcomings, King concedes that "Rauschenbach had done a great service for the Christian church" by insisting that it concern itself with both the spiritual and secular sides of humans, an interpretation of the social and economic responsibility of religion that was to remain with him.[34] For example, at the beginning of the Montgomery bus boycott, King criticized the African-American community for "the factionalism among the leaders, indifference in the educated group, and passivity in the uneducated."[35] But he specifically scolded the Negro ministers because most of them were content to remain aloof "from the area of social responsibility." King admits that much of their indifference "stemmed from a sincere feeling that ministers were not supposed to get mixed up in such earthly, temporal matters as social and economic improvement; they were to 'preach the gospel' and keep men's minds centered on the 'heavenly.' " But however sincere the intent, King felt that this view was "too confined." Such a religion King viewed as a "dry dust religion" and the kind that the Marxists call an opiate of the people.[36]

King does not state systematically what he learned from the great Western philosophers; however, their influence on his ideas is omnipresent, as demonstrated in his writings and speeches. While speaking in a sermon on the importance of courage, King concludes that courage "is the power of the mind to overcome fear."[37] He reaches this conclusion by synthesizing the ideas of Plato, who considered "courage to be an element of the soul which bridges the cleavage between reason and desire";[38] Aristotle, who "thought of courage as the affirmation of man's essential nature";[39] and St. Thomas Aquinas, who said "that courage is the strength of conquering whatever threatens the attainment of the highest good."[40] King states that he sees the fostering of love as the highest good, a view that he admits puts him at odds with most of the great Western thinkers.[41] But the fact that he saw himself engaged in a comparable quest to find life's ultimate purpose places him in the same Western philosophical and theological tradition as that of Plato, Aristotle, Aquinas, Augustine, the Epicureans and Stoics, and so on. In summary, a close reading of King's writings shows that although he found them wanting in certain areas, he actively used the thoughts of the great Western thinkers to work out his own answers to both intellectual and social questions.

The philosophy that had a catalytic effect on King's thinking on social problems was Marxism. King says that in 1949 he read Karl Marx's *Das Kapital* and Marx and Friedrich Engels's *Communist Manifesto*, while also reading "some interpretive works on the thinking of Marx and Lenin."[42] As a result of his reading, he came away with a negative impression of communism that was to remain with him throughout his life. He rejected the materialistic view of history on which communism is premised because in his view, "history is ultimately guided by spirit and not matter." Furthermore, King states that he strongly disagreed with communism because of its ethical relativism, for since the communists do not believe in a divine government or an absolute moral order, almost anything is justifiable as a "means to a millennial end." Finally, King opposed communism because in the communist ideology, "the individual ends up in subjection to the state."[43] On the other hand, King felt that the communist ideology was positive in that it "pointed to the weakness of traditional capitalism, contributed to the growth of a definite self-consciousness in the masses, and challenged the social conscience of the Christian Churches." In fact, King concluded that the "Kingdom of God" is found in neither pure communism nor pure capitalism, but in "a synthesis which reconciles the truth of both."[44] (Apparently, King preferred a mixed economy or a democratic socialist economic system to a purely capitalist one.)[45] After his reading of Marx, King's intellectual quest next focused on finding a method that would preserve respect for God, enhance individualism, foster Christian love, and not be materialistic. To satisfy his yearning, King first turned to pacifism.

While at Crozier Theological Seminary, King was exposed to the pacifist position in a lecture given by the famous pacifist Dr. A. J. Muste. King was impressed by Muste's lecture and came away from it hating war and insisting that it "could never be a positive good." On the other hand, King wondered whether war may not be a "negative good," meaning that despite its horrors, war might be preferable "to surrender to a totalitarian system—Nazi, Fascist or Communist."[46]

This question troubled King; in fact, it troubled him so much that he began to lose faith in the efficacy of a nonviolent method. While he was questioning the viability of pacifism, King read Friedrich Nietzsche's *Genealogy of Morals*, in which Nietzsche criticizes the Christian virtues of piety, humility, otherworldliness, its attitude toward suffering, and so on, and calls for the development of a superman who would "surpass man as man surpassed the ape."[47] Nietzsche's critique of nonviolence was so "effective and disturbing" to King's pacifist outlook that King began to seriously ask himself, Can nonviolence really work as an effective method of protest?[48]

On a Sunday afternoon in Philadelphia around 1950, King took a giant step toward the resolution of his dilemma regarding a nonviolent and pacifist method, for at this time he was exposed for the first time to the philosophy of nonviolence as practiced by Mahatma Gandhi. For Gandhi, as King interpreted him, love was not only a salve for individual conflict but it was also "a potent instrument for social and collective transformation."[49] Especially impressed by Gandhi's Salt March to the sea and his numerous fasts, Dr. King states, "The whole concept of 'satyagraha' (Satya is truth which equals love, and graha is force; 'Satya-graha,' therefore, means truth force or love force) was profoundly significant to me."[50] At last King felt he had found a possible way out of his dilemma regarding the efficacy of nonviolent protest.

His encounter with Gandhi's conception of nonviolence did not immediately end his perplexity on the question of the relationship between love, violence, and nonviolence. King writes that soon after being exposed to Gandhi, he read Reinhold Niebuhr's *Moral Man and Immoral Society*, in which Niebuhr argues that although nonviolence may be a more effective instrument for social change than violence, there is no intrinsic difference between them because both accept the principle that coercion is necessary for social change. For Niebuhr, nonviolence is preferable to violence mainly on the pragmatic ground that it is more likely to preserve the moral state of the individual involved in a social confrontation, and it is less physically harmful than violence. King admits that Niebuhr's critique of nonviolence left him "in a state of confusion." Only much further reading convinced him that this critique was fallacious because, as King explains it, nonviolence does not necessarily mean "non-resistance to evil but nonviolent resistance to evil." In nonviolence, one combats evil with love, "for it is better to be the recipient of violence than the inflicter of it." He goes on to say that by the practice of nonviolence one seeks to "develop a sense of shame in the opponent, and thereby bring about a transformation and change of heart." Thus, in King's view, Niebuhr missed the essence of nonviolence: resistance by love and not coercion.[51] This does not mean that King did not learn anything from Niebuhr. King states that Niebuhr has "an extraordinary insight into human nature, especially the behavior of nations and social groups."[52] Also, he lacks the false optimism of "a great segment of Protestant liberalism," which to King was a virtue. Thus, while disagreeing with Niebuhr's critique of pacifism, King admits that Niebuhr's theology "is a persistent reminder of the reality of sin on every level of man's existence."[53]

In King's own words, "The next stage of my intellectual pilgrimage to non-violence came during my doctoral studies at Boston University."[54] Here he was influenced most through his studies in philosophy and theology under Edgar S. Brightman and L. Harold De Wolf. Under these men King studied what he calls "personalistic" philosophy. Personalistic philosophy is premised on the notion "that only personality—finite and infinite—is ultimately real"; thus, the meaning of ultimate reality is found in personality. As King describes it, personalistic philosophy did two things for him: "It gave me the metaphysical and philosophical grounding for the idea of a personal God, and it gave me a metaphysical basis for the dignity and worth of all human personality."[55]

The final stage in King's intellectual odyssey came when he read the works of the philosopher Hegel, especially his *Phenomenology of Mind, Philosophy of History,* and *Philosophy of Right.* King admits that there is much in Hegel that he could not agree with, for example, "his absolute idealism" that "tended to swallow up the many into one." On the other hand, he agrees with Hegel's argument that "truth is the whole," a contention that led him "to a philosophical method of rational coherence." King adds that Hegel's analysis of the "dialectical process, in spite of its shortcomings, helped me to see that growth comes through struggle."[56] By 1954, King had reached the point where he could put all these experiences into a coherent philosophical framework with a method for action. As he describes it himself, "In 1954 I ended my formal training with all of these divergent intellectual forces converging into a positive social philosophy. One of the main tenets of this philosophy was the conviction that non-violent resistance was one of the most potent weapons available to oppressed people in their quest for social justice."[57] At this time, however, King had merely an intellectual understanding and appreciation of the position, with no firm determination to organize it in a socially effective situation. The opportunity to do so was to come sooner than he expected.

King's Philosophy of Nonviolence

Since nonviolence is the key characteristic of King's political theory and practice and remained so from 1954 to his death in 1968, one must examine it in some detail to fully appreciate King the political activist. As described by King, his philosophy of nonviolence has six characteristics.

First, nonviolent resistance is not a method for cowards "for it does resist." As King speaks of it, "If one uses this method because he is afraid or merely because he lacks the instruments of violence, he is not truly non-violent."[58] Admittedly, the nonviolent resister may be passive "in the sense that he is not physically aggressive toward his opponent." Yet, "his mind and emotions are always active, constantly seeking to persuade his opponent that he is wrong." Or, in other words, to King the method is passive physically but extremely active spiritually.[59]

Second, nonviolence "does not seek to defeat or humiliate the opponent but to win his or her friendship and understanding." Often, King points out, the nonviolent resister protests with noncooperation like boycotts and sit-ins. These are not considered "ends themselves," however, for "they are merely means to awaken a sense of moral shame in the opponent. The end is redemption and reconciliation."[60]

Third, nonviolence is directed against the "forces of evil" or the system "rather than against persons who happen to be doing the evil." King made clear to the people of Montgomery, as he did in all the locales where he protested, that blacks are "out to defeat injustice and not white persons who may be unjust."[61]

Fourth, the nonviolent resister accepts suffering without retaliation and is prepared to accept any punishment that his offense entails. As King expresses this facet of nonviolence, "The non-violent resister is willing to accept violence if necessary, but never to inflict it. If going to jail is necessary, he enters it 'as a bridegroom enters the bride's chamber.'"[62] As is well known, King and his followers were jailed many times for violating laws that they perceived to be unjust, but they always willingly accepted the punishments involved.

Fifth, the nonviolent resister avoids not only "external physical violence, but also internal violence of the spirit." Indeed, King repeatedly cautions the nonviolent resister against hating, for he believed that "along the way of life, someone must have sense enough and morality enough to cut off the chain of hate. This can only be done by projecting the ethic of love to the center of our lives."[63]

Sixth, and reminiscent of the faith of both Marcus Garvey and Frederick Douglass, the nonviolent resister holds that "the universe is on the side of justice." According to King, the nonviolent resister is optimistic in even the darkest of times, because he or she knows that there is some force that will ultimately rectify wrong: "Whether we call it an unconscious process, an impersonal Brahmin, or a personal being of matchless power and infinite love, there is a creative force in this universe that works to bring the disconnected aspects of reality into a harmonious whole."[64] In retrospect, it can be argued that it was this strong faith in ultimate justice that gave Dr. King the courage to survive the bombings, slanders, beatings, and jailings of the civil rights struggle and that enabled him to march triumphantly from Montgomery to Selma to Memphis.

The concept of love is central to the philosophy of nonviolence. According to King, there are three types of love. First, there is "Eros" or what in Platonic philosophy means "the yearning of the soul for the divine." This type of love is most often seen as a "sort of aesthetic or romantic love." Second, "there is Philia which means intimate affection between personal friends." As King defines it, "Philia denotes a sort of reciprocal love; the person loves because he is loved." The love involved in nonviolent resistance, however, is neither *Eros* nor *Philia* but "a love which is expressed in the Greek word *agape*."[65] In a summary definition, Dr. King says, "*Agape* means a recognition of the fact all life is interrelated. All humanity is involved in a single process, and all men are brothers. To the degree that I harm my brother, no matter what he is doing to me, to that extent I am harming myself."[66] In short, "Agape" or love for all humanity, is in King's view the highest form of love.

The Political Thought of King

King's View of People

It is impossible to understand King's political thought unless one examines his view of people. This is especially necessary in King's case because he argued that "the whole political, social and economic structure of a society is largely determined by its answer to this vital question." King begins his discussion by asking whether people are free and creative beings "capable of accepting responsibility," or whether they are cogs or pawns in some overarching process. Before presenting his own position on this question, however, King quickly surveys and critiques three conceptions that differ from his own: those of the materialist, the humanist, and the realist. King says that to the materialist, a person is simply a small part of a vast impersonal nature whose "whole life may be explained in terms of matter in motion." He goes on to say that because of their philosophy the materialists are often driven to "dark chambers of pessimism" about people, for at times they depict them as "cosmic accidents" and at other times as comparable to the "pernicious race of ominous vermin" spoken of by Jonathan Swift.[67] King rejects outright the materialist conception.

To King, the humanist conception, based on a belief "neither in God nor in the existence of any supernatural power," affirms that people are "the highest form of being which has evolved in the natural universe." In effect, humanism is a variation of materialism. At the same time, King contends that unlike the materialists, who tend toward pessimism, the humanists have a glowing optimism, an optimism that is captured well in Hamlet's declamation that begins, "What a fine piece of work is man."[68] King sees such glowing optimism as yet another oversimplification of human nature that is not only erroneous but unwarranted. In effect, humanism can be as injurious as materialism, because it completely overlooks people's capacity for sin.

The realists' conception, as described by King, is, despite its shortcomings, closer to the truth than either the materialist or the humanist position. According to King, the realists "wish to reconcile the truth of these opposites, [humanism and materialism] while avoiding the extremes of both." In effect realists "contend that the truth about man is found neither in the thesis of pessimistic materialism nor the antithesis of optimistic humanism, but in a higher synthesis."[69] King stresses that unfortunately many varieties of realism fall short because they also see people as but a part of nature and, like the humanists and materialists, fail to recognize the true human essence, which is found not in the material but in the spiritual realm.

King's view of people is what he terms "a realistic Christian view," which says that God has made people "a little less than God, and dost crown [them] with glory and honor."[70] This means that Christian realism "recognizes that man is a biological being having a physical body,"[71] for "in any realistic doctrine of mankind we must be forever concerned about his physical and material well being."[72] However, to "contend that the whole life of man is nothing but a materialistic process with a materialistic meaning" is from a Christian realist perspective incomplete. If people are so, King asks somewhat rhetorically, how can one explain "the literary genius of Shakespeare, the musical genius of Beethoven, and the artistic genius of Michaelangelo" or "the spiritual genius of Jesus of Nazareth"? King argues that such qualities "cannot be explained in chemical and biological terms," but only in spiritual ones.[73] Thus, to the Christian realist, "man is a being of the spirit."[74] To Dr. King, however, the characteristic that most distinguishes people is freedom, because unlike the animals, "man is man because he is free to operate within the framework of his destiny. He is free to deliberate, to make decisions and to choose between alternatives."[75] King warns that many people have accepted the view that people are both spiritual and physical beings but have refused to recognize that "engulfing human nature is a tragic, threefold estrangement by which man is separated from himself, his neighbors, and his God." In short, they have refused to acknowledge that "there is a corruption in man's will," that "man is a sinner in need of forgiving grace," and that such a recognition is not a "deadening pessimism, it is a Christian realism."[76] In essence, it is because Christian realism recognizes the potential for both human evil and human good that King adopts it.

How does King feel the West has used the freedom just described? He believes it has done so to embrace "secularism, materialism, sexuality, and racial injustice," which have brought Western civilization "a moral and spiritual famine." King stresses that "to return home" to God, westerners must first grant justice to those exploited colonial peoples whom they have "deprived [of their] sense of personal worth." Second, America itself, "which has oppressed nineteen million of your negro brothers," must return to its "true home of democracy, brotherhood and fatherhood in God." If America can do this, King prophesizes that God will give it, "a new opportunity to be a truly great nation."[77] In summary, the belief that people are children of God consisting of both spiritual and physical elements, the belief in people's free will, and the recognition that people are tragic beings are the major features of King's view.

King's Theory of State

Unlike Marcus Garvey, who articulated a vision of his ideal state, one searches in vain for a comparable vision in King's teachings. King strongly believed in the efficacy of America's values and institutions

as presently articulated, and he saw the challenge to America as making social practice conform to national ideals, not the construction of
new national ideals. Writing in 1963 when reflecting on the the centennial of the Emancipation Proclamation and limited black progress,
King stressed that the centennial should not be perceived as a celebra-
tion but rather as the commemoration of the one moment in the country's history when a bold start had been made. King went on to ask the
America of 1963 to resume by supporting the demands of the black
and poor, "the noble journey towards the goals reflected in the Pream-
ble to the Constitution, the Constitution itself, the Bill of Rights and
the Thirteenth, Fourteenth and Fifteenth Amendments."[78] This citation illustrates King's faith in America's ideals very clearly. Similarly,
in 1968 while reflecting on how white racism had distorted the American dream, King affirms that in spite of the distortion, "[America's]
pillars were soundly grounded in the insights of our Judeo-Christian
heritage: All men are created equal; every man has rights that are neither conferred by nor derived from the state, they are God-given. What
a marvelous foundation for any home! What a glorious place to in-
habit! But America strayed away."[79] Once again the complete acceptance of the American ideal emerges. One might say that King saw his
entire crusade not as one to reconstruct America but as an attempt to
return her to her own ideals of justice. This devotion to America's
ideals places King in the tradition of great articulators of the American
creed like Jefferson, Franklin, and Franklin Roosevelt.

The conclusion that King did not project a new political vision but
accepted the existing American ideal is also reached by the political
theorist Sam Cook. In this regard Cook argues that "the basis of Dr.
King's dream and practical efforts was a model of simplicity: to make
the American dream as relevant, meaningful, and applicable to Black
Americans as to White Americans. He looked beyond the darkness of
current reality to the light of limitless possibilities; beyond the chaos,
injustice and division of 'being' to the ordered liberty and equality,
justice and unity of becoming."[80] Similarly, African-American essayist
Julius Lester, commenting on the death of Dr. King, declares that
Americans, whatever their criticisms of him, cannot argue that he was
not totally committed to the society's ideals. As Lester puts it, King
"loved America as if he had sewn the first flag, and he articulated a
dream for America more forcefully than any man since Thomas Jefferson."[81] Thus, like Frederick Douglass, King can be described as a
moral reformer of the American system, and also like Douglass, he can
be characterized as one who never gave up on the American creed.

Other Characteristics of King's Political Thought

In spite of King's advocacy of moral suasion as the best means by which to effect change, one finds Legalist, Reformist, and Accommodationist strains in his political thought also. As an example of his Legalism, during the Montgomery bus boycott he was charged with "operating an illegal car pool" by the local authorities and was taken to court.[82] In spite of some initial setbacks in the local courts, however, King felt that ultimately the Supreme Court would declare segregated busing unconstitutional. After a long delay the decision was made in his favor. He states that his heart "began to throb with inexpressible joy." In fact, King and Birmingham's population all seemed in agreement with a black person in the courtroom, who said, "God almighty has spoken from Washington."[83] The most extreme Legalist could not have had more confidence in the integrity of the U.S. court system than did King at this time.

Like the NAACP with its Reformist approach to social change, King was not averse to manipulating the political system to pressure political representatives into using their positions to further the cause of equality. In 1968, while telling of his plans to lead a "camp-out" in Washington later in the year, he made it clear that he saw this as a way to aid America's poor by prodding the legislators and "the administrators, and all the wielders of power until they faced this utterly imperative need."[84] This demonstrates that although King's message was mainly one of moral suasion, he realized that the message increased in effectiveness to the degree that the issues it raised became a part of the national political agenda.

An Accommodationist side to Reverend King's philosophy can also be seen. After the Montgomery bus boycott had ended and blacks had achieved their goals, King warned blacks not to be satisfied with a court victory or to embarrass Birmingham's whites because they had lost. Instead, he tells blacks to face up to their own shortcomings and "act in such a way as to make possible a coming together of white people and colored people on the basis of a real harmony of interest and understanding."[85] King concludes his admonishment by saying that blacks must "turn their enemy into a friend" and "move from protest to reconciliation."[86] King's call for a harmony of interests between black and white is reminiscent of that of Booker T. Washington.

King's Legalism and Accommodationism will be misunderstood, however, if one fails to note a distinction that he made between "negative peace" and "positive peace," for it is with this criterion that he judged all laws, customs, and practices of a given society. In King's view, "negative peace" occurs when there is no overt conflict between groups and individuals, but there is acquiescence based on the passive acceptance of injustice. For example, while leading the bus boycott in Montgomery, King was accused by his conservative critics, both religious and secular, of "disturbing the peace." King responded angrily by stating that Montgomery never had "real peace." What had hitherto existed in Montgomery was, "a sort of negative peace in which the Negro too often accepted his state of subordination. But this is not true peace." True peace does not exist where social tensions are submerged; it can only occur where there is "the presence of justice," whether tensions or acquiescence are present or not.[87] Referring specifically to Montgomery, King argued, "The tension we see in Montgomery is the necessary tension that comes when the oppressed rise up and start to move toward, a permanent positive peace."[88] King's requirement that all accommodations with the system be based on a positive peace clearly distinguishes his Accommodationism from that of Washington. Further distinguishing King's Accommodationism from that of Washington is his conception of law. King argued that the citizen had an obligation to obey the law as long as it was consistent "with the moral law of God," which he identified with justice. On the other hand, when laws were unjust, he insisted that "just as the prophets of the 8th century b.c." resisted unjust laws, the citizens in twentieth-century America had a duty to resist them also.[89] In summary, although there is present in King's political thought a moralist preeminence, there are strong strains of Reformism, Legalism, and Accommodationism also.

King's Tactics

Dr. King's tactics follow logically from two fundamental tenets of his philosophy. The first tenet is King's acceptance of the values of the American system. The second is his belief in morally uplifting both oppressor and oppressed, thus his eschewing of violence because it could never uplift. In other words, in all his actions, King insists that "means and ends must cohere, because the end is pre-existent in the means, and ultimately destructive means cannot bring constructive ends."[90] Given these requirements, nonviolent protest is the only acceptable tactic.

If King's tactics were put into a time frame, the record suggests that they were typified by a move from a more Accommodationist and Legalist stance in the early years to the politics of confrontation in the later years. When he began in Montgomery in 1954, he insisted that blacks and whites of that city peacefully settle the dispute, and he went to great pains to ensure that long-standing traditions there were not upset too radically by the bus boycott. King also talks at this time about the need to "establish credit unions, savings and loan associations and cooperative enterprises," and in tones reminiscent of Washington he urges African-Americans to lift themselves up by their own bootstraps from the practice of segregation and the scourge of economic deprivation.[91] Finally, like Washington, King, especially in the early years, did not shrink from criticizing the African-American community itself about the negative features of its life that could not be directly attributed to white oppression. For example, he condemned the high crime rates, the lack of cleanliness, and the waste of money on nonessentials that typified some segments of the community. These were drawbacks that the African-American community could eliminate itself without the white community's leadership.[92]

During the days of the Montgomery bus boycott, King also began the practice of mobilizing national support for his cause by focusing attention on a local racist practice or institution that would arouse the consciences of Americans of all ideological persuasions. The latter strategy is reminiscent of the Reformist and Legalist approach of the NAACP. For example, to fight the specific bus segregation problem in Montgomery, King obtained national support from many churches and the support of "labor, civic and social groups." King also received support from blacks all over the United States, and Roy Wilkins urged all the members of the NAACP "to give moral and financial support to the movement."[93] It was at the time of the Montgomery bus boycott that King also identified the constituency of northern white liberals, the federal government, and blacks to which he would direct appeals for support until his death. To the northern white liberals, King said he expected their support, because "a true liberal will not be deterred by the propaganda and subtle words of those who say, 'slow up for a while; you are pushing things too fast.' "[94] Regarding the federal government, King continually argued that for the racial problem in America to be solved, the federal government had to assert "strong and aggressive leadership."[95] It can be argued that most of King's gains were made during the times when this coalition of white liberals, federal government, and blacks was strongest.

By 1963 the Accommodationist and Legalist elements were not stressed as strongly in King's tactics as they had been. At this time, mass demonstrations, various types of sit-ins, and civil disobedience were more heavily emphasized. The march on Washington in 1963 was the biggest of the mass demonstrations. Similar demonstrations and protests were held in all the major cities, especially in the South, where racism was most marked. An important ingredient of these meetings were the Freedom Songs. To King these songs were more than "clever phrases designed to invigorate a campaign." They were instead "adaptations of the songs that slaves sang—the sorrow songs, the shouts of joy, the battle hymns, and the anthems of our movement.[96] By 1967, perhaps in response to the growing influence of the Black Power Movement, the traditional marches were deemphasized and open confrontations with what was described as "the establishment" advocated. At this time, King suggested that if large numbers of Negroes and their supporters decided to protest by marching "in a major city to a strategic location," they could make it difficult for the city to function.[97] This type of demonstration, as King saw it, would "retain the dignity and discipline of the marchers" while drawing attention to their grievances.[98] At the time of his death, King was planning a march on Washington that was designed to function in this fashion, but he was assassinated before he could carry it out.

King and the Black Power Challenge

In his fight for an equalitarian and color-blind America, Martin Luther King, Jr., especially considering his early death, accomplished more in his lifetime than any single African-American leader since Frederick Douglass. In many respects King surpassed Douglass, for he eschewed physical violence, never served the government in any capacity, and exhibited a talent for love and forgiveness that rivals that of Gandhi. However, although twelve years of Moralist protest brought some improvement in the lives of the African-American masses, in 1966 great disparities still remained. At that time, many African-Americans began to argue that the prevalence of white nationalism prevented any significant changes from being made in their lives, and what was needed for improvement was an equally strong movement for Black Nationalism. On the Meredith March in June 1966, King, the preacher of nonviolence and universalism, was directly challenged by the adherents of the Black Power movement, the subject of the next chapter.[99]

VII

What Is Black Power?

The term *Black Power* has a range of related but distinct meanings. Because of this it is impossible to find any one summary definition that encapsulates the essence of the movement as a whole.[1] To seek the latter would at best yield a lowest common denominator of the Black Power ideologies, which if done well would describe that which is common to them, but at the same time such a definition would be so schematic that the unique value of each expression of Black Power would be lost. Instead of attempting to arrive at a summary definition of the Black Power Movement, I will develop a conception of Black Power by delimiting the factors that link the movement into a "family resemblance" or unity and from that show the uniqueness of each of the types of Black Power.[2] The chapter will be organized in the following fashion. First, a description of the range of meanings that have been suggested for the term *Black Power* will be given. Second, some of the characteristics that bind the meanings into a rough "family resemblance" will be articulated. Third, the ideological differences between Dr. Martin Luther King, Jr., and his Black Powerite opponents will be reviewed to illustrate the perennial conflict and competition between Black Nationalist expressions and those of their integrationist competitors in the African-American experience.

The Range of Usages of the Term *Black Power*

The views of Professor Charles Hamilton, one of the few scholars and Black Power activists who has attempted to categorize systematically the meanings of the term *Black Power*, underscores very well the difficulties involved in such a process. Hamilton correctly points out that to some people the Black Power Movement was associated with violence and an effort to "destroy the political and economic institutions" of the United States;[3] in other circles it was seen as an effort "to rid the Civil Rights Movement of whites who had been in it for years"; some saw it as black hatred of whites; others saw it as using "pressure group tactics" in the accepted tradition of American politics; yet others saw it as an "attempt to instill dignity and pride in Black People." Hamilton, writing in the late 1960s, concluded, "Ultimately, I suspect, we have to accept the fact, that in this highly charged atmosphere, it is virtually impossible to come up with a single definition satisfactory to all."[4]

Instead of one authoritative definition, Hamilton sees the individuals and organizations that espouse Black Power falling into roughly four categories. The first category, the "political bargainer," conforms to the established political process, because he or she can "work within the two party system," and has as a major goal "equalizing opportunities to produce goods and services." Individuals like ex-Congressperson Shirley Chisholm, Representative John Conyers of Michigan, ex-state representative Julian Bond of Georgia, and black political organizations like the Black Congressional Caucus are excellent "real world" examples of the political bargainer category. The second category, called the "moral crusader," is more interested in "saving the soul of society" than in goods and services, is usually nonviolent, is not averse to making deals with the status quo, and because of a willingness to compromise is frequently "open to the charge of 'sell-out.' "[5]

The third category and the one in which Hamilton includes himself, is that of the "alienated reformer."[6] The alienated reformer is "cynical about the possibilities of effecting change through the existing system," supports the concept of black control of black communities, and wants a transformation of society, but one premised on a revitalized black community. The alienated reformer is also interested in "bread and butter issues" like the political bargainer, but unlike the latter, is "contemptuous of 'white middle class values' " and takes pride in black culture worldwide.

The final category is the "alienated revolutionary." Like the alienated reformer, the alienated revolutionary is also "cynical about existing power structures" but argues that progressive change can only come by the use of "calculated acts of instrumental violence." Hamilton argues that the alienated revolutionary is likely to start out as an adherent of one of the other approaches but "is pushed by traumatic defeats into the category of 'alienated revolutionary.' " Hamilton suggests that this latter type of Black Powerite is likely "to call for a black separate nation."[7] The Student Non-Violent Coordinating Committee (SNCC), especially as exemplified in the lives of its two former leaders, Stokely Carmichael (now Kwame Turé) and Hubert (Rap) Brown (now Jamil Abdullah Al-Amin), is a good example of this change. The SNCC began with a moral-crusader stance in the early 1960s. By the early 1970s it had moved to a revolutionary ideology in which both Black Separatism and the idea of a revolutionary transformation of the United States by any means necessary played a prominent part. In fact, the ideological permutations and political clashes involved in this process destroyed SNCC.[8]

As stated, Hamilton is one of the few scholar–Black Power activists who has attempted to deal systematically with the various usages of the term *Black Power*, and despite the weaknesses in his analysis, it serves as an excellent starting point for developing a more precise conception of the Black Power ideologies. To begin, one may ask some critical questions about the usages as Hamilton has categorized them. For example, how well do his categories encapsulate the range of meanings of the term *Black Power*? How meaningful and operational are the distinctions that his categories purport to make? How can the categories or usages be improved?[9]

The political bargainer category seems the least vague of the four usages. Very clearly, organizations like the Black Congressional Caucus and the many black politicians in state and local office all over the country represent this kind of Black Power. Representative John Conyers of Michigan sums up the position of the political bargainer well when he warns blacks that "politics is important," and especially with the increasing black voting power stemming from legislation like the Voting Rights Act of 1965 it would be folly for blacks to "give up" on the political process. As Conyers sees it, through their voting power "black people can exert strong influence on state governments, can pressure Capitol Hill and force quite a bit of listening at the White House." To Conyers this represents Black Power.[10]

And yet, even this category is not as clear as it at first seems. For example, Hamilton says that the moral crusader will also bargain at certain points with the establishment, although his or her main concern is with changing the society's soul. Does this mean that the political bargainer is not concerned with the soul of society also? And if it is conceded that both the political bargainer and moral crusader do in fact bargain and that these bargains are conducted with the established order, how in practice can the two be distinguished? Through the kinds of bargains, the extent of the bargains, or in some other criterion that Professor Hamilton fails to reveal to us? The distinction between political bargainer and the moral crusader is quite vague, and it becomes even more vague when a political bargainer like Conyers says in regard to the relationship between black politics and society's soul:

> I am talking about politics from our point of view . . . from the Black point of view. Our own intelligence about the oppressiveness of the kind of society which would like to forget us along with other historical "mistakes" should give Black people a unique force in effecting change in America. *An infusion of Blacks into the political arena might provide the moral force of "soul" which America either lost or never had.* No longer will we be content to stand on the sidelines and rail against the forces that shape our lives. Instead, we propose to enter the political arena and wrest for ourselves a share of decision-making power (emphasis added).[11]

Given attitudes like those expressed by Conyers, it seems that the separation of the political bargainer and the moral crusader mainly on the grounds that one is less interested in goods or services than the other, or that one is more concerned with the "soul of society," does not make much "political sense." Obviously, Conyers is as aware of the moral questions as is, say, the Reverend Dr. Nathan Wright, Jr. (a moral crusader by Hamilton's definition), and since both regard political bargaining within the American system as a necessary strategy for blacks, politically there is no objective way to differentiate between the two. Indeed, what politician ever argues that his or her actions are not concerned with the "state of society's soul?"

Distinguishing the alienated reformer from the political bargainer is even more difficult. The alienated reformer is cynical about effecting change through the existing structures but at the same time will accept the payoffs derived from participating in these structures when pragmatic considerations dictate. The difficulty is that it is impossible to demonstrate how this attitude of cynicism toward the system while seeking to receive certain rewards from it differs essentially from the position of the political bargainer. Conyers certainly works within the American political system, but as for having uncritical faith in it he says, "But let us make no mistake. Beneath this thin veneer of this supposed highly civilized nation, there exists a potential for violence without historical precedent."[12] Given feelings like these, one can justifiably conclude that the alienated reformer and the political bargainer are indistinguishable from each other, for both are simultaneously cynical and pragmatic toward the American system. Finally, the usages become even more indistinguishable when Hamilton describes the alienated reformer as "standing hard for local control of Black communities and demanding equal distribution of decision-making power." But the political bargainer Conyers also believes in the same goals, for he insists that America will not fulfill its promise until there is a redistribution of power "at all levels of government so that ordinary citizens can gain control over their lives."[13] The same a agreement holds in matters like "the contempt for white middle class values," the interest in black culture, and the hope that transformed black communities will change America that Hamilton expresses as an alienated reformer. The three categories that have been discussed so far are in fact all variations of the political bargainer's position, and at many points the positions are indistinguishable.

The alienated revolutionary's position is clearly distinguishable from the other three positions that have been discussed. Like them, the alienated revolutionary is cynical about existing conditions but argues that violence is the only means by which the black social condition can be qualitatively changed. At this point, Hamilton's treatment of this category also becomes vague, for he goes on to say that "this sort of Black Power advocate is apt to call for a separate nation." As will be shown, however, the Black Panthers are cynical of the system and believe that violence may be used legitimately at points to effect change; yet they *do not* call for a separate nation. Indeed, the Panthers depict themselves as the vanguard party of the oppressed that is leading the fight to bring into being a more just and truly integrated American society for all races. The Panther position is clearly distinguishable from that of the Republic of New Africa (RNA), which is similarly alienated from the American system but which argues that black liberation will come not from a transformation of the system but by a separation from it.[14] It is obvious then that Hamilton's fourth category of Black Power, the alienated revolutionary, fails to accurately describe the expressions of Black Power that are cynical of the system, that do not rule out violence as a tactic in the quest for change, but that differ radically on solutions. Thus, to more accurately convey the full range of meanings of the term *Black Power*, a rethinking and reshaping of Hamilton's usages should be carried out.

Reshaping the Categories of Black Power

To begin this task, it seems obvious that there are no real political differences between his first three categories, those of the political bargainer, the moral crusader, and the alienated reformer, because they all advocate what is called in political science a "pluralist" approach to politics. Based on this, the first "reshaped" category of Black Power will be termed the "Pluralist Approach." The following discussion will demonstrate why such a categorization is justified.

Pluralism challenges the notion that within a state there is only a single sovereign power that is one and indivisible. Or as Professor Carl Friedrich expresses it:

As against such statist notions, the prevailing tendency in democratic thinking has been "pluralist." Pluralism challenges the notions of a "Monopoly of Force" and "indivisibility" of power, the latter associated with the Bodinian concept of a "highest" and "perpetual" power from which it logically derives. It stresses, on the basis of an empirical observation of political reality, that even in a rather centralized state there are several centers of power, but that more particularly in a *constitutional and democratic order a plurality of groups divide power among themselves without it being possible to identify any of them as the highest* (emphasis added).[15]

The Black Power Pluralists argue that power in the United States is not centralized but is divided among a number of competing ethnic groups that conform to similar "rules of the game." While admitting that individual success in America is still possible, the Pluralists insist that success for an ethnic group as a whole depends on that group's ability to pressure its competitors into conceding the legitimacy of its demands. Only when a group is able to do this can it speak of having power. The Pluralists go on to argue that blacks, unlike the other ethnic groups in America, have sought to compete by stressing individualism over ethnocentrism, with the result that while some individual blacks have succeeded spectacularly, the gains for blacks as a group have been minimal. Within the Pluralist context, the Black Power Movement is seen as the black awakening to the crucial interrelationship between individual and group power and as a counterbalance to the individualistic political strategy that has been the preferred method for black protest since the Garvey Movement of the 1920s.

A statement by the National Committee of Negro Churchmen addressed to Negro citizens—a group Hamilton would call moral crusader—expresses this Pluralist philosophy quite well. It says in part:

" 'We must not apologize for the existence of group *power, for we have been oppressed as a group, not as individuals.*' We will not find the way out of that oppression, 'until both we and America accept the need for Negro Americans as well as for Jews, Italians, Poles and white Anglo-Saxon Protestants among others, to have and to wield group *power*' " (emphasis added).[16]

Shirley Chisholm, a congresswoman from New York in the 1960s and another example of the political bargainer as defined by Hamilton, says in regard to the need for a black ethnic strategy, "There is no longer any alternative for Black Americans but to *unite and fight together for their own advancement as a group.* Everything else has been tried and it has failed" (emphasis added).[17] To those who believe that instrumental violence is the only real way to eliminate black powerlessness and that strategies that stress political bargaining are sellouts, Chisholm replies, " 'I'm fighting,' I tell them. I know I'm here in Congress, part of the establishment, but you can see I haven't started to conform. I haven't sold out. I'm fighting within the system. There is no other place to fight, if you only understood it. There's no other way for us to survive, because we really don't have anything."[18] Finally, Hamilton sums up the Pluralist Approach in almost classic terms when he describes the challenge to the black community in America. He says at one point, "The Black community was told time and again how other immigrants finally won acceptance: that is by following the Protestant ethic of work and achievement. They worked hard; therefore, they achieved. We were not told that it was by building Irish Power, Polish power or Jewish power that these groups got themselves together and operated from positions of strength."[19] One can see from these examples that regardless of their differing metaphysical and cultural emphases, Hamilton's "political bargainer," "moral crusader," and "alienated reformer" usages are without a doubt forms of political Pluralism.

Earlier it was stated that Hamilton's alienated revolutionary category does not adequately explain the differences between the black Separatists and black revolutionaries who are both cynical of the American system but who have different solutions to the racial problem. Let us now suggest a new category that better explains these differences. Friedrich argues that one way of looking at the political community is to see it as consisting of a number of people holding values, interests, and beliefs in common. If one accepts this position, it could be argued that when the intensity of loyalty to the values, interests, and beliefs of a specific community approaches zero, the community

is in danger of disintegration. In Friedrich's terminology by way of
Aristotle, the community in such a state is threatened by "anomie."
But Friedrich argues further that aside from being threatened by anomie, the community may be also threatened by "disnomie," "a state
of affairs wherein some substantial number of the community are attached to given value 'A,' while a substantial number cherish its opposite 'B.' " Friedrich suggests that such conflicting "value attach-
ments" transform forces "A" and "B" into "gladiators fighting for
supremacy," with the result that what he calls an "anticommunity"—
and what will be called here a "counter-community" and it adherents
"Counter-Communalists"—develops in the existing order.[20]

Unlike the Pluralists, who seek to work within the present American system, or the Separatists, who "disvalue" the present system and
desire to separate from it as a result, Counter-Communalists, exemplified by the Black Panthers, seek to replace the values, interests,
institutions, and beliefs of the present system with different ones.
Huey Newton, leader of the Black Panthers, disvalues the present governmental and institutional arrangements in America when he speaks
in the following way: "The Black Panther Party feels that the present
government and its subsidiary institutions *are illegitimate because
they fail to meet the needs of the people. Therefore, they have no right
to exist. The Black Panther Party feels that in the interest of the people new institutions, both political and economic, should be established, and that old institutions disappear*" [emphasis added].[21] Newton goes on to say that the present values in America are "capitalist
values" that legitimize the economic and political exploitation of the
masses, including blacks, for the benefit of a few. He calls for a new
system in which "the production of goods (and provision of services)
[is] based upon the needs of the people [and does not function] for
profit making purposes." Finally, Newton stresses that in capitalist
America, "the masses of the people do not participate in the decisions
as to what products shall be produced, what services offered, or where
either are to be distributed. This makes for unequal distribution which
in turn makes for suffering and privation for millions of people."[22] In
short, Newton's disvaluation of the present system is total. Similarly,
another Counter-Communalist, black political theorist James Boggs,
argues that for one to legitimately claim to be a "Black Nationalist" or
"socialist" in the America of the 1960s, "he must be for a total change
of this society by revolutionary means and the construction of a society which eliminates the exploitation of all other races, classes, and
nations which is inescapable from capitalism and democracy." Boggs
concludes by saying that "majority rule" in present-day capitalist

America will always tolerate the "continued repression" of substantial minorities like blacks, "through whose super-exploitation this affluent society was built."[23] It thus becomes clear that the term *Counter-Communalism* better describes the philosophy and tactics of the non-Separatist radical black critics of the American system than does Hamilton's *alienated revolutionary*.

The Black Separatists, like the Counter-Communalists, also disvalue the values, interests, and beliefs of present-day America and seek to introduce new values *into the black community*. For example, as black poet Imamu Baraka (formerly LeRoi Jones) describes the spiritual challenge to blacks, "A cultural base, a Black base, is the completeness the Black Power Movement must have. We must understand that we are replacing a dying culture, and we must be prepared to do this, and be absolutely conscious of what we are replacing it with."[24] Unlike the Counter-Communalists, however, the Separatists view the disvaluing process as the first stage in the creation of a separate and distinct black community, and their focus is on how to establish such a community. Consequently, they are concerned with the broader matters that affect the United States only to the degree that those matters enhance or detract from their Separatist goals, and they have no plans for a total societal transformation. A statement by Milton Henry, ex-president of the RNA is very representative of this position. When responding to the question of whether or not independent black cities would be a satisfactory alternative or even substitute for his demand for a separate nation, Henry says, "No. We could get bogged down in that for another hundred years and eventually find we would have to get out anyway. So the thing to do is to do it now. That is the only answer: get out."[25] And unlike any of the other categories of Black Power, the Separatists see permanent black-white separation as the best way to eliminate the imbalances discussed in Chapter I.

In conclusion, as a result of the above discussion, it is now clear that the new terms: *Pluralist*, *Counter-Communalist*, and *Separatist* are not only more precise than Hamilton's categories, but they are excellent tools with which to explore the variety and depth of the Black power Movement as a whole.

Commonalities in the Usage of Black Power

Now that the types of Black Power have been described, the next challenge is to delimit the major characteristics that bind them into a "family resemblance" as variations on Black Power.

Agreement on the Meaning of Power

The first characteristic is the almost identical use of the term *Power* in relation to blacks as a group. Perhaps the best way to approach the question of the meaning of the term *Power* as used in the context of the Black Power Movement is to present several ways in which a variety of Black Power advocates have attempted to define the term and develop a more elaborate definition from that. Stokely Carmichael defines *power* as the ability to define oneself and one's relationship to society and to have that definition acknowledged. As Carmichael notes, to achieve *black power,* "we [blacks] shall have to struggle for the right to create our own terms through which to define ourselves, and our relationship to society, and to have these terms recognized."[26] Black theologian James Cone defines *power* as simply the ability to determine one's destiny. Cone states that "Black Power means Black Freedom, Black self-determination, wherein Black people no longer view themselves as without human dignity but as men, human beings with the ability to carve out their own destiny."[27] Boggs defines *power* as the ability to construct and reconstruct society along desirable lines. Boggs suggests that " 'Black Revolutionary Power' means the power to reconstruct the total society, giving everyone in this society an equal opportunity to the best that society can offer both materially and politically."[28] Finally, Huey Newton says in regard to *power,* "For us the true definition of power is not in terms of how many people you can control, to us power is the ability to first of all define phenomena, and, secondly, the ability to make these phenomena act in a desired manner."[29]

All these definitions have several common themes. All imply that a certain amount of change or motion is involved in a power equation, meaning by this the ability to move from one state of affairs, "A," to another, "B." All imply that "power" involves the ability to "control" the phenomena with which one is dealing. Furthermore, they all hint that in the Black Power context "control" implies three things: (1) the ability of blacks to define states "A" and "B," (2) the ability of blacks to determine if states "A" or "B" or their combinations are desirable, and (3) the ability of blacks to institute that which has been deemed desirable. Finally, all imply that the agent (the black community) does not have power until it can carry out the operations that have just been described as concomitant with control.

It is apparent, however, that the equation sketched above is incomplete. What has been said is that when blacks have achieved "power," they will be able to control their "environment." What has not been explained, however, is the nature of power itself, or in other words, the kinds of relationships that constitute power relationships.

Friedrich agrees with the political philosopher John Locke in saying that "power is not primarily a thing, a possession, but rather a relation, as Locke insists in his *Essay Concerning Human Understanding*, where he states that powers are relations, not agents. Indeed, power is primarily a relation." Friedrich goes on to say that the longer the time span over which one looks, the more obvious the relational quality of power becomes clear: "For it is in the rise and decline of political power, whether of individuals or larger groups, that the relational quality, the fact that power is always over men, becomes evident."[30] But Friedrich suggests that to argue that power is solely a relation would be unjustified, for "due to the institutionalization of power relationships . . . the power attached to a certain office is a thing, a possession to have and to hold. To be sure, the office may be lost as a result of the way power is used, but while the office is held, the power is in the hands of him who holds it. Therefore, it is appropriate to say that power is to some extent a possession (p^1) and to some extent a relation (p^2)."[31] Friedrich summarizes his discussion of power by suggesting that "power . . . is the relation among men which manifests in the behavior of following. Following means typically that A's, B's, C's do what L wants." Even more relevant to our discussion, Friedrich restates the same conclusion on power in another way, for as he describes it, "One might say that when the behavior of a certain group of men conforms to the wishes of one or several of them, the relation between them shall be called the power of L over A, B, C. It is evident that such power is not only characteristic of the kind of relation we just sketched, but it is likewise found in stable offices where it is possessed by him who holds office."[32]

How does one achieve this power relationship in which "the behavior of a certain group of men conforms to the wishes of one or several of them"? According to Friedrich there are two main ways of doing this, with a combination stemming from them. One can establish such a relationship either by consensus or by coercion, or by combining the two. In the case of consensus, the parties are persuaded to cooperate; in the case of coercion they are forced to cooperate. In an important caveat to his consensus-versus-coercion dichotomy, Friedrich cautions, "The expressions 'coercive' and 'consensual' or 'cooperative' power are misleading if taken as exclusive and separate phenomena. . . . In many actual power situations, however, either the

coercive or the consensual aspect predominates to such an extent that
it is permissible for the purpose of concrete analysis to neglect the
minor aspects and thus simply speak of coercive or consensual
power."[33] In summary, Professor Friedrich is arguing that power is
that relationship among people that manifests itself in following. Or,
to put it another way, power is that relationship among people in
which A's, B's, and C's do that which L wants, by consensus or coercion, but in actuality most often by a combination of the two.

The discussion has now reached the stage where we can proceed
to more adequately define how the word *power* is used in the context
of the Black Power Movement. Common to all usages of the term
Black Power is the notion that blacks will only have power in America when L, meaning blacks, can have the other groups in America,
the A's, B's, and C's do that which L desires, either by consensus or
coercion. The Pluralists are more likely to stress consensus, while the
Separatists and Counter-Communalists are more likely to stress coercion. It must be noted, however, that in practice all the types may use
a particular means or a combination of means at various times.

Self-Determination for Blacks as a Group

The second characteristic, which sharply distinguishes Black
Power from integrationist strategies like that of Martin Luther King,
Jr., is the repeated insistence that the primary goal is not individual
black equality in America, which was the major (although not exclusive) emphasis of King, but self-determination for blacks as a group,
either inside or outside of the present American system. (As we shall
see, Dr. King felt that this emphasis on racial self-determination was a
negative feature of Black Power, not only because of the dubious morality of a group ethic, but because it alienated many sympathetic non-
blacks who supported the cause of black equality.)[34] Unlike any of the
other types of Black Power, the Pluralists stress that such black self-
determination can be achieved by working within the American system, whereas the Counter-Communalists declare that it can only come
in a transformed America, and the Separatists see true self-determination as synonymous with the creation of a separate black nation. Yet
despite their differences in strategies and visions of the future, all
types of Black Power insist that self-determination for the black community is their highest aspiration.

It is useful in this regard to compare the Black Power versions of
black self-determination with past expressions of the same goal. It is
clear that the Pluralist insistence that black self-determination can be

achieved inside the American system is a radical departure from Black Nationalist theory of the past—from the Pan-Negro Nationalists to Bishop Turner to Marcus Garvey—all of whom insisted that such a goal was impossible and even contradictory. Thus, Pluralism represents an authentically new version of Black Nationalism. In their stated goal of creating a noncapitalist America within which genuine black self-determination can take place, the Counter-Communalists come close to the communists of the 1930s in their call for the same. The Counter-Communalists differ radically from the Communists, however, in that they see the exploited black minority, not the American working class in general, as the catalyst for the transformation. Orthodox communist theory sees this latter view as a nationalist blurring of the class struggle.[35] Finally, the Black Power Separatists, by insisting that the formation of a separate black nation is the sole way to solve the inequities between black and white lives in the United States, stand clearly in the orthodox tradition of Black Nationalism that had its most famous exponent in Marcus Garvey. The difference is that in Garvey's time there was not a Pluralist version of Black Power. The existence of such an option starting with the Black Power Pluralists of the 1960s, however, means that orthodox Black Nationalism of the Garveyan variety may never reappear in the United States.

A "Realistic" Approach to Politics

The third characteristic is the political realism that typifies their analyses and strategies and that sharply distinguishes them from the idealist theory and tactics of King. What is meant by *political realism*? The theologian Reinhold Niebuhr provides an excellent context for this discussion when he says, "In political and moral theory 'realism' denotes the disposition to take into account all factors in a social and political situation which offer resistance to established norms, particularly the factors of self-interest and power."[36] Citing Machiavelli (the classic articulator of the realist position), Niebuhr says that "the purpose of the realist is to 'follow the truth of the matter rather than the imagination of it; for many have pictures of republics and principalities which have never been seen.' This definition of realism implies that idealists are subject to illusions about social realities, which indeed they are."[37] The realist, to summarize, is one who at all times is "aware" of the realities of a particular situation, and the realities rather than the ideals determine his or her disposition toward it. Regarding idealism on the other hand, Niebuhr notes:

"Idealism" is, in the esteem of its proponents, characterized by loyalty to
moral norms and ideals, rather than to self-interest, whether individual or
collective. The idealists believe that self-interest should be brought under
the discipline of a higher law, which is correct, for evil is always the assertion of some self-interest without regard to the whole, whether the whole be
conceived as the immediate community, or the total community of mankind,
or the total order of the world. The good is, on the other hand, always the
harmony of the whole on various levels.[38]

The idealist is thus the opposite of the realist, for whatever the realities of a situation, the idealist's disposition is determined by certain
moral imperatives. It seems very clear that the various usages of Black
Power, whatever their eventual goal, or to put it another way, whatever their respective degrees of idealism, all stress that blacks must
exercise the highest degree of realism when dealing with the rest of
American society. They recognize that the self-interest of the various
American ethnic groups always take precedence over the more abstract American ideal and that blacks must mobilize as a collective to
realize their self-interest. Thus the cry of "Black Power!"

The Black Community Takes the Lead

The fourth characteristic is the general agreement that the black
community itself must take the lead in alleviating the legacies stemming from racism. The Black Power ideologies reject the notion that
by appealing to the consciences of the rest of society blacks can bring
about the necessary changes. All insist that the latter approach has
been tried and has proved a failure. Shirley Chisholm sums up this
feeling quite succinctly when she says, "At one time a lot of us hoped
that all it would take was to convince the white majority of the simple
truth and justice, and the day of equality would dawn. That was the
faith that created and sustained the Civil Rights Movement of the
1950s and early 1960s. The Movement was a failure."[39] Later, while
arguing that blacks must take the lead in gaining power for themselves, she says:

Closer inspection reveals that white minorities are not yet melted into the
society even after two or three generations. The care that politicans take to
balance their tickets figuring on the Irish Catholic vote, the Jewish vote, the
Polish vote and so on, proves the point. These groups are, obviously, more
assimilated than the stubborn, refractory element of the Black population.
But before they began to blend in, they had first to raise themselves to a
level fairly equal to that of the rest, economically in particular. To do so,

they had to advance not as individuals but as groups. They built political and economic power structures of their own within the larger society . . . stores, banks, businesses of all sorts, and a professional class of doctors, preachers and teachers. Then they truly became enfranchised when they had the power to wield.[40]

Thus, to Chisholm the need for the black community's own initiative in solving the race's problems in America is painfully clear. Similarly, Julius Lester, in the 1960s a Counter-Communalist, expresses the identical sentiment when he says that white sympathizers can help blacks best by fighting racism in their own communities. Regarding the black community's need for its own intiative, he says, "We must organize around blackness because it is with the fact of our blackness that we have been clubbed. We therefore turn our blackness into a club. When this new world is as totally necessary for whites as it is for blacks, then maybe we can come together and work on some things side by side. However, we will always want to preserve our ethnicity, our community."[41] Finally, the Honorable Elijah Muhammad of the Black Muslims, a Separatist in our usage, says regarding blacks taking the lead in solving their own problems, "Love yourself and your kind. Let us refrain from doing evil to each other as brothers, as we are the same flesh and blood. In this way, you and I will not have any trouble in uniting. It is a fool who does not love himself and his people. Your Black skin is the best, and never try changing its color. Stay away from mixing with our slave master's children. Love yourself and your kind."[42] In conclusion, all the Black Power usages see the initiative for doing away with the imbalances falling upon blacks themselves.

Confidence That Strategies Emphasizing Blackness Can Succeed

The final characteristic is the confidence that strategies that emphasize blackness can succeed. This is yet another characteristic that opened up the Black Power ideologies to intense criticism, especially from proponents of integration like Dr. King. King advances three major criticisms of this strategy, criticisms that are typical of the kind given by blacks and whites who shared his vision. First, a black-based policy is doomed to failure because it ignores the fact that blacks are a minority in the United States and need substantial white support to make progress. Second, the Black Powerites view white society as a racial monolith and overlook the fact that many whites are sympathetic to the black cause. Third, the Black Power movement seems blind to the fact that whenever blacks have progressed in America, the progress has been achieved by a multiracial strategy and not a racially exclusive one. (These detailed criticisms of Black Power are treated in the next section.)

The pollster Richard Scammon, in somewhat the same language as King uses, describes what to him are some of the limits of a black political strategy that emphasizes group interests over multiracial interests. Scammon says that in the first place an appeal on the basis of blackness will ensure that blacks remain minority candidates, since blacks form only 11 percent of the population. Scammon continues: "The lesson of the success of two well known Black officeholders, Senator Edward Brooke of Massachusetts and California [School] Superintendent Wilson Riles is that they campaigned simply as candidates pitching their appeal to voters of all races."[43] Second, Scammon argues that since America's electoral system is not a proportional one, this "means that there is no guarantee that parties or groups will be represented according to their degree of electoral support." He concludes that "to be successful a politician must put together a broader coalition than his opponent. For the Black politician in most districts success means getting as much as he can by working within the winning coalition."[44]

Scammon goes on to say that coalition building by black politicians is especially difficult, because by seeking to hold his black constituency "the Black politician may push the larger coalition to a breaking point," yet to win, the black politician must please his black constituency. As Scammon theorizes, "A Black politician running in a district comprising both [black] ghetto voters and white suburban voters would win Negro support by campaigns for low cost housing in suburbs . . . but in present day America such a tactic would surely alienate a large part of the suburban vote."[45] In essence, Scammon is saying that the need for coalition politics in America makes an all-black political strategy a questionable one. At the same time, despite this pessimistic analyses, even the Pluralists, the most system-oriented of the Black Power strategists, support electoral strategies that emphasize blackness. (It should be noted in retrospect that the numerous successes of blacks since the 1960s in winning electoral offices testify to the fact that if handled skillfully, a black-based strategy will not automatically turn off whites. For example, Mayor Harold Washington's victories in Chicago and David Dinkins's 1989 defeat of the once-popular Mayor Edward Koch in the Democratic primary for the New York mayoralty, and subsequent victory in the mayoral election itself, where white votes were needed to win, would not have been possible without a black-based strategy that simultaneously appealed to whites.)

In summary, a common agreement on the meaning of the term *power*, the faith that black self-determination is a viable strategy of racial uplift, a realistic approach to politics, the belief that the black community must take the lead in its own development, and the confidence that black political strategies can succeed are the commonalities that make it legitimate to speak of a general Black Power Movement despite the variations in tactics and strategies.

Martin Luther King, Jr., and Black Power

At the beginning of this book it was argued that ever since blacks have been of significant numbers in the United States there has been constant conflict and competition between the strategies of black protest that seek a solution to the racial imbalances by working within the American system and those that do not. This can be seen in the controversy between the Pan-Negro Nationalists and the early integrationists like the Reverend Peter Williams, in the differences in protest style between giants in black history like Bishop Henry M. Turner and Frederick Douglass, and in the dynamic but ultimately debilitating struggle between Marcus Garvey and his integrationist opponents. When black aspirations soared in the late 1950s and early 1960s as a result of civil rights gains, it seemed as if the call for a radical Black Nationalism had been permanently muted. In the late 1960s, however, when it became clear that the progress in civil rights would not be matched by significant advances in removing the material imbalances that existed between black and white lives, the struggle between the radical Black Nationalists and their integrationist opponents occupied center stage once again. In the 1960s, the integrationist Martin Luther King, Jr., and his approach to civil rights were main targets of the new wave of Black Nationalism. A review of the clash between King and the Black Powerites brings the 1960s version of this perennial competition in African-American history into full relief.

The Setting

Dr. King was first confronted with the cry of "Black Power" in June of 1966 when he was part of a civil rights team assembled to complete an abortive march through Mississippi that was started by James Meredith, the first black to attend the University of Mississippi. Meredith had started on a solo antiracist protest march through his home state earlier in the month, but he was shot by a white segregationist and hospitalized. Thus the team consisted of "stars" in the Civil Rights Movement like Stokely Carmichael of SNCC, Floyd McKissick of the Congress of Racial Equality (CORE), and even the conservatives Roy Wilkins of the NAACP and Whitney Young of the Urban League, the latter two eventually leaving the march in disgust at Carmichael's militance.[46] In his book *Where Do We Go from Here?* King states that when Carmichael and others started to use the slogan "Black Power" as a rallying cry on the march he objected to its usage. He believed that the slogan was inflammatory and "would confuse our allies, isolate the Negro community, and give many prejudiced whites, who might otherwise be ashamed of their anti-Negro feeling, a ready excuse for self-justification."[47] Eventually, after bitter acrimony between King and the Black Powerites, he admitted his failure to convince them to drop the term, and in his own words, "Black Power is now part of the nomenclature of the national community."[48] King was an ardent but constructive critic of the Black Power Movement, and his views convey the flavor of the conflict between these competing social outlooks, helping to explain why the Black Power Movement became popular and its positives and negatives.[49]

"Black Power" as a Cry of Black Disappointment

King begins by saying that the cry of "Black Power" is a regrettable but understandable reaction by American blacks who for centuries have "been caught up in the tentacles of white power," which has "left the Negro empty handed."[50] To King, the Negro has a multitude of reasons to be disappointed in the American system, and even critics of the Black Power Movement like himself must acknowledge them. First, King states that even in the Civil Rights Movement it seemed that white lives counted more than black ones. He notes that when Rev. James Reeb, a white Unitarian minister, was fatally clubbed to death in Alabama, President Johnson mentioned his name in a speech and sent flowers to his wife. When a young black, Jimmy Lee Jackson, was killed under similar circumstances, however, the "parents and sisters of Jimmy received no flowers from the President."[51] To King, the president's behavior is typical of the double standard that America often practices towards blacks and gives credence to the Black Power charge that blacks are discriminated against on both the individual and the institutional level in this country.[52] Next, King argues that the Black Power Movement represents black America's legitimate disappointment with the failure of the federal government to implement the

Civil Rights laws on the statute books. He notes that when the Voting Rights Act of 1965 was passed, many blacks in the South felt that they could now freely exercise their right to vote. But King notes that instead of appointing hundreds of registrars to insure black voting freedom in a violent and racist South, the federal government sent an inadequate force of "fewer than sixty registrars."[53]

Another reason why American society lost credibility in the eyes of many blacks according to King was the Vietnam War. As King saw it, many whites praised the nonviolence used in the Civil Rights Movement in places like Albany, Birmingham, and Selma, but blacks watched in amazement as the very society and government that was so reluctant to use force to guarantee the rights of black American citizens almost gleefully sent not only whites but blacks to Vietnam "to slaughter, men, women and children." As King saw it, this double standard of morality led many black and white Americans to ask, "What kind of a nation it is that applauds non-violence whenever Negroes face white people in the streets of the United States but then applauds violence and burning and death when these same Negroes are sent to the fields of Vietnam." To King, such unadulterated hypocrisy, "represents disappointment lifted to astronomical proportions."[54]

Finally, King says that the cry of "Black Power" is a cry of disappointment with the following groups in America: the white moderates who tried to set "a timetable for the Negro's Freedom"; the federal government, which was more concerned about winning in Vietnam than winning the "war against poverty" in America; the Christian church, which was in many cases silent on the issue of black rights; the Negro clergymen who valued the acquisition of materialist symbols over "service to the Negro Community"; and the Negro middle class who had forgotten their "brothers" who were "still drowning." Thus, although a strident critic of the Black Power Movement, King saw it as a genuine cry of disappointment by the black masses and an understandable vote of no confidence in the status quo.[55]

Positive Aspects of Black Power

King believed, however, that in addition to being a regrettable but understandable reaction to white racism, the Black Power Movement was also a positive corrective to many of the strictures that keep blacks down in the United States. King felt that the Black Power call for blacks to amass political and economic strength within the system was not only a necessary one but was consistent with the fact that every race to "achieve its purposes" must begin by establishing a firm economic and political base. King stresses that insofar as Black Power was an attempt to transform the Negro's "condition of powerlessness into creative and positive power," to that degree he supported it.[56] King also argues that Black Power is welcome in that it represents an effort by blacks to shake off the feelings of inferiority that have been forced on them in the United States. King was of course sad that too often the "Black Power" slogan degenerated into a "kind of taunt" against whites, but to the extent that it represented a "psychological call to manhood" on the part of blacks, King states that he welcomed it.[57] Finally, King argues that the Black Power Movement was positive culturally, because it was true that too often aesthetic and cultural standards in America discriminated against blacks. In fact, King notes that even the English language, which is replete with associations of "black" with "foul," "devil," "grime," "soot," and the like, indirectly helps to downgrade blacks as a people.[58] And King notes that American history books have either omitted or minimized the contributions of blacks to art, science, business, and so on, and even to American history itself. Thus, to King, Negroes needed to assert the positiveness of blackness to offset "the cultural homicide" that American culture had inflicted on them.[59] In short, insofar as Black Power was a call for the development of black political and economic strength, psychological manhood, and cultural pride, King argues that he supported it. Nevertheless, King felt that the Black Power Movement had some troubling characteristics that would prevent its becoming "the basic strategy for the Civil Rights Movement in the days ahead."[60]

Negative Aspects of Black Power

In spite of its positive features, King argues that "Black Power is a nihilistic philosophy born out of the conviction that the Negro can't win."[61] Such an attitude given the black experience in America may be understandable says King, but "a revolution degenerates into an undiscriminating catchall for evanescent and futile gestures if hope is dead."[62] King compares the Black Power Movement to the Garvey Movement in this regard because for King both of them represent "a dashing of hope, a conviction of the inability of the Negro to win, and a belief in the infinitude of the ghetto."[63] (From the discussion of Garvey we know that his theory of racial nationalism was far more complex than this depiction of it.)

Another negative feature of Black Power for King is its "implicit and often explicit belief in Black Separatism" and its insistence that "there can be a separate Black road to power and fulfillment." King feels that few ideas are more unrealistic than this one, and he dismisses the separatist solution out of hand.[64] King makes clear, unlike some other critics of Black Power, that he does not see the movement as racist,[65] because despite its distortion of reality, its advocates "have never contended that the white man is innately worthless." (King is not exactly accurate here, because as we have seen, the Black Muslims under Elijah Muhammad preached both pacifism and white inferiority.) We may note that in his critique of Black Separatism, King does not spare the Pluralist Black Power advocates, some of whom saw the attainment of black political power in the cities where blacks are the majority as the first step on the road to self-determination. First, King argued that in these black enclaves, the vast majority would be left "outside of the mainstream of American political life."[66] Second, King warns that black politicians can be as corrupt and opportunistic as white politicians, so even the attainment of black political power "is no more insurance against social injustice than white power."[67] Third, King notes that what is needed to solve blacks' dilemma is a coalition of "Negroes and liberal whites that will work to make both parties truly responsive to the needs of the poor," not an exclusive movement for Black Power.[68] In this regard, King felt that a slogan like "Power for Poor People" would be much more appropriate than "Black Power," because economic inequality affected both blacks and whites, and the racist edge would be taken out of the protest if the former was used.[69] The former slogan would also take into consideration the fact that "within the white majority there exists a substantial number who cherish democratic principles above privilege and who have demonstrated a will to fight side by side with the Negro against injustice."[70]

However, the most destructive feature of the Black Power Movement to Dr. King was "its conscious and often unconscious call for retaliatory violence."[71] As King describes it, the Black Power advocates do not "quote Gandhi or Tolstoy. Their bible is Frantz Fanon's *Wretched of the Earth*."[72] Fanon was a black psychiatrist from Martinique who defected from the French Army in the Algerian War to join the Moslem rebels. In his book he argues that for people who have been oppressed to attain liberation, violence must not only be used but that it is a positive force, because it is both "psychologically healthy and tactically sound" as a method for reasserting the humanity of the oppressed.[73] To many Black Powerites, Fanon was summing up the plight of blacks in America perfectly. King opposed the Black Power sanction of the "legitimate use of violence" on both pragmatic and moral grounds. Pragmatically, King says that the Negro is a minority in America, and to envision a poor and badly armed minority confronting "a well armed, wealthy majority with a fanatical right wing that would delight in exterminating thousands of Black men, women and children" is nonsensical.[74] When the Black Powerites attempted to counter this argument by saying that they are a part of the Third World and could expect sympathy and support from that source, King counters by explaining that most Third World countries including China are so involved in their own struggles to fight poverty and illiteracy that they simply do not have the resources to help any other countries, "much less the American Negro."[75] Also on pragmatic grounds, King points out the vast strides that blacks made in America in the late 1950s and 1960s by using nonviolent methods. As King put it, "Fewer people have been killed in ten years of non-violent demonstrations across the South than [were] killed in one night of rioting in Watts."[76]

Morally, King states that he is in total disagreement with the Black Power Movement's eschewing of an appeal to the American conscience and their castigation of it as irrelevant. In this connection, he cites one exponent of Black Power as saying to him, "To hell with conscience and morality. We want power!"[77] King reiterates his constant theme that for humane change to come about, "power and morality must go together, implementing, fulfilling and ennobling each other." As a result, King laments the fact that in their quest for their elusive goal of power, the Black Powerites were emulating one of white society's major flaws, viewing power as an end in itself.[78] King warns that as much as he is dedicated to blacks' struggle for equal citizenship in America, he is more concerned that blacks sustain their "moral uprightness and the health of [their] souls."[79] It is because in his view the Black Power Movement deemphasized these higher aspirations of humankind that he most opposed it.

In summary, its ethos of despair, its advocacy of Black Separatism, its sanctioning of violence as a tactic and its deemphasis of morality, are the negative features of the Black Power Movement that led Dr. King to oppose it. The forthcoming chapters, which contain case studies of the types of Black Power, will treat in more detail the Black Powerites' views of King's integrationist philosophy.

VIII

The Counter-Communalists: A Comparison and Analysis

The Counter-Communalists are those proponents of Black Power who do not advocate a separate state for blacks but who argue that progressive change must come for the majority of the American people of all colors when the present system is restructured along more democratic lines. (As previously noted, for Counter-Communalists more "democratic" usually means more "socialist.") In the 1960s, certainly the most visible, if not the most articulate, advocate of Counter-Communalism was Huey P. Newton, the leader of the Black Panther Party. Thus, to capture the essence of Counter-Communalism, we will compare the ideas and tactics of Newton with those of other well-known figures of the black Left. These figures are the radical black theologian James Cone, the left-wing black civil rights activist James Forman, the left-wing black sociologist Robert Allen, the radical black essayist of the 1960s Julius Lester, and James Boggs the black worker-socialist writer and activist based in Detroit, Michigan.[1]

In terms of literary quality, Newton's pronouncements lack the rhetorical brilliance of King's, are devoid of the fire and originality that we have seen in the works of Marcus Garvey, and are bereft of the spirit of destiny that characterizes the teachings of the Pan-Negro Nationalists. As one reviewer of Newton's works wrote in 1972, his teachings "are more didactic and tactical rather than scholarly," and he lacks the ability to develop his ideas and place them into "an appropriate theoretical context."[2] On the other hand, Newton was undoubtedly the most forceful, the best-known, and the most ambitious theorist-practitioner of left-wing Black Power, and for these reasons alone his profile is a small-scale representation of the entire Black Power Left.

133

Huey Newton's Background and Intellectual Influences

Huey Newton (1942–1989), born in Monroe, Louisiana, February 17, 1942, was one of seven children of his sharecropper and Baptist preacher father.[3] In his autobiography Newton points out that his father constantly worked three jobs to make ends meet for his family but in spite of this always wound up in debt.[4] The constant work and continual indebtedness made an indelible impression on Newton. Unlike his father, who accepted this condition without question, Newton, who helped to pay the family's bills as a youngster, queried this paradox from his earliest years.

After his family moved from Louisiana, Newton grew up in the ghettoes of Oakland, California. Like many ghetto youth, Newton found high school boring and irrelevant and at the age of seventeen discovered that he could barely read. In response to his older brother's severe criticism, Newton resolved to do something about his illiteracy. Newton's autobiography tells how he struggled through Plato's *Republic* the first time, a task that took him seven months. He was to reread the *Republic* seven or eight times until he mastered it. The new world that it opened to him so excited Newton that he went on to become a voracious reader and a literate high school graduate. Oddly enough, Newton feels that despite the drawbacks of his long-standing illiteracy, it gave him one advantage: When he started reading, his mind was "not cluttered and locked by the programming of the system," so he could view matters in a new light![5]

Despite the skepticism of his high school teachers as to his ability to do college work, Newton enrolled at Merritt College in Oakland. There he became a political activist, joining groups like the Student Non-Violent Coordinating Committee and Merritt's Afro-American Association and then left them because they lacked community links. In the search for a fitting organization, Newton soon teamed up with Bobby Seale, a Merritt student who shared his aspirations, and together they founded the Soul Students Advisory Council and in 1966 the Black Panther Party for Self-Defense.

Newton describes how his intellectual quest that started with his reading of Plato continued. He speaks of how he devoured works on the black experience, especially those of W.E.B. Du Bois, Ralph Ellison, James Baldwin, Malcolm X, Frantz Fanon, and Booker T. Washington.[6] He was fascinated by the history of Western philosophy, especially the works of the logical positivist A. J. Ayer, and he read widely in literature ranging from Franz Kafka to the Bible. However,

Newton and the Panthers felt that they benefited most from reading the works of Che Guevara and Mao Tse-tung, although their theories evolved out of revolutionary practice in a non-American context: "We read these men's works because we saw them as kinsmen; the oppressor who had controlled them was controlling us both directly and indirectly."[7]

Unlike the previous organizations of which Newton and Seale were a part, the Black Panther Party was designed to educate African-Americans about the nature of the oppression they faced and also to work in the community to build institutions to which oppressed African-Americans could relate. Thus, the party under its "Minister of Defense," Huey Newton, "started out with a ten-point platform and program that detailed the needs for housing, jobs and the right of the community for self-defense."[8] The Panthers also organized community patrols to ensure that the police force, which they depicted as anti-black, would not violate the constitutional rights of African-Americans. The fact that the participants in the Panther patrols carried arms—they insisted that as American citizens they had a constitutional right to do so—became a source of great controversy, and eventually it led to brutal clashes between the Panthers and the police.[9]

Newton had a violent side as well as an intellectual and humanitarian side. He had been jailed for assault in 1964 even before the Black Panther Party was formed, he was imprisoned for murder in 1968 but won on a 1970 appeal and was released, and he was charged with murder and assault in 1974 but fled to Cuba to avoid standing trial. After his return from Cuba in 1977 he was acquitted of the murder charge but was subsequently jailed in 1978 and 1988 on charges of gun possession and assault, and in 1982 was accused of embezzling state funds allotted to the party's free school in Oakland. Despite his criminal activity, Newton continued to study, and in 1980 he received a doctorate from the University of California at Santa Cruz. (Newton's thesis was entitled "War Against the Panthers: A Study of Repression in America.") Apparently seriously addicted to drugs, Newton was killed in a drug dispute on August 23, 1989, in Oakland, California, and left a mixed legacy. Some, including the essayist David Horowitz, who had championed the Panther cause in the early years of its formation, feared his violence. (On Newton's death, Horowitz remarked "Today is a day of release for me. As long as he was alive a lot of people were in danger.")[10] Others praised him, like William Kunstler, one-time Black Panther lawyer, who stated that Newton "has a place in history."[11] An examination of the elements of his political thought will help explain why Newton made so powerful an impression on both his supporters and critics, and will tell much not only about Newton himself, but also about the Black Panther Party's political ideology.

The Political Thought of Huey Newton

A review of Huey Newton's ideas reveals that his political theory can be conveniently broken down into four parts: his view of nature and change, his view of people, his theory of state, and his stage theory of American history. We will deal with each segment in turn, starting with his views on nature and change.

Newton's View of Nature and Change

V. I. Lenin in the Soviet Union, Mao Tse-tung in China, and Amilcar Cabral in Africa are considered three of the leading theorists of the Left in this century, and to understand how Huey Newton attempted to evolve a philosophical basis for his political thought and action, it would be instructive to briefly summarize how these thinkers dealt with the same problem. First, Lenin, in his classic *Materialism and Empirio-Criticism*, attacks the notion that ideas are primary and matter secondary, a notion that he claims is advanced by his philosophical opponents the Machists. Instead, he strongly argues for the Marxist world outlook, which stresses that matter is primary and ideas are derived from it. Lenin insists that if one states that "all knowledge comes from experience, from sensation, from perception. That is true! But the question arises, does objective reality 'belong to perception,' i.e., is it the source of perception?" Lenin concludes that if one answers that objective reality is the source of perceptions, then one is a materialist. If one answers no, one is a subjectivist or idealist who denies the primacy of matter.[12] Within this context, "freedom" to Lenin, "does not consist in the dream of independence from natural laws" but in the knowledge of these laws and "making them work toward definite ends."[13] In Lenin's view, the method to use to correctly understand these laws is the Marxist dialectic, a "scientific method" predicated on the belief that in all phenomena there is a unity of opposing forces, and change comes when one force overcomes the other to create a new unity. The dialectical materialists insist that the struggle of opposites is both universal and eternal.

Mao Tse-tung, in his famous essay on contradictions, follows Lenin in asserting the primacy of matter, and he also argues that the dialectical method teaches how to observe the movement of opposites (contradictions) in both nature and history. But Mao, even more than does Lenin, constantly reiterates in his works the theme that the phenomenon of contradiction is universal and insists that Engels was correct when he said that "motion itself is a contradiction," that is, a unity of opposites.[14]

In a less elaborate manner than Lenin or Mao but just as explicit, the African leader Amilcar Cabral when speaking of Africa's cultural and spiritual development also gives a materialist explanation for Africa's reality. Speaking of the origins of culture, Cabral says, "Culture has as its material base the level of productive forces and the mode of production."[15]

Huey Newton characterizes himself as a dialectician and materialist similar to these figures, but he is far less systematic than they are in explaining his method. As one example, Newton says that a useful philosophical method must be premised on the view that an external world, characterized by flux and change (dialectic) exists and that it is independent of us.[16] Newton fails, however, to "demonstrate" in argument the "superiority" of the materialist notion over the idealist conception as Lenin tries to do; nor does he try to relate the nature of change to the dialectic as does Mao. (Of course, neither Lenin, Mao, or Newton demonstrate why contradictions are necessarily the basis for all change and transformations in the universe. In fact, the political philosopher George Sabine sums up this general criticism of the dialectical method well when he says that "even in science or philosophy, new discoveries and the emergence of new points of view cannot plausibly be construed as always due to self-contradiction in earlier systems of ideas.")[17] As another example, Newton argues that a prerequisite for mastering nature is the use of the scientific method, which he defines as the exercise of "disinterest" while examining, measuring, and analyzing nature and society.[18] But Newton never clearly distinguishes between "uninterest," which he says means a total lack of interest in a scientific method, and "disinterest," which he sees as requisite for successfully practicing the scientific method. In other words, Newton never clearly explains how an attitude of disinterest can be exercised toward a problem or process one is "interested" in investigating. He simply leaves this intriguing paradox unexplained. As a final example, Newton argues that a successful ideology must be based on a philosophical method that combines both theory (the scientific method) and practice (the subjective), and he sees the dialectical method of Marx as possessing the correct mix. Newton then relates

that Marx's genius as the first great ideologist of dialectical materialism stems from the fact that he successfully integrated Kant's theory
of pure reason with the rules of the scientific method. Newton is even
incorrect in his chronology regarding the origins of dialectical materialism in Marx's work, for as Sabine points out, Marx's first statement about "dialectical materialism" was made between 1844 and
1848, "under the stimulus of Fuerbach's materialist interpretation of
Hegel."[19] The foregoing are samples of the problems that one encoun-
ters in Newton's explicitly philosophical comments. In them, he ex-
hibits the weaknesses of the typical and not greatly talented auto-
didact.[20]

Newton's Method Compared with the Methods of Other Counter-Communalists

While there are problems with Newton's usage of the dialectic to
explain nature and change, he is one of the few thinkers on the Black
Power Left who attempted to provide a philosophical basis for his
actions. For example, Boggs insists that ethnic groups must lead
America in discovering a new humanity and calls for a socialist revolution in this country, which he characterizes as "the last stronghold
of capitalism."[21] Yet nowhere does Boggs attempt to justify these beliefs philosophically as Newton does. Similarly, Robert Allen speaks
of the need to transform both black and white America "into a humanistic society free of exploitation and class division."[22] However, Allen's ideas, like those of Boggs, are devoid of a philosophical method.
Forman also argues for a socialist America and stresses that "only under socialism can the problems of black people and all humanity be
solved."[23] At the same time, Forman also neglects to justify his positions philosophically. Finally, Lester speaks of Black Power as being
"a highly moral point of view," but a moral force that does not ignore
the truth that morality is always grounded in the particular "economic
and political realities of life."[24] But like the others, Lester never tries to
grapple with the question of why certain values as opposed to others
are used to structure the realities.

On the other hand, James Cone, while failing to develop a philosophical method for understanding reality, does present a theological
belief that he insists does the same. According to Cone, historical affairs are ultimately subject to God's grace, and Christ always inter-
venes in history on the side of the oppressed. Cone goes on to suggest
that if Christ is the friend of the oppressed, "then it would seem that
for 20th century America the message of Black Power is the message

of Christ himself."[25] Cone thus finds justification for his conception of Black Power in God's divine plan. In summary, Huey Newton's system, with all its weaknesses, represents an effort to place the African-American struggle in the wider context of twentieth-century leftist thought, and Cone is one of the few black leftist thinkers other than Newton who even broaches the question of ultimate order.

Newton's View of People

Huey Newton's view of people is premised on two seemingly distinct but related notions: Newton insists that although people are part of a natural and material universe, they are distinguished by their spiritual attributes, which alone make them what they are. Newton argues that the next distinguishing characteristic of people is their constant quest for answers to the unknown, a quest that will go on as long as humanity exits. ·

Although a materialist like Lenin, Mao, and Cabral, Newton insists that it is erroneous to conceive of people as simply physical beings devoid of spiritual attributes or as beings whose spiritual attributes are somehow diminished because of their materialist origin. In Newton's view, "the dignity and beauty of man rests in the human spirit which makes him more than simply a physical being. This spirit must never be suppressed for exploitation by others."[26] Consistent with this sentiment, a review of Newton's writings reveals that although he stressed that the Panther program was designed to uplift the *material* conditions of the black masses, he also saw the Panthers as engaged in a fight to assert the *spiritual* dignity of themselves and other African-Americans. In his autobiography *Revolutionary Suicide* Newton suggests that when individuals commit suicide because they are no longer prepared to fight oppressive social conditions, their deaths constitute reactionary suicide. He cites an article by Dr. Robert Hendin in a 1970 issue of *Ebony* that referrs to the high proportion of black youth who were committing suicide as compared to white youth.[27] To Newton, these young blacks did not die fighting the oppressive social and economic conditions that the African-American community faces; they succumbed to reactionary suicide. Counterpoised to reactionary suicide is revolutionary suicide, which is premised on the view that "it is better to oppose the forces that would drive me to self-murder than to endure them."[28] Newton saw his personal fight in America as an engagement in revolutionary suicide, to him the highest form of spiritual self-assertion and freedom. In practicing it, Newton insists, "Although I risk the likelihood of death, there is at least a possibility, if not the probability, of changing intolerable conditions."[29] (In retrospect, it is ironic that Newton died in a rumored drug deal, which by his own definition is a prime example of reactionary suicide. However, despite the circumstances of his death, Newton's stress on the importance of the spiritual side of people is clear.)

It should be noted that unlike Martin Luther King, Jr., who saw freedom as stemming from the practice of a morality that is consistent with God's (eternal) law, Newton saw freedom as existing where the individual is committed to a social practice that enhances the interests of the majority of people. At one point when commenting on the mission of the Black Panther Party, Newton says, "The ideas which can and will sustain our movement for total freedom and dignity of the people cannot be imprisoned, for they are to be found in the people. As long as the people live by the ideas of freedom and dignity, there will be no prison which can hold the movement down."[30] In short, fighting for the interests of the majority of the people is the basis of a freedom.

The word people is very prominent in Newton's rhetoric, and it is necessary to explain his usage of it. Newton accepts the Marxist idea that under the capitalist system a minority ruling class exploits the working class majority, or the "people," and that the laws and institutions of capitalist society rationalize this exploitation. He looks at the United States from this perspective and insists that it was the mission of the Black Panther Party to lead the fight for majority control, or people's control, of the laws and institutions of American society. According to this view, acts, institutions, and laws are considered "moral" if they facilitate "majority" or "people's" control, and they are considered "immoral" if they do not. Thus, we find Newton consistent with this belief saying that in the United States, "law should be made to serve the people. People should not be made to serve the laws. When laws no longer serve the people, it is the people's right and the people's duty to free themselves from the yoke of such laws."[31]

Newton is almost theological in tone when he speaks of the second distinguishing characteristic of people which is the "drive to explain the unknown." Newton argues that people are not only the sole entity in the universe that is constantly engaged in this quest but also the only agent capable of finding solutions to the questions that surround the unknown. To Newton, it is this "X" factor, or unknown, that constitutes the mystery of "God." However, Newton's view of God is more relative and naturalistic than the more personalistic God of both Dr. King and Cone. As Newton explains his view of God's essence, "As soon as the scientist develops or points out a new way of controlling a part of the universe, that aspect of the universe is no longer God."[32] In short, the mystery of "God" is to Newton ultimately knowable and explainable.

In light of his view of God, what is the role of the Church in Newton's system? Newton suggests that its role is to make people aware of the potential for knowledge and of the capacity to eliminate the spiritual and material obstacles that confront them. It is also to make them aware of "heaven." However, when people achieve perfect knowledge, they will have attained heaven. Once this happens, Newton opines, there will be no need for the Church, because since there is no "need for the church in heaven," the Church will have negated itself.[33] Finally, Newton sees the Black Panther Party as having a similar consciousness-raising role as the Church, and when the party, like the Church, has brought people to "truth," Newton insists that the party "will not need to exist because we will have already created our heaven right here on earth."[34]

Newton's Theory of State

Unlike Marcus Garvey, who saw nations based on races as the building blocks of civilization, Newton's writing reveals that he has a more evolutionary and universal view of the state and the nation. Based on concrete experience as a Panther, Newton sees the state as evolving in five distinct but connected stages: the Nationalist, the Revolutionary Nationalist, the Internationalist, the Inter-Communalist, and eventually the stage of the withering away of the state. Newton states that when the Black Panther Party was formed in 1966, its members felt, as Marcus Garvey did, that "nationhood was the answer" to the black dilemma. He goes on to say, however, that the Panthers soon found the Nationalist stage inadequate and moved on to the stage of Revolutionary Nationalism. Newton does not give concrete reasons for the shift, but the general impression one gets from reviewing the Newton literature is that although the Panthers saw the black community as being in the vanguard of the struggle to change America, like most of the other Counter-Communalist Black Powerites, they came to the conclusion that blacks and other minorities needed the support of the white majority to succeed. Newton defines this stage as a more inclusive combination of "nationalism plus socialism," yet after more deeply analyzing its implications the Panthers found that it too was "impractical and even contradictory."[35] Without really explaining what these impracticalities and contradictions were, although one would surmise it had to do with the seeming contradiction of one race—blacks—being depicted as the vanguard of a nonracial socialist revolution, Newton says that the Panthers entered the third stage, that of Internationalism. In the Internationalist stage, the Panthers saw their struggle in the United States as not only necessary for the liberation of blacks and other oppressed people in America, but as a struggle whose success was critical for the liberation of exploited nations worldwide, especially developing nations. Newton says that unfortunately, because of the dominance of Western imperialism in the world, especially U.S. imperialism, the Panthers found that most of the nations of the world lacked the genuine "criteria for nationhood." Instead, they found that the world consisted of a large number of communities all dominated by imperialism. This realization forced the Panthers to move to the stage of Inter-Communalism.[36]

At this point, Newton makes a distinction between what he terms the stage of "Reactionary Inter-Communalism," in which the imperialists dominate the world's communities as they now do, and "Revolutionary Inter-Communalism," when such domination will cease. Newton suggests that the stage of Revolutionary Inter-Communalism will come about "when the people seize the means of production [presumably of the entire imperialist system] and distribute the wealth in an equalitarian way to the many communities of the world."[37] However, this is a long and drawn-out process. The present socialist states claim that they are the building blocks of the future Inter-Communalist system, but Newton insists that because of the existence of Western imperialism there are no genuine socialist states in the world, only liberated territories like North Korea, North Vietnam, and the provisional government of South Vietnam. Although existing in an imperialist-dominated world, they are considered "liberated territories" because they have started a process of building their societies in an Inter-Communalist framework, which makes them pioneers for the future world order.[38] Newton insists that it is only when the Inter-Communalist Revolution is complete that the world will become "a place where people will be happy, wars will end, the state itself will no longer exist, and we will have communism."[39] Much like Marx, Engels, Lenin, and the utopian socialists, Newton sees the future communist world as a stateless one.[40]

Newton's Theory of the State Compared with the Theories of Other Counter-Communalists

While the other Counter-Communalists are in agreement with Newton that the United States should be transformed, and several make suggestions about how to alleviate specific features of the U.S.

system, their conceptions of the state and the good society are less developed than Newton's. Boggs talks of the need for an America where technology serves the people. He suggests that black control of black communities will set the stage for a more humane America, argues for a health system that can serve the needs of the people, and is confident that changes like the foregoing would change America for the better. Nevertheless, Boggs has no comprehensive vision of the good society and does not deal with the question of the state.[41] Similarly, Julius Lester is in agreement with Newton that the capitalist system is oppressive, and he insists that "Black Power is not a move to have the power of the country, as it presently organized, more evenly distributed. It is a move to destroy power as it now exists."[42] He also criticizes imperialism, calls for the "cooperative concept in business and banking," advocates the right of self-determination for all races, and hopes for "a society in which the spirit of community and humanistic love prevail."[43] At the same time, like Boggs, he fails to develop a theory of state in his writings. Cone posits that true reconciliation between blacks and whites in America can come about only when "the black community is permitted to do its thing," and he insists that it is the duty of white Christians to help it do it.[44] Cone, however, also fails to discourse on the nature of the new society or on the kind of state system that would guarantee black self-determination.

Finally, Allen and Forman likewise agree with Newton's criticisms of capitalist society, and they also call for a form of socialism for America. Again, they lack a theory of state. Allen insists that the socialist system in America will not work if it does not include both blacks and whites, and he warns against the illusion of a successful all-black approach. However, on questions of how these changes will come into being or how they will affect international relations Allen is silent.[45] Forman insists that America is run by "seven sources of capital: The U.S. government, banks, business enterprises and corporations, foundations, churches, and people,"[46] and he suggests that blacks will not achieve self-determination until the society is run by the last factor—the people. Forman does not sketch how people's control will come about, however, nor does he theorize on the kind of state that is consistent with people's control. It is apparent that aside from Newton, the theory of the state has not been seriously addressed in Counter-Communalist literature, and the lack of such a theory may account for the many schisms that typified the Black Power Counter-Communalist Left in the 1960s.

Newton's Stage Theory of American History

Newton bases his call for a restructuring of American society along socialist lines on a stage theory of American history that to him makes this change inevitable. He argues that in the first stage of American history, which ended at the end of the eighteenth century, the United States was a small and relatively homogeneous nation with an agricultural base. Within this context, democratic capitalism flourished and the "people" of that time, who were mostly white, could "advance according to their motivation and ability."[47] Newton suggests that even at this stage, however, American society was typified by a basic contradiction, for "while the majority group achieved their basic human rights, the minorities achieved alienation from the lands of their fathers and slavery."[48] In other words, the United States of the late eighteenth century was typified by "majority freedom and minority oppression."[49]

The second stage of American history occurred during the industrial age of the nineteenth and early twentieth centuries. It was during this period that the United States expanded from the eastern seaboard to the rest of the continent, attracted millions of immigrants from all continents to build its industrial machine, and developed an economy controlled by giant corporations. At this time, the initial democratic capitalism of the past was replaced by the "bureaucratic capitalism" of today, a capitalism in which corporations run by a minority of the people increase their profits at the expense of the majority, especially the racial and ethnic underclass.[50] Newton goes on to say that in the second stage of American history another important change took place, one that had fateful consequences for the Civil Rights Movement of the 1960s. During this stage, the descendants of the eighteenth-century citizen class, whose forefathers constituted the majority of the population or "the people," went on to enjoy full citizenship and were among the major beneficiaries of the advances made under the bureaucratic capitalist system. Today, however, instead of being a majority of the population, they constitute a privileged minority, a minority that oppresses the mass of dispossessed workers and minorities who make up the new majority or "the people" of our time. Newton adds that the United States of the bureaucratic capitalist age is the United States that practices imperialism against other nations "so that the profits of American industry can continue to flow."[51]

Newton suggests that the Civil Rights Movement failed because its adherents were trying "to complete the promise of an 18th century revolution in the framework of a 20th century government."[52] The most legitimate way to guarantee mass rights today though is not struggling for civil rights, but to fight to restructure the system along socialist lines. Under socialism, the work and rewards of society will be equally shared by all the "people," and at that stage "all men will attain their full manhood rights."[53] Needless to say, the Black Panther Party constituted the vanguard force that was pioneering the move from civil rights to socialism.

Huey Newton and the Tactics of Counter-Communalism

Consistent with the ideology of Marxism–Leninism from which he borrowed so much, Newton argues that the tactics of the mass movement should not be spontaneous but must be guided by a disciplined vanguard party. As Newton expresses the goal, "The main function of the party is to awaken the people and teach them the strategic method of resisting a power structure which is prepared not only to combat with massive brutality the people's resistance, but to annihilate totally the Black population."[54] According to Newton, the tools the party should use to make the masses conscious of their oppression are propaganda, especially the newspapers and the electronic mass media; educational programs; children's breakfast and lunch programs like those the Panthers established in Oakland, California; electoral politics; and black–white alliances. Newton also stresses that the party must work aboveground and not underground, because among other things voluntary underground or secret activity shows cowardice and hypocrisy, and it also leads people to say that "revolutionaries want the people to say what they themselves are afraid to say, to do what they themselves are afraid to do."[55] Newton adds that the proponents of a secret organization ignore the fact that the successful Cuban and Chinese communist revolutionaries operated openly before they were forced to go underground.

Newton advises that in the process of politicizing the masses, one should use the dialectical method in making alliances and carefully balance the negatives and positives of each phenomenon as the method demands. For example, Newton argues that black capitalism is like all capitalism fundamentally an exploitive economic form. Newton says that in the same way that the native bourgeoisie of the colonies often support the anti-colonial struggle because they see the colonial system as thwarting their highest ambitions, African-American capitalists can be led to see that the "corporate capitalists who control the large monopolies" are thwarting their economic ambitions. Converted businesspeople would then view a group seeking to eliminate the stranglehold of the corporate trusts over the entire system as actually working in their interests in the short run, and thus would support it.[56] Newton says, nevertheless, that black capitalists must be handled diplomatically, because the black community views black capitalist institutions as legitimate parts of their environment and would react against unfocused criticisms of them. In short, Newton concludes that if black capitalists can be persuaded that they have a progressive role to play in the struggle for liberation, "Black Capitalism will be transformed from a relationship of exploitation of the community to a relationship of service to the community, which will contribute to the survival of everyone."[57] It is this realistic assessment of possibilities and historical settings that distinguishes the dialectic approach from idealistic approaches.

At the height of their notoriety in the late 1960s, the Panthers were criticized by Black Nationalists and others for three of their tactics: their participation in electoral politics, their refusal to categorically rule out the use of violence as a liberation tool, and their advocacy of black–white alliances. The criticism regarding the use of electoral politics deepened as several Panthers ran for office over the years. How did Newton respond to these critics? Dealing with the first criticism, Newton argued that until the United States is transformed, "everybody is in the system" and even if one is in prison he or she is still in the system. Newton suggests that to enlighten the masses the contradictions in the system need to be "heightened," and at times electoral politics may be the most legitimate way to do this.[58] Regarding the second, Newton comments that all people who have struggled for socialism have had to use violence at some point, and the Panthers also "feel that only with the power of the gun will the bourgeoisie be destroyed and the world transformed."[59] More importantly, however, Newton reminds his critics that "politics is war without bloodshed, and that war is politics with bloodshed."[60] Thus, those who distinguish between them in an absolute sense, as his critics were doing, fail to discern the true nature of the political.

In responding to the third charge, Newton first criticizes the Nationalists for dismissing the fact that there are many young whites "who are sincere in attempting to realign themselves with mankind, and to make a reality out of the high moral standards that their fathers and forefathers only expressed."[61] He points to white criticism of U.S. involvement in Vietnam and the Dominican Republic as examples of this sincerity. Second, Newton says that whites play a progressive role when they turn against the establishment and when they decide that they are a friend of his rather than "a friend of Lyndon Johnson." But Newton adds that "when whites take this stand, they have a duty and responsibility to act."[62] Subsequently, Newton was asked the question, If you support black–white alliances, why are the Black Panthers an all-black party? Newton responds by saying that "the Black Panther Party is an all Black Party, because we feel as Malcolm X felt that there can be no black–white unity until there is first black unity."[63] He then says that blacks have their own specific and unique problems, and the Panthers will accept aid from the "Mother Country" (white America) "as long as the Mother Country radicals realize, that we have, as Elridge Cleaver says in *Soul on Ice*, a mind of our own." Newton adds that since blacks through the Black Revolution have "regained" their minds, "we'll make the theory and we'll carry out the practice. It's the duty of the white revolutionary to aid us in this."[64] In summary, participation in black–white alliances, the use of violence, the manipulation of mass media, and participation in electoral politics span the range of tactics that Huey Newton and the Panthers advocated in their efforts to achieve black liberation.

Other Counter-Communalists on Tactics

The other Counter-Communalists advocate tactics that are roughly similar to those of the Panthers. Boggs argues, like Newton, that blacks must be in the vanguard of the struggle for change because blacks have the vision "of the new society that only Black Power can create in the U.S.A."[65] Similarly, Boggs dismisses the idea of a spontaneous American revolution and speaks of the need for a "revolutionary organization of serious, dedicated, and disciplined Blacks who have recognized the need for Black Power to revolutionize America and who are prepared to work patiently among the masses to mobilize them for the struggles that will, stage by stage, create pockets of power."[66] Boggs adds that the cadre must use all relevant tactics to achieve this goal and that violence cannot be categorically excluded.[67] A question that was frequently asked advocates of black vanguardism was, Is the Black Panther Party the realization of the black vanguard? Boggs concedes that the Panthers represented the first step toward that goal, but they fell short because they made many mistakes. First, Boggs states that the fanfare with which the Panthers announced their formation "reveals democratic illusions about the rights a revolutionary party contending for power can expect to enjoy in this country."[68] Second, Boggs argues that the original name—"Black Panther Party for Self-Defense—" "shows that its central focus is confrontation with, reaction to, and defense against white oppression, particularly in the form of the police occupation army, rather than an offensive strategy leading to the conquest of power."[69] Thus, to Boggs the Black Panther Party as it was then constituted had fallen far short of fulfilling the goal of a black vanguard force. At the same time, Boggs agrees that the Black Panthers were correct in their strategy of seeking alliances with progressive whites, or those whites who recognized the bankruptcy of America and who "look to the Black Revolutionaries as their only salvation."[70] Boggs feels that progressive whites can make other whites aware of the "legitimacy of Black Power" and neutralize opposition to it, and they can also demonstrate to other whites that there are needs that both blacks and whites have and that the black liberation struggle is addressing these needs. Finally, Boggs concludes, as does Newton, that "only after revolutionary whites have taken some power from other whites now in power can they sit down with revolutionary blacks who have also wrested some power from some whites and as equals with power lay the basis for the relationship of new social forces in the United States."[71]

Julius Lester is in agreement with the others that a "cadre of organizers" to politicize the masses is needed and that this vanguard force should mobilize them for action.[72] He goes on to say that since blacks have been educated by the Panthers into accepting the notion of self-defense, "the next step in the evolution of the revolutionary process will be the movement from self-defense to aggressive action," an aggressive action that cannot exclude absolutely the use of violence.[73] Furthermore, Lester like the others also sees black–white alliances as essential, although he counsels that sympathetic whites "must evolve an approach to their own communities" and then join with blacks who are fighting for change.[74] In short, the need for a black vanguard force and the necessity of joining with sympathetic whites were common characteristics of the Counter-Communalist Ideology of the 1960s.

To further illustrate this conclusion, when one looks at the works of Robert Allen and James Forman, one finds the same ideas expressed. Allen speaks of the need to develop "an independent Black political party capable of providing militant leadership";[75] he insists that the party "devise a strategy of calculated confrontation, using a mixture of tactics to fit a variety of contingencies";[76] and he supports alliances with whites, especially those like the student radicals, who "are capable of initiating skirmishes, which then mobilize thousands of non-radical whites."[77] In fact, Allen suggests that the black vanguard will not succeed until it finds a way to induce the masses of white labor into becoming more receptive to multiracialism and socialism. Finally, in tones reminiscent of Newton's Revolutionary Inter-Communalist ideal, Allen calls for an alignment between the poor struggling in the United States and the poor in the rest of the world.[78] However, Allen, unlike Newton, Boggs, and Lester, warns against the party becoming an elitist organ that is not "solidly based upon the masses of ordinary black working people" as vanguardist parties have a tendency to become.[79] He is also skeptical especially of members of the black middle class and black intellectuals assuming direction of the party, for they "are as likely to be reactionary as they are to be revolutionary, and for this reason they must always be somewhat suspect."[80] Forman also supports the concept of "an independent political organization" dedicated to serving the people, he also argues that it should organize the masses by "whatever means necessary," and he is strongly for the idea of black–white alliances.[81] Furthermore, regarding the idea that blacks must be the catalyst for change and the leading force for revolution in America, Forman is as militant as Newton. As Forman expresses it, "We, as Black people in this country, understand we are the revolutionary force which is going to be the Vanguard in the final destruction of this system of government under which we live. We understand that, and we are not going to abdicate our leadership to anybody."[82] In summary, Forman, Newton, Boggs, Allen, and Lester are in essential agreement on the tactics of Black Power and on the need for a vanguard party.

Perhaps because he is a theologian and not a political tactician, Cone, unlike the others, does not call for the formation of a cadre organization to lead the masses to liberation. On the other hand, like the others he does see Black Power as an instrument—in his view a Christian instrument—to articulate the demands of the oppressed, and like the others he also does not categorically reject violence as an instrument of change. For example, Cone saw the black riots of the 1960s not as contradictions of Christian love but "as the Black man's attempts to say yes to his being as defined by God in a world that would make his being into a non-being." Furthermore, Cone says that if the violence is the black man's way of affirming himself "as a creature of God . . . then violence may be the black man's expression, sometimes the only possible expression, of Christian love to the White oppressor."[83] In short, all the Counter-Communalists reject the existing American system and advocated the building of a new America by any means necessary. The new America would be a socialist one, an America without imperialism, and an America that sees itself as a part of a broader humanity.

IX

The Black Power Pluralists: A Comparison and Analysis

The Pluralists are those advocates of Black Power who argue that power in the United States is divided along interest and ethnic group lines, and the inability of African-Americans to obtain their requisite portion of economic and political power stems from their failure to mobilize themselves into an effective "ethnic-interest group" that stresses collective success over individual achievement. The Pluralist version of Black Power is designed to correct this deficiency. It should be noted that unlike the Counter-Communalists or Separatists, who argue that liberation cannot be achieved within the American system, the Pluralists believe that by working within the system and by skillfully using the strategies and techniques sanctioned by it, African-Americans can achieve the level of success that other ethnic groups have attained. Charles Hamilton, by this definition a Pluralist, expresses the position well when he says that "black people will gain only as much as they can win through their ability to organize independent bases of economic and political power—through boycotts, electoral activity, rent strikes, work stoppages, pressure group bargaining."[1] It follows that given their orientation, Pluralists view the advocacy of violence as counterproductive in the African-American's quest for liberation. The categorical rejection of violence differentiates the Pluralists from the Counter-Communalists, and, as we shall see, from those Separatists who do not rule out violence as a legitimate instrument for social change.

Outstanding African-American legislators like Barbara Jordan and Shirley Chisholm, who served in Congress with eloquence and distinction, are popular with Americans of all races and creeds and were successful to the degree that they were because they were not perceived as having an ideological agenda. However, it is because they represented their constituencies with pragmatism and ingenuity and never failed to act in the interest of their African-American constituency when the situation warranted it that they are excellent real-life examples of Pluralism. Chisholm, the first black woman member of Congress, is highlighted throughout this chapter because in the 1960s she was undoubtedly the most articulate and forthright practitioner of the kind of politics that in this book has been termed Pluralist. Indeed, from the vantage point of the 1990s, it would not be unfair to call her the pioneer in the field, because since the 1960s, black politicians ranging from the mayor of Detroit, to the mayor of Los Angeles, to the governor of Virginia, to the Reverend Jesse Jackson in his two presidential races have all used the strategies of coalition building, black–white alliances, and effective mobilization of the black vote that Chisholm advocated so strongly. Indeed, Jackson's two attempts at the presidency were presaged by Chisholm's running for the same office in 1972.[2] As the exposition proceeds, her thoughts will be compared with those of other Pluralists, like Hamilton, Nathan Wright, Jr., Sir Arthur Lewis, and others.[3]

Shirley Chisholm's Background and Intellectual Influences

Shirley Chisholm (b. 1924) was born in Brooklyn, New York, of West Indian parentage. Her father, Charles St. Hill, was a native of British Guiana (now Guyana), who had grown up in Barbados; and her mother, Ruby Seale, was a native of Barbados. Both of Shirley's parents later migrated to the United States, where they were married. During the depression, economic conditions were so bad that the St. Hills doubted whether they would be able "to buy a house and provide education for their girls."[4] After some deliberation, it was decided that Shirley and her two sisters would be sent to Barbados, where they would remain until their parents had saved enough to take care of them in the United States.

Returning to the United States from Barbados in 1934, Chisholm finished high school in New York, attended Brooklyn College from 1942 to 1946, and graduated cum laude in Spanish and sociology. Her interest in social affairs also emerged during her college years, and she joined the Brooklyn chapter of the NAACP and worked with the Urban League. After graduation, Chisholm obtained a master's degree from Columbia University, directed the Mt. Calvary Child Center in Harlem for seven years, and until 1960 headed the large Hamilton–Madison Child Care Center in Harlem.

Deeply influenced by her Garveyite father, who in Chisholm's view stressed a race pride to his children "that was not fashionable at that time as it is today,"[5] she became involved in Democratic politics in New York and soon rebelled at the machine's practice of "don't rock the boat!" politics.[6] Frustrated by the Democratic Party's tactics, Chisholm "formed the Unity Democratic Party Club as an alternative to the existing political machine in Brooklyn."[7] This multiracial pressure group scored a major success in 1965 when Chisholm was elected to the New York legislature. After serving four years there, the outspoken Chisholm was elected to the U.S. Congress in 1969. While in Congress, she distinguished herself in the House of Representatives by consistently opposing the Vietnam War, always standing up for the rights of blacks and other minorities, pioneering in the advocacy of women's rights, and stubbornly refusing to automatically adhere to the prerogatives of the seniority system. In 1972, she tried to gain the Democratic nomination for the presidency, failing when the nomination went to Senator George McGovern. She retired from politics in 1982.

The Political Thought of Shirley Chisholm

Unlike Huey Newton and Martin Luther King, Jr., who have written elaborate descriptions of their intellectual and spiritual development, Chisholm's works are less intellectually structured. She is the pragmatist and activist rather than the political and social theorist. As was the case with Booker T. Washington and Frederick Douglass, her political theory must be gleaned from her speeches and writings rather than from formal essays on the subject. The lack of a systematic political theory does not mean however, that Chisholm's political views are any less challenging or engaging than those of the other thinkers that we have discussed.

Chisholm and the American Creed

It was argued that Dr. King accepted most of the premises of the American creed and that his political activism may be viewed as an attempt to bring its promise to fruition. In many respects the same can be said of Chisholm, for like King, she strongly believed in the American system, emphasizing that "it is her belief that the basic design of this country is right."[8] Of the values of the American creed, Chisholm especially cherished the belief that the fostering of the individualism is the highest good. She argues that one of the weaknesses of contemporary America is the tendency for individuals to place class or race loyalties before their obligation to respect the individual. As an example of this narrow-mindedness, Chisholm tells of the criticism she received following her visit with Governor George Wallace of Alabama after he was wounded in an assassination attempt during his 1972 campaign for the presidency. Wallace was seen by blacks as a racist, and many blacks criticized Chisholm for carrying out what she terms a "private expression of human sympathy and concern."[9] In fact, Chisholm says that "one Black man from Texas, a delegate pledged to me, was so angry that he threatened to withdraw his support."[10] Chisholm said that she visited Wallace for two reasons. First, it was the humane thing to do. Second, despite his racism, Wallace, in his call for a more responsive government, a fairer tax structure, a less concentrated wealth distribution in America ("Roughly 2% of the people of this country control 80% of resources and wealth"), and the like, was echoing sentiments that millions of Americans of all colors and classes shared.[11] In short, to Shirley Chisholm human decency came before ideology.

Another example, of Chisholm's commitment to the American creed can be seen in her reaction to the criticism leveled against her presidential bid at a Black Political Convention in Gary, Indiana, in 1972. The convention was called to hammer out a common black strategy for the presidential election of 1972. At the convention Chisholm was criticized by many of the black politicians assembled there for going off on an ego trip, and she received little support from them for her campaign. One of the conference's organizers, black poet and separatist Imamu Baraka (LeRoi Jones), was especially critical of her position, and he argued that blacks should participate in the system only to the degree that such participation aided them in building a base for future black separation. (Baraka has since become a Counter-Communalist.) Chisholm praised Baraka's eloquence and persuasion, "which many black elected officials cannot match." Yet she goes on to say that "I cannot understand how someone who holds such strong Separatist views keeps trying to associate himself with those of us who still believe that, in spite of the inequities and grievances that persist, America can become a just, democratic and multifaceted society."[12]

Chisholm's Dream for America

Dr. King frequently spoke of his dream of an America without racism and inequality, and although not expressed as poetically as that of Dr. King, Shirley Chisholm had a similar vision. To Chisholm, when all groups that make up America participate in its decision making, and when all the people of America receive a decent proportion of its goods and services, this is when the country will have laid the basis for achieving its true potential. However, for America to do this, she insists that "the Blacks alone can't do it. The young people can't do it. The women alone can't do it. But together all these groups can rise up to get their share of the American dream and participate in the decision making process that governs our lives."[13] Chisholm opined that she probably was naive, but she viewed her candidacy as an effort to aid in this process.

During her campaign for the presidency, Chisholm states that she saw a miniature enactment of her American dream at a program at Hamline University in Minnesota. As she describes it, the audience was one of the biggest and warmest she had during the campaign. On the agenda they had in addition to her speech, "a program of student poetry readings and music by a Black vocal group and the Hamline University Jazz Band." Chisholm remarks that "as I looked out over them I could not help feeling that I was seeing the future of America as it should be, as it must be—Black and White youth together, Black and White adults, women, children, Indians, Hispano-Americans, the alienated and left-out—joined with the mainstream of the nation at last, all reaching out to be included in the democratic process."[14]

Other Pluralists on the American System

It should be pointed out that not all Pluralists possessed the same faith and optimism in the American system and its processes that Chisholm exhibited. Charles Hamilton, for example, while commenting on the unrest of the 1960s, depicts them not as riots but as revolts. He uses the word *revolt* because to him "they were acts which deny the very legitimacy of the system itself." Hamilton goes on to explain that the unrest was in reality a challenge to such negative features of the American system as "a value structure which supports property rights over human rights," a system of law and order that means "the perpetuation of an intolerable status-quo," and "traditional political procedures for alleviating one's ills that were not sufficient."[15] Despite his skepticism of the system, Hamilton suggests that blacks work within its confines, but he cautions that black strategies should not be clouded by visions of what America ought to be, and that they "should depend entirely on a hard nosed, calculated examination of potential success in each situation—a careful analysis of cost and benefit."[16] Similarly in 1966, Stokely Carmichael, while arguing that blacks use their political power within the system to attain "proper representation and sharing of control," makes it clear that he is not advocating that blacks join the American mainstream.[17] As Carmichael saw it, true inclusion of blacks in the present-day United States involves so radical a change that it "is impossible under present circumstances." Furthermore, he notes that he was in complete agreement with a Brooklyn College faculty member who stressed that when blacks talk about participating in the mainstream, "they don't realize that the mainstream is the very cause of their troubles."[18]

Black Power Pluralist Dr. Nathan Wright, Jr., on the other hand is closer to Chisholm in his view of the American system than he is to Carmichael and Hamilton. Like Chisholm, Wright believes that the United States has the potential to become a great nation, and Wright is at one with Chisholm when he says in regard to Black Power that "the thrust of Black Power is toward freeing the latent power of negroes to enrich the life of the whole nation."[19] In summary, despite the fact that all the Pluralists agree that blacks should work within the American system and use its tools to obtain their goals, they differ regarding the degree of their faith in the system.

Shirley Chisholm on the Obstacles to True Pluralism in the United States

Although Chisholm sees a multiethnic and open society as the goal for the United States, based on her governmental experiences she sees three major political obstacles to the development of this dream: the Machiavellian nature of congressional politics, Congress's general inability to respond to the needs of the voters, and the decisive importance of money in American politics.

The Machiavellian Nature of U.S. Politics

Chisholm argues that the core of U.S. politics is "don't rock the boat" and that this "maxim," which she always defied, lies at the root of our political problems. Chisholm relates that after she was elected to the 91st Congress, she expected to be put on a committee like the Education and Labor Committee, because in an urban area like Brooklyn, education and labor matters are of primary importance. To her consternation—and in line with the prevailing notion of the time that freshman congresspersons accept the committee assignments that the senior congressmen designate for them—she was assigned to the Subcommittee on Rural Development and Forestry.[20] Chisholm objected vehemently to this assignment, and after refusing to accept an alternative slot on the Agricultural Committee she broke tradition and appealed to the "full Democratic Majority at a caucus."[21] Finally, after much debate and embarrassment, Chisholm was placed on the Veteran Affairs Committee, a post far more in line with her own experience and the needs of her district. Chisholm relates that subsequently both members of Congress and outside observers lectured her that one does not advance in Congress by proposing one's own measures, but by "blocking measures others want enacted or by supporting measures others oppose." One reporter told her that if she had used the proposed post on the Agricultural Committee to "scuttle price supports and other farm programs—farm belt Congressmen would have been knocking on her door asking for favors."[22] Chisholm saw this type of political trading, which she calls "Machiavellian," as harmful in two ways. First, it prevents the issues that confront the public from being openly and seriously debated by their representatives. Second, the moral questions surrounding what is right or good always become secondary to the queries, Why did he say that? or, Where does he expect that to get him? or, Who put him up to that?[23] Chisholm says that with some notable exceptions, the liberal bloc of congresspersons from whom she expected more "moral fight" were particularly disappointing in this regard. As she describes it, "The liberals in the House strongly resemble liberals I have known through the last two decades in the Civil Rights conflict. When it comes time to show on which side they will be counted, they suddenly excuse themselves."[24] Chisholm concludes that without "a deeper and more sincere commitment by some of its members," Congress will become more and more unable to solve America's problems.[25] It is worth remembering that Chisholm was speaking before the Watergate scandal almost brought the American system of law and governmental checks to its knees, which serves to further prove how sharp and insightful an observer of American politics she actually was.[26]

Congress's Inability to Respond to Voter Needs

In addition to a Machiavellian mindset that prohibits Congress from responding more directly to the needs of the public, Chisholm saw the seniority system, which allots committee chairmanships to legislators based on the time they serve in Congress, as another roadblock to a more democratic political process. Chisholm maintains that as a result of the seniority system, Congress is "ruled by a small group of old men"[27] who are frequently elected from "rural backwaters" where the broad issues that face urban America are absent.[28] As a result, "competence, character, past performance, background or orientation" are not necessarily the requisites for office, but rather one's ability to "stay alive and keep getting re-elected."[29] To correct the abuses of the system, Chisholm suggests that the age of congresspersons should be limited to sixty-five, the committee system be shaken up by moving members around, that "six or eight terms in the House or three or four in the Senate should be the limit regardless of age," and that all congresspersons be required to avoid conflicts of interest while making complete financial disclosure of their assets.[30] If actions of this kind were taken, Chisholm predicted that a great step will have been taken toward making America a truly Pluralist and Democratic society. (During and since Chisholm's tenure in Congress changes have taken place in the seniority system. The political scientist James Q. Wilson points out that in 1971 House Democrats agreed "to elect committee chairmen by secret ballot," in 1975 "they used the procedure to remove four committee chairmen who held their posts by seniority," and "in 1985 they removed the chairman of the House Armed Services Committee." Thus, although seniority is still a factor in committee selection, it is not as overriding as it used to be.)[31]

Money as an Obstacle to Democratic Politics in the United States

According to Chisholm, the third obstacle to a truly multiclass and multiracial democracy in the United States, and which became patently clear to her during her campaign for the presidency, is the decisive importance of money in determining who participates in U.S. politics. In Chisholm's view, it is tragic that "everywhere in this country there are men and women who have real ability and new solutions to offer, but they will never have a chance to serve in public office because they do not have the money to run and win." Chisholm suggests as a solution that campaigns be shorter and more "tightly regulated and financed by public funds."[32] If campaign funds were made more available, Chisholm believes that more capable and varied representation would be the result. (A step in the direction that Chisholm articulated was taken in 1972 when a law was passed that enabled the federal government to give matching funds to party presidential candidates and nominees. The law did not help Chisholm, but it did help the Reverend Jesse Jackson in his 1984 and 1988 campaigns for the presidency. The issue of matching funds also illustrates Chisholm's pioneering role in raising issues that would later affect other Black Power political Pluralists.)[33]

Progress in Removing the Obstacles to Democratic Politics

To Chisholm, the effects of the obstacles to democratic politics on black and other minority participation in the electoral process were devastating.[34] She laments that although blacks and minorities at that time made up nearly 30 percent of the electorate, they "do not vote because they see no salvation for them in either political party or candidate. They know that the parties represent the White majority, and they are not true participants in the political process."[35] (Since this statement there has been an increase in black political participation. For example, the African-American historians Mary Frances Berry and John W. Blasingame point out that in 1974 there were around 200 blacks in 37 state legislatures and 17 in Congress including Chisholm. In May 1975, there were 3,503 blacks in elective office.)[36] Chisholm notes that starting in 1972, the Democratic Party began to reform its rules "to open up the party to all kinds of people, old and young, white and black, men and women."[37] Chisholm still saw the effort as inadequate, however, and she insists that the Democratic Party politics of 1972 remained a white man's politics."[38] (Despite its limits, the Democratic Party reforms of 1972 initiated a process of change in the party that had its biggest effect during the Jackson presidential campaign of 1984, when Jackson won scores of delegates. Today, the rules are far more liberal than before, and Jackson used them to his advantage again in 1988. Her raising of the matter of rule changes within the Democratic Party once again points out Chisholm's role as a Black Power Pluralist pioneer.)[39] Reflecting on the black minority political predicament in America, she concluded that the sole hope for the black minority was to rethink the integrationist approach used hitherto and try a new strategy. Now, they must use their ethnic power or Black Power to achieve their desires instead of relying totally on the conscience of American society. (Chisholm's case for Black Power is discussed after the next section.)

Other Pluralists on the Obstacles to Democracy

A review of the Pluralist literature reveals that most Pluralists are in general agreement with Chisholm on the failings of the American political process. Carmichael, for example, when commenting on the efforts of his organization, the Student Non-Violent Coordinating

Committee (SNCC), to organize the black sharecroppers of Alabama into a political force in 1966, notes two features of the American political system that could thwart the effort. First, he cautions that the American political process tends to stifle grass-roots expressions of democracy. Second, he wonders if "perhaps power politics will eventually overwhelm the freedom parties," and "the would-be Negro sheriffs that they were trying to elect."[40] In other words, Carmichael, like Chisholm, was well aware of the limits of the American political process as it functioned at the time. Finally, although Carmichael is far more sweeping in his criticism of the American system than is Chisholm, it should be noted that he agrees with her that the power of the minority that controls Congress must be broken if America is to fulfill itself. As Carmichael sees it, the minority that controls Congress is representative of the tiny minority that monopolizes the economic system in the United States, and he is of the opinion that black liberation could not be achieved until "the economic foundations of this country" are shaken.[41] Carmichael adds that mass democracy will not work effectively until this powerful political and economic minority that has enriched itself "at the expense of the poor and colored masses" both in America and around the world has been removed.[42] Unlike Huey Newton, however, in the mid-1960s Carmichael felt, as did Chisholm, that the goal could be achieved by using the American electoral process.

Shirley Chisholm and the Case for Black Power Pluralism

To put Chisholm's case for Black Power in its proper perspective it is necessary to carry out three tasks. First, her opinion of the Civil Rights Movement, its origins, successes, and failures must be considered. Second, her analysis of the various types of Black Power must be described. Third, her vision of the good society must be compared in more detail with the visions of other Pluralists.

From Civil Rights to Black Power

In tracing the change from civil rights to Black Power, Chisholm she sees the modern Civil Rights Movement as starting with the Montgomery bus boycott of 1955, broadening its focus in 1960 when four black students in Greensboro, North Carolina, began the nationwide sit-in movement with their efforts to be served coffee at a segregated Woolworth lunch counter, and becoming a nationwide mass movement with the freedom rides of the mid-1960s.[43]

In spite of its enthusiastic start, Chisholm states that the Civil Rights Movement "did not achieve its lofty goals," for aside from integrating hotels and buses and later obtaining a more liberalized vote, most blacks found by the mid-1960s that they were not much better off than before. As some blacks expressed the dilemma, "What good is it to sit in the front of the bus when you haven't got the fare."[44] It was these kinds of realizations and the feeling by black students that even in the Civil Rights Movement they were "still subtly being treated as inferiors by white students," that led to the breakup of the black–white alliance.[45] Chisholm saw the same "master–slave" relationship that typified Frederick Douglass's relationship with William Lloyd Garrison characterizing black–white relationships in the Civil Rights Movement. In reaction to this unequal status, young blacks who had at first been "integrationist and non-violent—became separatist and militant." It was after the decline of the Civil Rights Movement that the era of Black Power began.[46] Why according to Chisholm did the Civil Rights Movement fail? First, it failed because it was an illusion to think that a black minority oppressed for three hundred years could move forward to full citizenship, "one by one, on the strength of individual talents and luck." That only worked for a few, and even for those few it most often meant that they became "probationary members of American society." Second, it failed because although blacks are proud of the achievements of fellow blacks like late U.N. representative Ralph Bunche, entertainer Sammy Davis, Jr., and New York politician Percy Sutton, their achievements do not "close or even appreciably narrow the gulf between them and the greater society." Finally, it failed because the entire integrationist strategy was the brainchild of a "small group of white idealists who did not understand their own society. They did not know the facts of life, that all Americans are prisoners of racial prejudice."[47] It is because of the pervasiveness of racial prejudice that Chisholm saw the rise of the Black Power Movement as inevitable.

Chisholm on Achieving Black Power

Chisholm comments that there are a variety of Black Power groupings ranging "from community-united black fronts to the Black Panthers and the Republic of New Africa." In her view, regardless of their tactics and in spite of her own differences with them, "each has an essential role to play in the cure." Chisholm admits that the Black Power Movement's calls for independence from white society, new styles of dress, behavior, and so on—in short, their stressing that blacks must become "beautiful, black, and proud"—struck "a deep chord in the soul of black Americans," who have traditionally been demeaned.[48] Chisholm supports these features of the Black Power Movement.

Instead of supporting the militant tactics adopted by some of the Black Power groups, however, Chisholm supports what she terms "a more sophisticated and forward looking concept of Black Power." She feels that the core of this conception of Black Power was summarized well by historian Christopher Lasch in his book *The Agony of the American Left*, which analyzes what other ethnic groups faced with similar conditions have done.[49] These other ethnic groups built economic and political power within their group, used their ethnic vote to achieve the political power that could stabilize their gains, and sought higher and higher offices within the American political system. For example, in the case of the Irish, "In less than four generations—the despised Boston Irish produced mayors, senators and at last a president."[50] If the Irish can do it, why can't the blacks? asks Chisholm. It is apparent that Chisholm supports what in this book is termed Black Power Pluralism.

Chisholm Versus Other Pluralist Black Powerites

Chisholm's view of how to achieve Black Power is shared by all the Pluralists including Charles Hamilton, Stokely Carmichael, Dr. Nathan Wright, Jr., and Sir Arthur Lewis, the Nobel prize winning black economist from St. Lucia. While admitting that Black Power involves a degree of self-segregation, Lewis does not see that as negative, because "all American minorities have passed through a stage of temporary self-segregation, not just the Afro-Americans."[51] Like Chisholm, Lewis sees the black challenge as one of performing well enough in the integrated world of workplace and business to be able to gain enough resources to build up black communities and, by skill, education, and the use of collective power, to successfully compete for a just proportion of America's goods and services. For Lewis, the accomplishment of these objectives would lay the basis for Black Power.

Black political analyst Chuck Stone expresses many of the same sentiments as Lewis and Chisholm. In Stone's opinion, "In no major political situation in America—since Reconstruction"—have blacks achieved their just proportion of power, largely because blacks deemphasized ethnic power. As Stone laments, "Ethnic bloc voting and ethnic political loyalty has been a feverish adjunct of every ethnic group in America except black people." Stone believes that Black

Power is a necessary corrective to this failing. What has prevented blacks from stressing their ethnicity before the 1960s? Stone claims that blacks have "been too busy trying to get integrated and listening to the Black surrogates of White racism such as Roy Wilkins, Whitney Young and Bayard Rustin instead of trying to build political bases."[52] Stone is clearly in agreement with Chisholm and Lewis in calling for the replacement of integrationist politics with ethnic politics.

Other Pluralist Visions of the Good Society

As previously mentioned, Chisholm believes that the good society in the United States will emerge when there is true representative democracy and when all our institutions reflect "the multi-faceted and multi-racial" makeup of the country. What are some other Pluralist visions of the good society? Dr. Nathan Wright Jr., sees it taking place in the United States when Black Power has become so intense and been accepted so widely that it renews America in all its facets. Charles Hamilton argues that to create the good society blacks must succeed on both the "internal" and "external" fronts in the United States. On the internal front, blacks must cure their own communities of exploitive merchants, absentee slumlords, bad schools, arbitrary justice, and political and economic disorganization. Hamilton continues, saying these problems "do not require the presence of massive numbers of whites marching arm in arm with blacks."[53] External problems, on the other hand, are those that must be dealt with outside the ghettoes. These problems include "jobs, open occupancy, medical care and higher education,"[54] and Hamilton insists that blacks are deluding themselves if they believe that they can solve them without white help. Blacks need white help because there are simply not enough resources in the ghetto "for a total, unilateral bootstrap operation."[55] Why should whites help blacks according to Hamilton? He answers that if black powerlessness continues, the United States will become an increasingly unstable society and an illegitimate one in the eyes of blacks. Whites must be made to see that an equitable distribution of power between blacks and themselves "is a matter of mutual interest," for if black degradation continues, it will ruin the future of not only those blacks affected but the entire society. Hamilton concludes that if blacks can succeed on the internal and external fronts, then true integration will become a realistic possiblility. This type of integration will however, involve blacks "who are psychologically and mentally healthy, with people who have a sense of their history and themselves as human beings."[56]

Finally, Carmichael, somewhat like Hamilton, sees the good society occurring when blacks become so politically and economically effective that they have "their own institutions with which to represent their own communal needs within the larger society." To Carmichael, "This is one reason Africa has such importance: the reality of Black men ruling their own nations gives Blacks elsewhere a sense of possibility, of power, which they do not now have."[57] In summary, all Pluralists see the achievement of Black Power in the United States as not only necessary for blacks, but as mandatory for the development of a truly multiracial society in the United States as a whole. In essence, the Pluralist vision is the American vision.

The Tactics of Pluralism

The tactics of Pluralism have been mentioned in so many places in this chapter that they can be portrayed quite succinctly by being summed up. First, all the Pluralists agree that blacks must effectively use "coalition politics." Coalition politics, as defined by Shirley Chisholm, means a form of black politics that "is issue oriented instead of party oriented. It draws together disparate groups, who combine temporarily, in all probability—around some issue of overriding importance to them at that time and place. By its nature, it confronts the traditional politics of expediency and compromise."[58] Richard Hatcher, mayor of Gary, Indiana, in the 1960s, agrees with Chisholm that blacks do not need to riot; instead, they need to "mobilize political strength around militant demands,"[59] which can be met by skillful performance in a coalition. Second, all the Pluralists agree that black control of community institutions, especially the educational institutions, is necessary for Black Power. For example, Chisholm notes that properly run black–controlled educational institutions can aid in the development of black political sophistication.[60] Yet other Pluralists like Wright and Hamilton suggest that blacks build economic cooperatives to lay the basis for black economic independence. Hamilton points to the success of the Congress of Racial Equality's (CORE) farming cooperatives in Opelousas, Louisiana, as a start in the right direction.[61] Wright, on the other hand, urges "cooperative buying."[62] Finally, all the Pluralists exclude violence as a legitimate strategy for social change in the United States. For example, Shirley Chisholm remarks that while she is aware that many blacks and whites support "individual violence or mass rebellion," she is not convinced "that such tragic heroism is the only course of action left."[63] Similarly, Charles Hamilton opposes the use of violence for four reasons. First, the history of the black experience demonstrates that "he who shouts revolution the loudest is one of the first to run when the action starts." Second, calls to violence "are a sure way to have one's ranks immediately infiltrated." Third, a violent revolution by blacks in the United States would fail because blacks are militarily powerless. Fourth, Hamilton stresses correctly that a black call to arms would pander to the wishes of the worst racists in the United States. As he summarizes this danger; "There are many White bigots who would like nothing better than to embark on a program of Black genocide, even though the imposition of such repressive measures would destroy civil liberties for Whites as well as Blacks."[64] Thus, for moral, pragmatic, and common-sense reasons, the Pluralists rule out the use of violence as an instrument for black liberation.

X

The Black Power Separatists: A Comparison and Analysis

The Black Power Separatists are those advocates of Black Power who, like the Counter-Communalists, disvalue the American system of values, interests, and beliefs, but who insist that liberation for blacks can come only in a separate state. In this regard, Black Power Separatism can be described as a 1960s version of Garveyism, although as will become apparent, most of its manifestations lack the back-to-Africa goal that typified the Garvey Movement. Because the Nation of Islam was the largest and oldest Black Power organization of the 1960s calling for separation, and because it was directed from the 1930s by one man, the Honorable Elijah Muhammad, a broad understanding of Separatist thought may be gained by examining the political theory of Muhammad and comparing it with the thoughts of other Separatists of the time, for example, Imamu Baraka (LeRoi Jones), Imari Abubakari Obadele I (Richard Henry) of the Republic of New Africa (RNA), and Yusufu Sonebeyatta (Joseph Brooks) of the RNA.[1]

Elijah Muhammad's Background and Career

Elijah Muhammad (1898–1975), formerly Elijah Poole, was born in Sandersville, Georgia, the son of a rural preacher. Muhammad was educated in the public schools there and never left the state until he was twenty-five years old. Unlike many of the persons highlighted in this study, Muhammad, by his own (admission, had the bare rudiments of a formal education, since at an early age "he had to go to the fields to help his family earn a living."[2] In April 1923, Muhammad, along with his wife and two children, moved to Detroit, where he

166

worked for the Southern Railroad and Cherokee Brick Company as "a tramroad foreman and builder."[3] It was in Detroit that he met Wallace D. Fard, whom the Black Muslims regard as God's incarnation and who converted Poole into the Black Islamic faith. One of the major tenets of Fard's Black Islamism was that by keeping white European names, blacks were denying their true identity, which was Muslim and Islamic. Consistent with this belief, Elijah Muhammad changed his name. As a reward for his religious devotion, Fard eventually made Muhammad the Apostle of Allah and sole interpreter of God's words (i.e., Fard's words) on earth. In 1934, when Fard disappeared, Muhammad became leader of the Black Muslim Movement.

Despite the Black Islamic belief in racial separation, Muhammad during his long career had but two clashes with the law. In 1934 he went to prison to protest the State of Michigan's charging the teachers in the private Black Muslims schools in Detroit with "contributing to the delinquency of minors." Eventually the charge was dropped and the teachers freed on the condition that the Muslim children be put back "in the public schools under Christian teachers."[4] Muhammad refused to comply with this request and instead moved his headquarters to Chicago.

Muhammad's other clash with the law ocurred on May 8, 1942, when he was charged with sedition against the United States for his advocacy of nonviolence during the war and for refusing to register for the draft. Muhammad argues that he refused to register on two grounds: "When the call was made for all males between 18 and 44, I refused (not evading) on the grounds that, first, I was a Muslim and would not take part in war and especially not on the side with infidels. Second, I was 45 years of age and was not according to the law required to register."[5] The charge of sedition was eventually dropped, but Muhammad was "convicted on the charge of encouraging draft resistance and sentenced to five years in the Federal Correction Institute at Milan, Michigan. He was released in 1946."[6] The sociologist E. U. Essien-Udom estimates that during the war years a hundred Black Muslims were arrested on similar charges. The Chicago temple was frequently raided because the government believed that the Black Muslims were "Japanese espionage agents." Udom notes that usually the "police did not 'molest' the women who were present at the temple," but the men who were arrested and convicted were "each sentenced to 3 years imprisonment and, upon release, placed on 9 months probation." In Udom's opinion, "although some Muslims could have avoided arrest during the raids, most were anxious to be

included among the 'persecuted' and submitted themselves volun-
tarily."[7]

After World War II, branches of the Nation of Islam were founded
in every major city of the United States and in some foreign countries.
In addition, the Muslims owned numerous farms, restaurants, businesses, and a newspaper with the largest circulation in the black
community in the 1960s. When writing about the Muslims in 1960,
African-American sociologist, C. Eric Lincoln, noted that "the Black
Muslims have come far under Muhammad. He has given them temples and schools, apartment houses and grocery stores, resturants and
farms. Most important of all, he has given them a new sense of dignity, a conviction that they are more than the equals of the white man
and destined to rule the earth."[8] During the 1960s and early 1970s, the
Black Muslims continued to make gains in all the areas described by
Lincoln, a success that lasted until Elijah Muhammad's death in 1975.
After his death, his son and successor, Wallace D. Muhammad abandoned the Separatist and antiwhite doctrine and moved the organization closer to the multiracial doctrines of orthodox Islam. Furthermore, "he called upon Afro-Americans to adopt the name 'Bilalians,'
and urged the hitherto apolitical Muslims to register to vote." (Bilal
was the first black convert of the prophet Muhammad.)[9] A segment of
the Black Muslims led by Louis Farrakhan split with Wallace Muhammad over these doctrinal changes and continues today the Separatist
tradition of Elijah Muhammad.

The Political Theology of Elijah Muhammad

Muhammad was not a socialist with a scientific socialist outlook
like Huey Newton, nor was he a Christian theologian with a universal
Christian perspective as was Dr. Martin Luther King, Jr. Muhammad
did, however, develop a somewhat elaborate theological system to explain Black Muslim political, social, and religious practice. A brief
look at that system will be helpful in understanding the group's behavior in these areas.

As stated in Chapter I, Muhammad argues that whites are the offspring of the inventive devil Yakub, who was at one point a rising star
in the world's first nation, which was a black nation. After causing
dissension in the Black nation, Yakub and 59,999 of his followers
were allowed to migrate to the island of Pelan (the biblical Patmos) in
the Aegean Sea, where he continued and succeeded in his biological
experiments to create an all-white race. God sent the prophet Muham-

mad to try to convert the new race to the Islamic religion and to civilized ways. However, according to Elijah Muhammad, whites reacted so violently to the prophet Muhammad's teachings that they "caused him heart trouble until his death (age sixty-two and one-half years.)"[10] Then, Moses tried to go into Europe to convert them after their "2,000 years of living as a savage."[11] Moses failed also, at one point dynamiting three hundred of the worst miscreants. Elijah Muhammad saw the white maltreatment of the prophets as ample warning to blacks like Dr. King who preached racial brotherhood that they were propounding a doctrine that was contrary to nature. In short, integration was destined to fail.[12] Finally, Elijah Muhammad preaches that he was told by God, or Wallace D. Fard, that white domination of blacks would last for six thousand years, a period that would end around 1914. When asked in the 1960s why the white race had not "fallen" as predicted, Elijah Muhammad replied that "depending on their treatment of the righteous" whites could get an extension; and he added "that there can be no judgement, until we (the so-called Negroes) hear Islam whether we accept it or not."[13]

What is the specific status of the African-American in Black Muslim theology? Muhammad states that African-Americans are members of the tribe of Shabazz, which was an integral part of the original black nation. In fact, the tribe was "the first to discover the best part of our planet to live on. The rich Nile valley of Egypt and the present seat of the Holy City Mecca." As Muhammad describes it, the African-American's exile and hair type came about because another dissatisfied scientist of the tribe of Shabazz about fifty thousand years ago "wanted to make all of us tough and hard in order to endure the life of the jungle of East Asia (Africa) and to overcome the beasts there."[14] After the rest of the tribe refused to agree, he took his family and "moved into the jungle to prove to us that we could live there and conquer the wild beasts, and we have." Black Muslim theology goes on to say that African-Americans are fated to be denied a true knowledge of themselves for hundreds of years, but with the coming of Islam they will "awake and know that Allah has revealed the truth."[15]

An Interpretation of Black Muslim Theology

Whatever the theological implications of Elijah Muhammad's system, the outlook has some psychological dimensions that have had a strong appeal to specific segments of the African-American community. For example, in the conventional interpretations of Christian theology, the Devil is portrayed as a powerful but evil spirit who is continually attempting to lead men astray. As a result, life for the Christian is seen as a struggle to overcome the Devil's blandishments and render good actions. The reward for having a surplus of good over evil is salvation in another life, a life in which men will be united with God. Black Muslim theology appropriates elements of Christian eschatology and turns them into a powerful quasi-secular doctrine. To start with, it teaches that man's existence—past, present, and future—will be in this world and not in an "immaterial world." It also insists that the devil for the African-American is not an immaterial spirit but is represented concretely through the "White devils" or the white race here in America.

By positing that the whites are devils to be continually fought, the theology has succeeded in incorporating several features into its world outlook that appeal to some blacks. First, it attempts to instill race pride in blacks by insisting that they are the chosen people, while whites are clever manipulators. Second, by arguing that despite the oppression blacks will eventually triumph over whites, it gives a measure of hope to blacks, especially those on the lower end of society, who feel that their condition will not be bettered in the present system. Third, by describing whites' origins in pseudoscientific terms, that is, as a result of Yakub's germ-theory experiments, it seeks to take the "mystery" out of white power and injects a self-confidence into African-Americans that is designed to enable them to perform effectively in a white-dominated society.

The Black Muslim view of history in which the white world is fated for destruction is also a very powerful ideological tool. Because of this belief, any natural or human disasters in America (or for that matter throughout the world) can be used to support the Black Muslim prediction of the fall of the United States. To illustrate, in Muhammad's writings, he sees the problems with the value of the U.S. dollar as proof that "the American government is falling to pieces" and that "she has lost her prestige among the nations of the earth."[16] Similar examples abound in his speeches. Also, by teaching that Allah will defeat the white world and that blacks should not practice aggressive violence toward this end, the theology enables the Black Muslims to focus on their internal religious development and avoid the kind of violent confrontations that decimated the Black Panthers. In short, the historian Theodore Draper is correct when he describes Black Muslim theology as "a potentially explosive mixture," and he is insightful when he insists that the reason that "it has not erupted more forcefully . . . partly lies in the theology itself."[17]

Black Islamism in the Context of Black Separatism of the 1960s

A review of the Black Power Separatist literature of the 1960s reveals that its adherents are in agreement with Elijah Muhammad in several key areas. First, they agree with him that African-Americans can only truly realize themselves in a separate nation and that that goal, not integration, should be the focus of their struggle. Imamu Baraka, for example, argues that nations are the vehicles through which peoples achieve their interests, and he adds that it is "just this concept which has allowed the Western peoples to remain for so long the richest and best fed in the world."[18] Thus, African-Americans, Baraka emphasizes, need a nation to solve their problems too. Similarly, Obadele I of the RNA argues that the African-American is in the same condition as the African peoples of Zimbabwe, Mozambique, and Portuguese Guinea, who are "captive nations" struggling for a land space in which to fulfill themselves. According to Obadele I, a land space is a "real part of our [African-American] struggle for that wonderful but amorphous state called freedom."[19] Other Separatists echo similar feelings.

Second, all the Black Power Separatists agree with Muhammad's depiction of American culture as inimical to African-American development. Baraka insists that a people can be free only when they have a set of cultural values relevant to their needs, values that blacks in Western culture lack. As a result, Baraka teaches that "Black Power is inimical to Western culture, as it has manifested itself within Black and colored majority areas anywhere on this planet. Western culture is and has been destructive to colored people all over the world. No movement shaped or contained by Western culture will ever benefit Black people. Black Power must be the actual force and beauty and wisdom of Blackness . . . reordering the world."[20]

Third, all the Separatists agree with the Black Muslims that the separate homeland for blacks should be on United States soil and not in Africa as Garvey preached. As Muhammad expresses it, since white people prevented the blacks from going to their original homeland, "then give us a place here to ourselves [in the United States]."[21] Baraka speaks in the same vein when he insists that Garvey's back-to-Africa conceptions must at this stage of black history remain mental, as "separation must come mentally before any physical movement [even within the United States] can begin."[22] Similarly, Obadele I, a lawyer by profession, argues that a recognized principle of land tenure in international law is that "if a people have lived on a land traditionally, if they have fought to stay there, the land is theirs. It is upon this rule of international law that Africans in America rest their claim for land in America."[23]

Fourth, although the Black Power Separatists as a whole rejected the back-to-Africa goal of Marcus Garvey, they all agreed that exploited people everywhere, especially blacks, had a common fight to overcome the legacies of colonialism and exploitation. For example, Baraka calls for a worldwide effort for unity among blacks;[24] Muhammad describes all non-whites as similarly oppressed as blacks;[25] and in his separatist polemics, Obadele I refers to the struggle of his African "brothers in Guinea or Mozambique against the Portuguese."[26] Such references confirm that Pan-Africanism and anticolonialism were still alive in the Black Power Separatism of the 1970s, but unlike Garveyism, it was a Pan-Africanism rooted in U.S. soil.

In one important respect, however, Black Islamism has more in common with Garveyism than it has with its Separatist competitors. Muhammad stresses, like Garvey, that as long as blacks are a part of the American system, they should exercise the virtues of thrift and hard work and seek to make economic and other gains within the system itself. These achievements would not only help blacks materially, but they would ensure that blacks had a cadre of trained people to administrate and run their own nation when the time came. The parallel to Garvey is obvious. The historian Howard Brotz suggests that Black Islamism's relationship to Garveyism may be more direct, for Brotz queries whether W. D. Fard, the founder of Black Islamism, may not have been Arnold Ford, once a high official of the UNIA.[27] And Professor Theodore Vincent has stated flatly that Muhammad was once a Garveyite.[28] Muhammad's writings yield no clues in either regard.

Elements of Elijah Muhammad's Political Theory

With an understanding of the fundamentals of Black Muslim theology, the major elements of Black Muslim political theory can now be examined, specifically, its view of people, its vision of the good society, and its case against integration.

The Black Islamic View of People

If the American creed is based on human equality, Black Islamism is in contrast based on human inequality in the sight of Allah. Black Muslim theology insists that people are born unequal, and the degree of inequality depends on the race to which one belongs and on whether or not, and to what degree, those who can qualify as Black Muslims accept Islamism. Given this view, if one were to construct a hierarchy based on Black Islamic theology, it would look something like this: Closest to Allah are

1. blacks and nonwhites who accept and conscientiously practice Islam.
2. blacks and nonwhites who have not been exposed to Black Islamism. (Since these latter have not had a chance to accept or reject Islam, judgment of the world will not come until they have had a chance.)
3. blacks and nonwhites who have been exposed to Black Islamism but reject it (although they can theoretically change their decision).
4. all whites. Whites are farthest away from Allah; also as children of the Devil, they are fated to reject him; thus, they are ultimately destined for destruction.

It should be noted that when Muhammad talks about human inequality, he refers primarily to people's ability to achieve spiritual merit and not to material inequities among them. He suggests that blacks will progress materially to the degree that they advance spiritually, and the theology predicts that when the millennium comes, people will live in both material and spiritual bliss; however, nothing in Black Muslim theology says that until Allah's final judgment there will not be whites or disbelievers who are materially better off than the faithful. Thus, material equality or inequality is not a key issue in the theology.

The construction of the hierarchy of spiritual grace leads to another problem when dealing with Black Islamism, that of the individual and freedom. If liberty is as Locke says, "The power a man has to do or forebear doing any particular action,"[29] then in Black Islamic theology, since all people regardless of their race have the power to carry out actions within a particular range of choices, all have freedom.[30] On the other hand, if to be free means that one has the capacity to make good choices over bad choices in the Christian sense, then all individuals from a Black Muslim perspective cannot achieve freedom, because good choices are excluded from the range of options open to whites. (The Christian view is succinctly summed up by St. Augustine: "Thus, good things without defects can sometimes be found; absolutely bad things, never—for even those natures that were vitiated at the outset by an evil will are only evil insofar as they are defective, while they are good insofar as they are natural.")[31] Thus, Black Islamic theology does not argue that blacks never make bad choices; it only teaches that whites never make good ones.

If one accepts the Black Islamic notion of choice, a question follows: If white choices are never good, how can one condemn whites for the maltreatment of blacks? Clearly it follows that one cannot. Elijah Muhammad, however, does not shrink from this conclusion, for regarding whites he says, "You cannot blame one for the way he or she was born, for they had nothing to do with that. Can we say to them why don't you do righteousness when nature did not give righteousness to them or say to them, why are you such a wicked devil? Who is responsible, the made or his maker? Yet we are not excused for following and practicing his evil or accepting him for a righteous guide just because he is not his maker."[32] It is clear that a determinism regarding white choices permeates Muhammad's view.

Other Separatist Views of People

Although pessimistic about black progress in white America, other Separatists are not as deterministic as Muhammad in their views on the peaceful coexistence of blacks and whites. Baraka, for example, agrees that "men are what their culture predicts [enforces]." Yet he concedes that in theory black–white coexistence is possible, "except the devils never want to tolerate any power but their own."[33] Dr. Robert Browne, a black economist, after making the case for a separate black nation, echoes the same sentiments as Baraka. To Browne, if the separation settlement between blacks and whites is satisfactory to both parties; "the basis for the present racial animosity would be removed by the very act of separation. Reciprocal tourism might very well become a leading industry for both nations, for the relations between the nations would finally be on a healthy, equalitarian basis. A confederation of the two states, perhaps joined by Canada, Mexico and other nations, could conceivably emerge at some future time."[34] In short, like Baraka, Browne does not rule out the theoretical possibility of future black–white friendship and cooperation.

The Black Muslim Vision of the Good Society

An examination of the writings of the Black Power Separatists reveals that while none of them possessed the powerful visions of the future that the Pan-Negro Nationalists and Marcus Garvey did, some did write in utopian ways. For example, the Muhammad argues that after the present world order is destroyed in "a religious war between the two great religions of the earth and their believers, namely, Islam and Christianity" (a war that Islam will win), a new and peaceful order will emerge.[35] In the new world there will be unlimited progress, peace, no wars or disagreements, and the earth will be transformed to such a degree that "people will think it is a new earth." Also, in the future kingdom of virtue, the present physical maladies of man will disappear: "No sickness, no hospitals, no insane asylums, no gambling, no cursing or swearing will be seen or heard in that life. Fear, grief and sorrow will stop on this side as proof."[36]

Can people ever see glimmerings of the "good life" before the Black Islamic Apocalypse? Muhammad responds that the true believer receives a feeling of what the good life is like at those times in this life when he or she is spiritually ecstatic: "You are so happy that you don't feel even the pain of sickness, no trouble or sorrows, and that is the way you will always feel in the next life." But to reiterate, life in the utopia will only be a "continuation of the present life. You will be flesh and blood. You won't see spooks coming out of the grave to meet God." Muhammad also saw "the present brotherhood of Islam" organization consisting of the Messenger—the Honorable Elijah Muhammad—at the top followed by the Ministers who head the individual temples, then the Supreme Captains both male and female who keep discipline among the two sexes, next the separate Black Muslim school system organization, and so on, as an imperfect model of the future kingdom of virtue. The difference is that "the brotherhood in the hereafter will enjoy the spirit of gladness and happiness forever in the presence of Allah."[37]

Other Separatist Visions of the Good Society

Other Black Power Separatists suggest visions of the future that parallel Muhammad's in some ways but differ with it in others. Baraka for example, repeatedly reiterates that the Black Nation must be based on black culture, but aside from advising that the first step to Black Power involves blacks obtaining political control of the cities in which they are a majority and building prototypes of the future black nation-state in them, Baraka's vision lacks the vivid detail of Muhammad's.

Sonebeyatta of the RNA is more concrete about his vision of the good society. Sonebeyatta argues that the new society will be a socialist society with "the major means of production and trade in the trust of the state."[38] He goes on to say that the socialism of the RNA will be comparable to the African socialism of Tanzania in which decisions, especially in the communal (or ujaama) villages, are made by the participants themselves. Initially, Sonebeyatta expects that the Republic will finance its activities by means of reparations from the United

States and that it will join the United Nations. He says that it will then
"cultivate support among Afro-Asians," and try to form "a common
market between the Republic and the Black Caribbean nations, with
Africa, Asia and South America." Finally, Sonebeyatta says that the
RNA will seek a political federation, perhaps "linking the Black state
on the continental U.S. with the Black controlled nations of the West
Indies and Guyana."[39] Unlike the Black Muslims, however, the RNA
does not prescribe a national religion for its members, although it does
stress the importance of possessing a national culture that can respond to the needs of blacks. In summary, the Black Power Separatist
notions of the good society range from a theocratic state (Elijah Muhammad), through a state based on a variant of African socialism
(Sonebeyatta), and to a state based on black culture (Baraka).

The Black Separatist Case Against Integration

Given their premise that blacks will never achieve liberation until
they form their own separate state, it is not surprising that all the
Black Power Separatists condemn efforts at integration. Elijah
Muhammad, for example, warns blacks that "they [the white race] are
people described as the 'beast' in the revelation of the Bible"[40] and
thus cannot be expected to "give us an equal chance."[41] He reserves
his strongest criticism for black advocates of integration, however, including Dr. King, and he blames them and their "few" white supporters for "the trouble that our people and the American whites are suffering." Muhammad goes on to say that "integration between the two
races . . . is opposed by God, Himself. It is time that the two people
should separate."[42] Elijah Muhammad argues that King foolishly
teaches that "God is not interested in the freedom of the White, Black
or Yellow man, but in the freedom of the whole human race." To
Muhammad, this statement demonstrates that King has not studied
the scriptures correctly, for they teach that "the world has been under
the rule of Satan for 6,000 years, and now separation must come between God's people and the devil so that the righteous can survive."
Castigating King's call for black–white brotherhood as a call for continued "black enslavement," Muhammad asks cynically, "I am just
wondering how many followers he [King] has after his last statements
[concerning human brotherhood]."[43]

Baraka's case against integration echoes Muhammad's criticisms.
For example, Baraka warns that because race pride and one's own
nation are both necessary for self-identity, racial integration "in America will not work because the Black man is played on by special

forces." Baraka justifies racial separation because "in order for the Black man in the West to absolutely know himself, it is necessary for him to see himself as culturally separate from the White man. That is to be conscious of this segregation and use it as a strength."[44]

Finally, Obadele I of the RNA argues that both blacks and whites imbibe America's "white Nationalist" values, and until blacks extricate themselves from this mental straitjacket, they will never be able to appreciate the fact that their case for a separate nation is justified by international law and by all standards of humanity. Thus, to Obadele I like the others, integration is an effort to prevent blacks from achieving a Black Nationalist consciousness.

In summary, the same disvaluation of the American system that is found in Counter-Communalism is found in Black Power Separatist political theory. However, while the Counter-Communalists desire to reconstruct the American system, the Separatists seek ways to develop a black nation of their own.

The Tactics of Separatism: The Black Muslims

Black Power Separatists use tactics aimed at facilitating an eventual withdrawal from the American system, and a review of the literature shows that the more immediate the goal of separation, the more likely that violence is viewed as a necessary tool for black liberation. On the other hand, the more distant the goal of separation, for example, as in the case of the Black Muslims, the more nonviolent and conventional are the tactics proposed. As stated earlier, the Black Muslims urge that blacks engage in economic self-help, exercise the values of hard work and thrift, eschew violence except in self-defense, and develop a separate educational system in which the new values can be inculcated into the members of the nation, especially the children. In addition, the Black Muslims also counsel that their adherents engage in frequent prayer especially in the Mosque, because in the Mosque "social relations between the different sections of the Moslem Community" are promoted.[45] The conservative nature of Black Muslim political tactics can be seen in Muhammad's advice to his followers on how to conduct themselves in American politics. He admits that it is difficult for him to advise his "followers on taking part in the corrupt politics of our enemies, who are in complete control of political affairs.[46] He does, however, concede that there are some black politicians like the late Reverend Adam Clayton Powell who are genuinely working for "equal recognition for themselves and their people."

Muhammad urges blacks to give such politicians "the total backing of our population."[47] In summary, it is mainly by prayer, thrift, hard work, a correct education, selective political activity, and by nonaggression that the Black Muslims hope to lay the basis for a separate nation.

Other Separatists on Tactics: Imamu Baraka and Imari Obadele I

Unlike the Black Muslims, Imamu Baraka urges blacks to use conventional political methods to achieve a separate black nation. As discussed, Baraka saw black control of the cities in which blacks are the majority as a short range goal and the first step on the road to an eventual black nation. Baraka insists, however, that such control will not come about or serve the cause of the future black nation unless black political activity is coordinated by a black political party. The party must set goals for blacks in the various communities and demonstrate how to achieve them, it must increase black voting power, it should teach blacks political sophistication, it must run first-rate candidates for office, and it must run and support only those candidates for office who support Black Nationalism and Pan-Africanism.[48] (Baraka himself was a very active participant in Black Nationalist politics in Newark, New Jersey, in the 1960s and early 1970s.)[49] To Baraka, only a political party that carries out these functions can provide black people wherever they are "with Identity, Purpose and Direction."[50] Regarding the use of violence, Baraka argues that "there is no instant revolution in America," so Africans in America should concentrate their efforts on building a value system that can survive white domination. Baraka is quick to point out that he is not "underestimating the military aspect of national liberation," but at this time in America "murder mouthing" will only get one murdered. In other words, Baraka sees the advocacy of violence as counterproductive to the cause of black liberation until blacks are "really organized, really trained, and practicing a value system that will constantly remind us who our real enemies are."[51] In essence, Baraka sees a black political party as the tool that will lay the basis for a future black nation, and that is why as Shirley Chisholm noted in the last chapter, he was so active at the National Black Political Convention in Gary, Indiana, in 1972.

Unlike Muhammad and Baraka, Obadele I sees a separate nation as an immediate goal for black people. As a result, one finds that Oba-

dele's tactics are more unconventional and involve a positive attitude toward violence. Regarding separation as an immediate goal, on
Sunday, March 28, 1972, Obadele stated that "the Republic of New
Africa consecrated lands in Hinds County, Mississippi, as the capital
of the Republic."[52] The lands were to be run as a corporation abiding
fully by the laws of the United States and Mississippi until the nation
is actualized. Obadele's strategy was centerd around the hope that the
RNA through the United Nations could force the United States to hold
a plebiscite that would enable African-Americans to choose from
three options. First, blacks who want to stay in the United States
would have an opportunity to express their preference for this option,
and the United States would be bound to respect their wishes. Second, blacks who want to migrate to Africa would be allowed to make
that choice, and the United States would assist in the migration. Finally, blacks who want a separate homeland on U.S. soil, and Obadele
feels that they constitute either a majority or close to it, would receive
assistance toward this goal. Obadele is certain that the RNA would get
a majority vote among the blacks in Louisiana, Mississippi, Alabama,
Georgia, and South Carolina, and he suggests that in the resulting negotiations between the RNA and the U.S. government, blacks might
very well agree to give up all claims to U.S. cities in return for the
United States' conceding the southern states.

However, Obadele states that it is naive to expect a "violent . . .
racist United States" to peacefully accede to such reasonable demands.[53] Therefore, "an important supporting strategy is the development of inherent viability: the creation of an over-ground army, properly motivated, properly equipped, and able to meet and succeed at
the kind of combat which may be forced upon us."[54] Obadele sketches
a rather elaborate military strategy for the RNA based on the assumption that if "Black guerillas" are active in U.S. cities, while at the same
time an RNA army is in the field fighting conventional warfare, the
United States will sue for peace rather than risk a destructive war. As
Obadele comments cynically, this would be the smart thing to do, and
whites will do it, since "all white people believe that they are smarter
than we are."[55]

Violence is an important tactic in Obadele's arsenal, but it is far
from the only one. Equally as important is the need for blacks to financially support the efforts of the RNA to build communities across
the South, communities that will be prototypes of the future black
republic there. In these model communities, the RNA hopes to house
five hundred families within a modern infrastructure with "schools,

shopping center, nursery, factory, farm equipment and [very impor-
tant] a prefab housing factory." All this will be owned by the community, with housing belonging "to the family without mortgage or rent."[56]

In summary, Obadele, like Muhammad and Baraka, advocates a
variety of tactics to achieve a separate black nation, but violence plays
a more prominent role in his overall strategy than it does in that of
Muhammad and Baraka.

XI

A Critical Assessment of the
Black Power Ideologies

The preceding chapters have described various Black Power ideologies, their antecedents, and their competitors and made comparisons among them. This concluding chapter presents a critical assessment of the Black Power ideologies and considers their permanent contributions to American society.

The Paradoxes in the Goals of the Black Power Ideologies

A frequent criticism that has been made of the Black Power ideologies, and a criticism having some merit, is that they are contradictory and vague. For example, the Counter-Communalists, especially the Black Panther version of the approach, see blacks as the vanguard for the transformation of America as a whole and insist that black gains can be made permanent only if the masses of the American people of all races are also participants in these gains. In the attempt to create their new version of the United States, the Counter-Communalists have been forced to emphasize more universal ideologies, frequently some form of socialism at the expense of an emphasis on Black Nationalism, and as a result have found themselves attacked from two sides. The Black Nationalists attack them because the Nationalists see race as the ultimate source of values and are suspicious of and even hostile to ideologies that put race values in a secondary place. With their positing of blacks as a vanguard, Counter-Communalists risk alienating groups who feel that race should be subordinated to values like class, capitalism, or the principles of American democracy, that are more universal in scope. The Black Panthers were aware of this danger, and the attempts of Huey Newton, for example, to reestablish Panther links with the black community by insisting on the relevance of both the black church and black capitalism to black liberation have previously been described.

The Pluralists hope to achieve Black Power by using the tools of the American system and by welding African-Americans into the kind of pressure group that can use these tools to maximum advantage. However, the Pluralists operate on certain assumptions, especially about African-Americans, that call their ideological system and strategies into question. First, the Pluralists assume that most African-Americans see or will see their collective self-interest as distinct from that of whites. This is an assumption without much grounding in fact, for poll after poll indicates that the majority of African-Americans are preoccupied with the same concerns and do not express their sentiments on these concerns significantly differently than do their white counterparts. Thus, to assume as the Pluralists do that unanimity can be gained on the majority of issues that confront African-Americans is an illusion.[1] Needless to say, there are some issues like high unemployment rates, fewer educational opportunities, higher crime rates, and so on, that affect African-Americans more than they do whites. These are certainly not distinct enough, however, to make African-Americans a permanent and united pressure group on all issues, and as a result it is fairly fragile ground on which to build a lasting movement. (A good example of an issue that splits both communities is the abortion question.) Second, the politics of racial self-interest is a politics fraught with danger for African-Americans. Martin Luther King, Jr., articulated the peril very well when he urged African-Americans to seek the good will of whites, for as King saw it, the practice of the politics of self-interest by the former may further encourage the continuation of a similar policy by the latter, a development that could condemn African-Americans to continued regression. Furthermore, King noted that African-Americans have made their greatest gains when they have had the support and sympathy of whites. These are some of the more important dilemmas that Pluralism will have to overcome if it is to continue to be acceptable to African-Americans.

Of the three Black Power groupings, the Separatists are the least contradictory and vague regarding their ultimate goal. As pointed out, they preach that different races can fulfill themselves only in their own separate nations; thus they conclude that African-Americans should attempt to create a nation-state of their own. In short, their ultimate goal is unambiguous and clear. The Separatists are, however, also confronted with a number of paradoxes, as a few examples will help illustrate. To begin with, numerous surveys show that the majority of African-Americans still see some form of integration as desirable. Thus, Separatism, which to work needs the support of the majority of the African-American population, is definitely the philosophy of a minority. What makes this position even more precarious is that a significant number of the minority that supports Separatism do so not because they reject the American system of values, interests, and beliefs, but because regarding African-Americans the United States has failed to live up to that system. If American society makes a turnaround in this regard, the Separatists' potential constituency would become even smaller.

The Separatists are acutely aware that as long as African-Americans accept the American creed Separatism is in a precarious position, so they have taken steps to deal with this. As the previous chapters have shown, all the Separatist groups seek to make their black converts into "new men and women," and they usually demand that the converts take on a new name, a new culture, and reject totally not only the practice but the creed of the present-day United States. In this respect, the Black Power Separatist challenge reminds one of the challenge the Stoics faced in the Hellenistic and Roman Empires, for the Stoics also constituted a militant minority seeking to convert radically different majorities into a new way of life. The Stoic philosophy, like Black Power Separatism, demanded much of its adherents, for example, a supreme discipline, a faith in reason, and an indifference to externalities. Yet while Stoicism was able to attract followers as dissimilar as the slave Epictetus and the emperor Marcus Aurelius, still largely because of its demands, it was unable to gain the allegiance of the popular masses.[2] Similarly, one may argue that Black Power Separatism demands so much and gives so little in immediate returns that it may have doomed itself to remain forever the ideology of a minority.

Malcolm X and the Dilemmas of Black Power

The life of the ex-Black Muslim minister Malcolm X (1925–1965), the most colorful and most quoted Black Power advocate of the 1960s, illustrates clearly some of the dilemmas faced by the adherents of Black Power, and it would be instructive to look at some of the highlights of Malcolm's life. Malcolm X's life is a case study of many of the practical problems that Separatists and Counter-Communalists face. After the deaths of his father and mother, Malcolm lived the life of a hustler and in 1946, at the age of twenty, ended up in Charleston State Prison.[3] In prison, Malcolm became a devoted Black Muslim and upon his release went to work for the organization, eventually becoming minister of the Black Muslim Mosque in Harlem. In 1963, however, Malcolm broke with the Black Muslims. According to Malcolm, he had reason to question Elijah Muhammad's sincerity, and he felt that the Muslims were shunting him aside quietly after he stated in public that blacks had little reason to mourn at President Kennedy's assassination.[4]

Until the time of his defection, Malcolm had accepted without question the Black Muslim theology. In 1964, however, he made a pilgrimage to Mecca and was so impressed by orthodox Islam's multiracialism that he rejected Black Islamism. As Malcolm describes his experience, "There were tens of thousands of pilgrims, from all over the world. They were of all colors, from blue-eyed blonds to black skinned Africans. But we were all participating in the same ritual, displaying a spirit of unity and brotherhood that my experiences in America had led me to believe never could exist between the white and non-white."[5] On his return, Malcolm became an orthodox Muslim and eventually a rival to Muhammad. Malcolm was assassinated by unknown assailants in 1965.[6]

The transformation of Malcolm X points up some very important challenges to the Black Power ideologies generally and particularly to the Separatist and Counter-Communalist versions. For the Separatists the questions are, Can their ideologies stand the test of variety in experience? Are they flexible enough to change in the light of new experiences? Can they afford the political price of change? Malcolm X left the United States a strong believer in Black Islamism. However, Malcolm insists, "Despite my firm convictions, I have been always a man who tries to face facts, and to accept a reality of life as new experience and new knowledge unfolds it. I have always kept an open mind, which is necessary to the flexibility that must go hand in hand with ovory form of intelligent search for truth."[7] As a result Malcolm came back from his pilgrimage changed beyond the limits of what could be reconciled with Black Muslim beliefs. The challenge to Malcolm X is also the challenge to Black Power Separatism. Malcolm changed to adjust to his new vision of truth. Is change possible for the Separatists? On the other hand, how far could Malcolm have proceeded in the direction of Islamic Counter-Communalism without losing his African-American mass following? This is especially critical when history shows the strong political potential of a specifically Black Nationalist appeal. Malcolm X was killed before any final conclusions regarding this question could be drawn from his life and thought, but the issue is still a critical one for Counter-Communalists.

The Life of Malcolm X and Its Meaning for the Black Power Movement

Since Malcolm X's assassination, he has become almost a cult figure in the United States, particularly in the African-American community. And, although he did not write extensively himself, a hagiography has developed around his life. The adulation of Malcolm X started soon after his assassination. For example, at his eulogy the African-American actor Ossie Davis referred to Malcolm as "our own black shining Prince."[8] Subsequently, the African-American sociologist of religion C. Eric Lincoln describes him as "the uncompromising symbol of resistance and the spokesman for the nonviolent 'black man' in America."[9] Professor Mburumba Kerina sees him as a "humble servant of his people,"[10] and James Boggs views Malcolm as "a brilliant organizer who had been chiefly responsible for building the Muslims into the most highly disciplined mass organization that the black community has ever known."[11] Why is Malcolm X seen as such an important symbol of Black Power? It is certainly not because of the uniqueness of his political program, because to the extent that he articulated one in his autobiography, it is the standard Pluralist program calling for blacks to form themselves into a powerful political lobby, so that "every morning, every legislator should receive a communication about what the black man in America expects and wants and needs."[12] (The same program of action is articulated in the basic statement of his political grouping, the Organization of Afro-American Unity.)[13] Indeed, Malcolm's Pluralist program does not come close to matching that of Shirley Chisholm in depth and insight. Furthermore, if one searches Malcolm's writings and speeches for a creative vision of the black future, a vision comparable to that of Marcus Garvey, one also searches in vain. In fact, aside from a vague Islamic Counter-Communalism, Malcolm X's works lack a concrete vision of the black future. Finally, if one seeks to find in Malcolm X an "organic intellectual" like Martin Luther King, Jr., or Frederick Douglass, both of whom successfully "linked the life of the mind to social change," one also searches in vain.[14] Malcolm's works lack an overarching theory, and, in fact, he became a famous organizer not in a system devised by himself but by Elijah Muhammad.

Given all this, why is Malcolm X seen as the most heroic symbol of the Black Power Movement of the 1960s? He is so recognized because despite his many limits, he developed into a fearless propagandist who hammered home to America the view that the attainment of civil rights without ethnic dignity for blacks was a violation of the African-American's "human rights."[15] He further stated what thousands of African-Americans, especially youth, also felt but often feared to articulate, that they had a right to use any means necessary—violent or nonviolent—to attain these human rights. As Malcolm stated in 1964, "If white America doesn't think that the Afro-American, especially the upcoming generation, is capable of adopting the guerilla tactics now being used by oppressed people elsewhere on earth, she is making a drastic mistake. She is underestimating the force that can do her the most harm."[16] This sample of Malcolm X's outspokenness illustrates the kind of rhetoric that made him the conscience and symbol of the Black Power revolution.

Black Power and Individualism

Another criticism that has been made of the ideologies of Black Power is that they do not look kindly on individualism, seeing it at least as practiced in the United States as a form of evil. Regarding modern individualism, Professor Ernest Barker states: "We start from the individual: We regard him as possessed of rights (only too often of 'natural rights' independent of social recognition) and we expect the state to guarantee those rights, and, by so doing, to secure the conditions of a spontaneous growth of character."[17] The Black Powerites, on the other hand, much like the ancient Athenians, view the "collective voice" of the black community as setting the parameters for its members. This is a characteristic that holds true whether that voice is expressed through a messenger, as the Black Muslims hold or a political party, as believed by the Panthers, Baraka, and Chisholm.

Barker goes on to argue, however, that in ancient Athens the pioneer experiment in Western style democracy, it was "precisely because the individual felt himself an influence in the life of the whole, that he did not endeavor to assert his rights against the whole."[18] Indeed, as Murray Bookchin notes, the Athenian Society because of its institutions like the Council of Five Hundred, the Ecclesia, and the Assembly,[19] and "despite the slave, patriarchal, and class features it shared with all of classical society, developed into a working democracy in the literal sense of the term."[20] Although in Black Power political theory one finds constant criticism of American individualism and a concomitant praise of collectivism, one finds little or no effort spent on trying to show how this collective spirit can be made to enhance individualism, as was apparently the case in the Athenian system.

Black Power and the Intellectual

Finally, it can be argued that the Black Power Movement at least up to now shares a common failing of past Black Nationalist ideologies in its inability to attract black intellectuals. Why is this so? Some intellectuals claim that the movement rejects them because the intellectual values of openness, flexibility, and change, are perceived as debits in a movement that is under constant attack and where loyalty and even dogmatism become prime virtues. Professor Edwin Redkey notes that in the past the failure to attract intellectuals distinguished Black Nationalism of the nineteenth and twentieth centuries from its European Nationalist counterpart. For while neither the black middle class nor the intellectuals "endorsed Black Nationalism," in Europe the chief spokesperson for European Nationalism were "the intellectuals and bourgeois leaders of Europe. They brought their talents as thinkers, writers, and teachers to the task of building a national spirit among their people as old empires were overthrown and old disunities mended." Redkey says that, like the blacks in the United States, "in the aristocratic societies of Europe, intellectuals were marginal men but they had abilities and aspirations which brought them success." In the case of Black Nationalism, because of the lack of intellectual support there was no real dialogue "between men who endorsed Separation." As a result "there was no sharpening of arguments, no clarification of strategies, no toughening of resolve."[21] This identical dilemma confronted the Black Power Movement in the 1960s.

In summary, the need for more well thought out strategies and tactics, the need to sharpen their ideological systems, the need to address the question of how to reconcile collectivism and individualism, and, finally, the need for more intellectual support, explain the past failings and indicate the necessary future goals of the Black Power Movement.

Permanent Contributions of the Black Power Ideologies

Despite these criticisms, however, the Black Power ideologies have made some permanent contributions to the African-American community and American society. Their first major contribution is that they started a debate in the black community and in the nation at large about the nature of American society and the place of the African-American in it. Regarding the African-American community, specifically, Bayard Rustin argues that "a full fledged debate has not taken place in the Black community since the monumental exchanges between W.E.B. Du Bois and Booker T. Washington which occurred over half a century ago." He goes on to say that "the intensity of today's dialogue is an indication of the aroused political awareness of Black people and an overall heightening of aspirations and militancy."[22] Although a critic of the Black Power Movement, Rustin gives it credit for sparking this debate and for elevating the quality of the dialogue.

This debate has covered almost every dimension of human experience from religion, science, and aesthetics, to economics, international affairs, and education; however, no dimension of human affairs has been more affected by it than black politics. Most advocates of Black Power have described themselves as gadflies seeking to bring into being a new black political autonomy. Although one may reject the ideas and proposals of a Shirley Chisholm or an Imamu Baraka or a Huey Newton, even their critics concede that their cases have been presented with vitality, variety, wit, and ingenuity and admit that any future efforts to deal successfully with America's societal problems must take their ideas into consideration. In the long run, this may indeed be the Black Power Movement's most lasting contribution to American society.

Finally, Black Power has helped to highlight the importance of ethnic identification even in an individualistic society like the United States. As the record has shown, giants in black history like Frederick Douglass, W.E.B. Du Bois and Martin Luther King, Jr., all tended to deemphasize race, but one could argue that these proponents of black individualism, however well intentioned, ignored the fact that Greek democracy, in many ways still a model for democratic living, took place in an environment where the citizens were highly conscious of their racial and community ties. The evils of the city-state—its support of slavery, its fratricidal wars, its chauvinism—are well documented by history, and it is to the credit of figures like Dr. King that they saw the potential for like evils stemming from an African-American racial chauvinism. In condemning the evils, however, King and others may have ignored the positive aspects of a balanced and humane ethnocentrism, and the Black Power Movement at its best desired to achieve such an equilibrium.

In his autobiography, Malcolm X tells how during one of his visits to an African country he spoke at length with a white American ambassador who told him that on the African continent "he never thought of human beings in terms of race, that he dealt with human beings, never noticing their color." In fact, this ambassador said that "he was more aware of language differences than color differences." To Malcolm, who investigated the ambassador's actions and found them consistent with his declarations, the ambassador's life proved "that the White man is not inherently evil," but that in regard to race American society "has produced and nourishes a psychology which brings out the lowest, most base part of human beings."[23] To Malcolm, the challenge was to create a new psychology, a psychology that would have "Black Power" and "White Power" merge into "Human Power." For this condition to be achieved, however, Black Power must be seen less as a bewildering slogan and more as a genuine cry for humanity. Sadly, despite its permanent contributions, the former view of the Black Power Movement even in the 1990s dominates the latter.

Notes

PREFACE

1. Gerd Tellenbach, *Church, State and Christian Society at the Time of the Investiture Contest* (Oxford: Basil Blackwell, 1959), p. 115.

2. Walter Phelps Hall, Robert Greenhalgh Albion, and Jennie Barnes Pope, *A History of England and the Empire-Commonwealth* Boston: Ginn, 1969), p. 242.

3. George H. Sabine, *A History of Political Theory* (Hillsdale, Ill.: Dryden Press, 1973), p. 452.

4. Mulford Q. Sibley, *Political Ideas and Ideologies* (New York: Harper and Row, 1970), p. 431.

5. Ibid., p. 4.

6. Ibid.

7. Ibid.

8. For a sample of the types of debates and discussions on Black Power, the following articles are instructive: Martin Bauml Duberman, "Black Power in America," *Partisan Review* 35, no. 1 (Winter 1968): 33–48; Michael Thelwell, "What Is to Be Done? A Review Article on, *The Crisis of the Negro Intellectual* by Harold Cruse" *Partisan Review* 35, no. 4 (Fall 1969): 619–22; Robert Coles, Ivanhoe Donaldson, Paul Feldman, Charles V. Hamilton, Abbie Hoffman, Tom Kahn, William Melvin Kelley, Norman Mailer, Jack Newfield, Fred Powledge, Stephen Thernstrom, and Nathan Wright, Jr., "Black Power: A Discussion," *Partisan Review* 35, no. 2 (Spring 1968): 195–232.

9. An excellent case study of the competition between the Black Power ideologies and the more mainstream forms of black protest can be seen in Clayborne Carson's study of the Student Non-Violent Coordinating Committee (SNCC) of the 1960s. Carson, *In Struggle: SNCC and the Black Awakening of the 1960s* (Cambridge, Mass.: Harvard University Press, 1981).

10. Mary Frances Berry and John W. Blasingame, *Long Memory: The Black Experience in America* (New York: Oxford University Press, 1982), p. 389.

11. Ibid., pp. 389–90.

12. Ibid., p. 391.

13. Ibid., p. 392.

14. Ibid., pp. 395–96.

15. For a recent discussion on the usage of the term *African-American*, see the article "African-American or Black: What's in a Name?" *Ebony* 44, no. 9 (July 1989): 76–80.

CHAPTER 1

1. Gunnar Myrdal, *An American Dilemma* (New York: McGraw-Hill, 1964), p. 281.

2. Myrdal cites as an example of this new southern ruling class a white contractor "who rose from the class of white building workers." Ibid.

3. Ibid., p. 282.

4. Ibid., pp. 291–92.

5. Ibid., p. 293.

6. Ibid., p. 142.

7. Tom Wicker, Introduction to *Report of the National Advisory Commission on Civil Disorders* (New York: Bantam, 1968), p. 251.

8. Ibid., p. 251.

9. Ibid.

10. Ibid., p. 252.

11. Ibid.

12. Ibid., p. 268.

13. Ibid.

14. Ibid., p. 270.

15. Ibid.

16. Ibid.

17. Ibid., p. 425.

18. Fred R. Harris and Roger W. Wilkins, *Quiet Riots* (New York: Pantheon, 1988), p. 176.

19. Ibid., p. 175.

20. Ibid., p. 179.

21. Ibid.

22. Ibid., p. 180.

23. For a disturbing description of the imbalances between African-American and white lives in the 1990s, see Bill McAllister, "The Plight of Young Black Men in America," *Washington Post National Weekly Edition* 7, no. 15 (12–18 February, 1990): 6.

24. Herrington Bryce, "Putting Black Economic Progress in Perspective," *Ebony* 28, no. 10 (August 1973): 59. The study by Wattenberg and Scammon to which Bryce is referring is Ben J. Wattenberg and Richard M. Scammon, *This USA: An Unexpected Family Portrait* (New York: Doubleday, 1965).

25. William Julius Wilson, *The Declining Significance of Race: Blacks and Changing American Institutions* (Chicago: University of Chicago Press, 1978).

26. For a critical study of the Wilson thesis and others, see Alphonso Pinkney, *The Myth of Black Progress* (New York: Cambridge University Press, 1984).

27. Stanley M. Elkins, *Slavery* (New York: Universal Library, 1963), p. 28.

28. Ibid., p. 34.

29. Ibid., p. 43.

30. Ibid.

31. Ibid.

32. Ibid.

33. Philip D. Curtin, *The Atlantic Slave Trade* (Madison: University of Wisconsin Press, 1969), pp. 86–93. The Elkins thesis has for years evoked a great deal of controversy among scholars of the black experience. Curtin is a good example of one group of scholars that questions the validity of Elkins's conclusions regarding the severity of slavery. Using statistical methods, Curtin estimates that roughly 1,665,000 slaves were imported into the British Caribbean, 1,600,000 slaves were imported into the Dutch Caribbean and Guiana, 28,000 were imported into the Dutch West Indies, and 3,000,000 were imported into Brazil. Of the total number of slaves imported into the New World, only 5 percent eventually came to the United States; yet Curtin argues that by 1950, the United States had more than a third of all the African-Americans in the world. At the other extreme, the Caribbean retained more than 40 percent of all the slaves imported into the New World, but in 1950 this area had only 20 percent of the world's African-American population. What were the factors that account for such a disparity? Tropical disease may have accounted for the decline of the Caribbean slave population, but even recognizing this, Curtin asks that if American slavery was as severe as conventionally depicted, would the disparity in population growth have been so great? A study of slavery by the statistical historians Robert William Fogel and Stanley L. Engerman entitled *Time on the Cross* (Boston: Little, Brown, 1974), supports Curtin's speculations. Fogel and Engerman argue that the statistical evidence reveals that the slave's diet, health standards, and life expectancy were considerably better than most traditional studies of slavery (like that of Elkins) indicate.

34. Melville Herskovits, *The Myth of the Negro Past* (Boston: Beacon Press, 1958). In his book, the late Dr. Herskovits argues that far more remained of African-Americans' African traditions than most scholars have, in fact, recognized. In reality, African-Americans' language, life style, religion, and so on, have all been structured by their African past; in fact, Herskovits at times seems to suggest that these traditions have been the crucial variables in African-Americans' ability to adapt successfully to the United States. Most young African-American historians and scholars tend to support Herskovits. On the other hand, an opponent of Herskovits's view is the eminent African-American sociologist the late E. Franklin Frazier. In his book *The Negro Church in America* (New York: Schocken, 1964), p. 6, Dr. Frazier argues that "in America the destruction of the clan and kinship organization was more devastating (than the destruction of the Fon in Dahomey) and the Negroes were plunged into an alien civilization in which whatever remained of their religious myths and cults had no meaning whatever." Later on, Dr. Frazier says, "It is our position that it was not what remained of African culture or African religious

experience but the Christian religion that provided a new basis of social cohesion."

35. Oddly enough, Elkins's view that African-Americans' position would have been better today if there had been more emphasis on evolutionary and institutional change rather than on total reconstruction is partially echoed in the Politics of Accommodation as enunciated by black leader Booker T. Washington. Washington, as we shall describe later on, emphasized to Negroes the importance of accommodating themselves to the status quo while at the same time building industrial, educational, and business bases.

36. Barrington Moore, Jr., *Social Origins of Dictatorship and Democracy* (Boston: Beacon Press, 1966), pp. 144–45.

37. For an excellent short discussion of the motives of the Radical Republicans, see Eric Foner, "Blacks and the U.S. Constitution 1789–1989," *New Left Review* 183 (September–October 1990): 63–75.

38. See Phillip S. Foner, *The Black Panthers Speak* (Philadelphia: J. B. Lippincott, 1970), p. 45.

39. Ibid., p. 46.

40. Ibid.

41. Ibid.

42. Harry Hoetnik, *The Two Variants in Caribbean Race Relations* (London: Oxford University Press, 1967), pp. 120–60.

43. Larry Neal, "Any Day Now: Black Art and Black Liberation," Ebony 24, no. 10 (August 1969): 54.

44. William H. Grier and Price M. Cobbs, *Black Rage* (New York: Bantam, 1968).

45. Elijah Muhammad, *Message to the Black Man in America*, no. 2. (Chicago: Muhammad's Mosque of Islam, 1965), p. 133.

46. Ibid., pp. 133–34.

47. Ibid., p. 333.

48. Ibid.

49. Ibid., p. 334.

50. Ibid.

51. Francis W. Coker, *Recent Political Thought* (New York: Appleton Century, 1934), especially pp. 309–32, 354–64.

52. Arthur Jensen, "How Much Can We Boost IQ and Scholastic Achievement?" *Harvard Educational Review* 39 (Winter 1969): 1–124. Psychologist Richard Herrnstein makes a similar contention. See Richard Herrnstein, "I.Q." *Atlantic* 228, no. 3 (September 1971): 43–65. The continued strength of white supremacist views in the United States is exemplified by the election of David Duke, an ex–Ku Klux Klan wizard and racial supremacist in the Stoner mold, to the Louisiana legislature from a New Orleans suburb in the fall of 1988. See Wayne King, "Bad Times on Bayou," *New York Times Magazine* 138, no. 47, 898 (11 June 1989): 56.

53. Jason DeParle, "An Architect of the Reagan Vision Plunges into Inquiry on Race and I.Q.," *New York Times*, Friday, 30 November 1990, sec. A.

54. Leonard Kriegel, "Academic Freedom and Racial Theories," *New York Times*, Thursday, 3 May 1990, sec. A.

55. Ibid.

56. Louis L. Knowles and Kenneth Prewitt, *Institutional Racism in America* (Englewood Cliffs, N.J.: Prentice Hall, 1969), p. 6.

57. Ibid., p. 9.

58. Ibid.

59. Ibid.

60. Ibid.

61. Ibid., p. 10.

62. Ibid.

63. Ibid., p. 11.

64. Ibid., p. 12.

65. Ibid., pp. 12–13.

66. Harold Cruse, *Rebellion or Revolution?* (New York: William Morrow, 1969), p. 113.

CHAPTER II

1. John Hope Franklin, *From Slavery to Freedom* (New York: Vintage, 1969), p. 238.

2. Martin R. Delany, "A Project for an Expedition of Adventure to the Eastern Coast of Africa," in *Black Brotherhood: Afro-Americans and Africa*, ed. Okon Edet Uya (Lexington, Mass.: D. C. Heath, 1971), p. 71. For a critical view of Delany's activities in Africa, see Earl Ofari, *The Myth of Black Capitalism* (New York: Monthly Review Press, 1970), pp. 11–47.

3. Delany, "Project for an Expedition," p. 71.

4. Mary Frances Berry and John W. Blasingame, *Long Memory: The Black Experience in America* (New York: Oxford University Press, 1982), p. 402. For a detailed discussion of the life of Bishop Holly and his commitment to the Pan-Negro Nationalist ideal, see David M. Dean, *Defender of the Race: James Theodore Holly, Black Nationalist Bishop* (Boston: Lambeth Press, 1979).

5. An excellent critical discussion of Lincoln's attitude toward colonization is given in W.E.B. Du Bois, *Black Reconstruction in America 1860–1880* (New York: Atheneum, 1977), especially pp. 145–49.

6. Franklin, *From Slavery to Freedom*, p. 159.

7. Ibid.

8. Ibid. Franklin states that by 1806 Cuffee owned "one large ship, two brigs, and everal smaller vessels, besides considerable property in houses and land." For a critical assessment of Cuffee's business activities, see Ofari, *Myth of Black Capitalism*, pp. 11–47.

9. Berry and Blasingame, *Long Memory*, p. 55.

10. Immanuel Geiss, *The Pan-African Movement* (New York: Africana, 1974), p. 81.

11. Franklin, *From Slavery to Freedom*, p. 238. Franklin tells how even slaveholding states "like Maryland, Virginia and Kentucky were among the states that approved the colonization society," and he adds that "North Carolina, Mississippi, and other states had local colonization societies." Ibid.

12. Edwin S. Redkey, "Bishop Turner's African Dream," in Uya, *Black Brotherhood*, p. 111. It could be that Turner's bitterness toward the American system stems from his disappointments at the lack of interest shown by the Georgia Reconstruction legislature in black rights. W.E.B. Du Bois tells us that despite Turner's serving as a chaplain in the Civil War, in fact, he was appointed by President Lincoln, "Turner was not liked by whites. The *Atlanta Intelligencer* called him an 'unscrupulous fellow, shrewd enough to deceive the poor, deluded Negro.' He had to withstand all sorts of attempts to involve him in difficulties" (*Black Reconstruction*, p. 499).

13. Redkey, "Bishop Turner's African Dream," pp. 109–10. For a superficial biography of Bishop Turner, see M. M. Ponton, *The Life and Times of Henry M. Turner* (Reprint. New York: Negro Universities, 1970).

14. William Bittle and Gilbert Geis, "Alfred Charles Sam and an African Return: A Case Study in Negro Despair," in Uya, *Black Brotherhood*, p. 114. Another short but good discussion of the Chief Sam Movement can be found in Geiss, *Pan-African Movement*, pp. 93–95.

15. Robert A. Hill, *The Marcus Garvey Papers*, vol. 1 (Berkeley: University of California Press, 1983), pp. 536–47.

16. Redkey, "Bishop Turner's African Dream," p. 112.

17. Ibid.

18. Leslie H. Fishel, Jr., and Benjamin Quarles, eds., *The Negro Americans: A Documentary History* (Glenview, Ill.: Scott, Foresman, 1967), pp. 146–47.

19. Ibid., p. 146.

20. Ibid., pp. 146–47.

21. Louis Mehlinger, "The Attitude of the Free Negro Toward African Colonization," in Uya, *Black Brotherhood*, p. 33.

22. Ibid., p. 36.

23. Ibid.

24. Edwin S. Redkey, *Black Exodus* (New Haven, Conn.: Yale University Press, 1969), p. 189. It is interesting that W.E.B. Du Bois also mentions Albion Tourgee as one of the "most honest of the carpetbaggers" of the Reconstruction period. Tourgee was active in the North Carolina Reconstruction legislatures. *Black Reconstruction*, p. 536.

25. Redkey, *Black Exodus*, p. 190.

26. Ibid.

27. Ibid.

28. Ibid., p. 187. Jesse Jackson is not a Separatist, but Sheila Collins, in her essay on Jackson's 1984 presidential campaign, tells how Jackson appealed to blacks and other minorities with slogans like "I AM SOMEBODY!" "DOWN WITH DOPE, UP WITH HOPE," and "RED, YELLOW, BLACK, WHITE, ALL ARE PRECIOUS IN GOD'S

SIGHT!" See Sheila D. Collins, *The Rainbow Coalition* (New York: Monthly Review Press, 1986), p. 153.

29. Ibid.

30. Hollis Lynch, "Pan-Negro Nationalism in the New World, Before 1862," in Uya, *Black Brotherhood*, p. 54.

31. Ibid.

32. Ibid., p. 60.

33. Ibid., p. 61.

34. Ibid., p. 60.

35. Ibid., p. 61.

36. Ibid.

37. Edward W. Blyden, "The Call of Providence to the Descendants of African in America," in Uya, *Black Brotherhood*, p. 84.

38. Ibid., p. 87.

39. Delany, "Project for an Expedition," p. 71.

40. Ibid.

41. Alexander Crummell, "The Relations and Duties of Free Colored Men in America to Africa," in Uya, *Black Brotherhood*, p. 66.

42. Ibid.

43. Blyden, "Call of Providence," p. 84.

44. Ibid., pp. 87–88. For a brief but good description of Blyden's historiography, see Geiss, *Pan-African Movement*, pp. 108–9.

45. Crummell, "Relations and Duties," p. 69.

46. Ibid.

47. Delany, "Project for an Expedition," pp. 73–74.

48. Ibid., p. 69.

49. Redkey, "Bishop Turner's African Dream," p. 102.

50. Ibid.

51. Crummell, "Relations and Duties," p. 66.

52. Ibid.

53. Ibid.

54. Ibid., p. 70.

55. Delany, "Project for an Expedition," p. 75.

56. Blyden, "Call of Providence," p. 91.

57. Ibid.

58. Redkey, "Bishop Turner's African Dream," p. 101.

59. Ibid.

60. Ibid.

61. See Hollis R. Lynch, *Edward Wilmot Blyden: Pan-Negro Patriot, 1832–1912* (New York: Oxford University Press, 1967). Blyden was born on St. Thomas in the Virgin Islands and migrated to Liberia. He eventually became a citizen of Liberia and in 1877 became its ambassador to London. Lynch states that by assuming the post Blyden became the first African diplomat to Europe.

62. Kola Adelaja, "Sources in African Political Thought—Part I" *Presence Africaine* 70 (2d Quarter 1969): p. 10.

63. Ibid., p. 10–11.
64. Ibid., 11.
65. Ibid., 13.
66. Crummell, "Relations and Duties," p. 67.
67. Delany, "Project for an Expedition," p. 77.
68. Redkey, "Bishop Turner's African Dream," p. 108.
69. Lynch, "Pan-Negro Nationalism," p. 62.
70. Delany, "Project for an Expedition," p. 82.
71. Ibid.
72. Blyden, "Call of Providence," p. 87. For a short, concise treatment of Blyden's views of Africa as a land of black regeneration, see Gordon K. Lewis, *Main Currents of Caribbean Thought* (Baltimore: Johns Hopkins University Press, 1983), pp. 315–16.
73. Redkey, *Black Exodus*, p. 6.
74. Ibid.
75. Ibid.
76. Ibid., p. 7.
77. Ibid.
78. Ibid., pp. 7–8.
79. Ibid., p. 15.
80. Ibid.
81. Ibid., p. 149.
82. Lynch, "Pan-Negro Nationalism," p. 45.
83. Ibid., p. 47.
84. Redkey, *Black Exodus*, p. 151.
85. Ibid.
86. Ibid., p. 195.
87. Lynch, "Pan-Negro Nationalism," p. 45.
88. Ibid., p. 57.
89. Ibid.
90. Ibid. Immanuel Geiss gives a short but comprehensive treatment of Delany's activity. See Geiss, "Pan-African Movement," pp. 86–89.
91. Redkey, *Black Exodus*, p. 195.
92. Ibid., pp. 174–75.
93. Ibid., pp. 279–80.
94. Ibid., p. 275.
95. Ibid., p. 175.
96. Theodore G. Vincent, "Black Power and the Garvey Movement (Berkeley, Calif.: Ramparts Press, 1973), pp. 13–14.
97. Redkey, *Black Exodus*, p. 16.

CHAPTER III

1. William Z. Foster, *The Negro People in American History* (New York: International Publishers, 1970), p. 48.

2. Ibid., p. 49.

3. Ibid.

4. Ibid.

5. Ibid., p. 60.

6. Ibid.

7. Ibid., p. 61.

8. John Hope Franklin, *From Slavery to Freedom* (New York: Vintage, 1969), p. 147.

9. Foster, *Negro People*, p. 61.

10. Ibid., p. 62.

11. Ibid.

12. Eugene D. Genovese, *The Political Economy of Slavery*, 2d ed. (Middletown, Conn.: Wesleyan University Press, 1989), pp. 313–14.

13. Ibid., p. 313.

14. Foster, *Negro People*, p. 62.

15. Ibid., p. 72.

16. Robert William Fogel and Stanley L. Engerman, *Time on the Cross* (Boston: Little, Brown, 1974), p. 24.

17. Foster, *Negro People*, p. 76.

18. Ibid.

19. To illustrate cotton's importance to the American economy, Foster states that in 1859 "it furnished 61% of all American exports, 3,533,000 bales being exported that year." He adds that "it was the centre of the whole economic, political and cultural life of the South." Ibid., p. 77.

20. Ibid., p. 90.

21. Ibid.

22. To cite a few examples, in 1831, 1832, and 1833 conventions were held in Philadelphia; in 1856, in Chatham, Ohio; in 1854, in New York; in 1853–54, in Cleveland. Ibid., p. 94.

23. Ibid., p. 107.

24. Ibid., p. 289.

25. Ibid., p. 108.

26. Ibid.

27. Ibid.

28. Ibid., p. 109.

29. For a further excellent discussion of the limits of Abolitionism, see W.E.B. Du Bois, *Black Reconstruction in America 1860–1880* (New York: Atheneum, 1977), especially chap. 1.

30. Foster, *Negro People*, p. 109.

31. Ibid., p. 100.

32. Vernon Parrington, *Main Currents in American Thought* (New York: Harcourt Brace and World, 1954), pp. 352–53.

33. Foster, *Negro People*, p. 110.

34. James M. McPherson, *The Struggle for Equality* (Princeton, N.J.: Princeton University Press, 1969), p. 3.

35. Ibid., p. 5.
36. Ibid.,
37. Ibid., p. 6.
38. Ibid.
39. Ibid.
40. Ibid., p. 8.
41. Julius Lester, *Look Out, Whitey!* (New York: Dial Press, 1968), p. 39.
42. Ibid., p. 43.
43. Mary Frances Berry and John W. Blasingame, *Long Memory: The Black Experience in America* (New York: Oxford University Press, 1982), p. 67.
44. Frederick Douglass, *The Life and Times of Frederick Douglass* (New York: Collier, 1962).
45. Ibid., p. 366.
46. Foster, *Negro People*, p. 96.
47. Du Bois, *Black Reconstruction*, pp. 11–28.
48. Frank S. Greenwood, "Frederick Douglass and U.S. Imperialism," *Monthly Review* 2411 (April 1973): 43.
49. Ibid.
50. Ibid.
51. Taylor Branch, *Parting the Waters: America in the King Years, 1954–63* (New York: Simon and Schuster, 1988). The continuing struggles between King, the leading Moralist, and Roy Wilkins, leader of the NAACP, for ideological dominance in the Civil Rights Movement of the 1950s and 1960s are legend. King's approach became more popular, but Wilkins's more legalist approach more than held its own. Taylor Branch's book illustrates the contours of the competition well.
52. Douglass, *Life and Times*, p. 546. The Civil Rights Law on March 1, 1875, prohibited discrimination in public accommodations, transportation, places of public amusement, and the like, North and South. It stipulated fines of up to $1,000 and no less than thirty days imprisonment for violations. See Foster, *Negro People*, p. 334.
53. Waldo E. Martin, Jr., *The Mind of Frederick Douglass* (Chapel Hill: University of North Carolina Press, 1984), p. 172.
54. Ibid., p. 173.
55. Douglass, *Life and Times*, p. 90.
56. Ibid., p. 275.
57. Ibid.
58. Ibid., p. 143.
59. Ibid.
60. Foster, *Negro People*, pp. 138–39.
61. Ibid., p. 139.
62. Martin, *Mind of Frederick Douglass*, p. 158.
63. Ibid., p. 151.
64. Ibid., p. 159.
65. Ibid., p. 161.

66. Ibid., p. 226.
67. Ibid., p. 231.
68. Ibid., p. 233.
69. Douglass, *Life and Times*, p. 354.
70. Foster, *Negro People*, p. 256.
71. Douglass, *Life and Times*, p. 352.
72. For an excellent short summary of West Indian history, culture, and politics, see Catherine A. Sunshine, *The Caribbean* (Ecumenical Program on Central America and the Caribbean, Washington, D.C.: 1470 Irving Street, NW, Washington, D.C., 20010, 1985), see p. 14 for citation on slavery abolition dates.
73. Douglas, *Life and Times*, p. 500.
74. Ibid., p. 501.
75. Ibid., p. 504.
76. Ibid.
77. Ibid., p. 550.
78. Ibid., p. 542.
79. Ibid.
80. Martin, *Mind of Frederick Douglass*, p. 220.
81. Douglass, *Life and Times*, p. 284.
82. Ibid., p. 285.
83. Martin, *Mind of Frederick Douglass*, p. 190.
84. Douglass, *Life and Times*, p. 285.
85. Ibid., p. 286.
86. Ibid.
87. Martin, *Mind of Frederick Douglass*, p. 206.
88. Ibid., p. 208.
89. Ibid., p. 211.
90. Ibid., p. 219.
91. Ibid., p. 95.
92. Ibid., p. 98.
93. Ibid., p. 96.
94. Ibid., p. 212.
95. The African-Americans were James G. Barbadoes of Massachusetts, Peter Williams of New York, and Robert Purvis, James N. Crummell, John B. Vashon, and Abraham D. Shadd of Pennsylvania. See Foster, *Negro People*, p. 111.
96. Lester, *Look Out, Whitey!* p. 46.
97. Douglass's later personal life was a testament to the fact that his belief in the equality of all races did not waiver. His second wife, whom he married in 1884, was Helen Pitts, a white from Rochester, New York. She had served as his secretary when he was Recorder of Deeds of the District of Columbia. Some blacks and whites criticized the marriage, but it lasted until Douglass died in 1895. See Douglass, *Life and Times*, p. 20.
98. Franklin, *From Slavery to Freedom*, p. 254.

99. Foster, Negro People, p. 130.

100. Ibid., p. 131.

101. Ibid., p. 112.

102. For a short, moving discussion of John Brown, see Foster, Negro People, pp. 176–86. For a classic study of Brown, see W.E.B. Du Bois, John Brown (New York: International Publishers, 1962.)

103. McPherson, Struggle for Equality, p. viii.

104. Ibid.

105. For a good description of the sometimes bitter struggles to pass these amendments, see ibid.

106. Franklin, From Slavery to Freedom, p. 323.

107. Du Bois, Black Reconstruction, p. 693.

108. Martin R. Levy and Michael S. Kramer, The Ethnic Factor: How American Minorities Decide Elections (New York: Simon and Schuster, 1973), p. 39.

CHAPTER IV

1. Martin Bauml Duberman, Paul Robeson (New York: Knopf, 1988), p. 30.

2. Ibid., p. 67.

3. Louis R. Harlan, The Booker T. Washington Papers. Vol. 1, The Autobiographical Writings (Urbana: University of Illinois Press, 1972), p. 425.

4. Booker T. Washington, Up from Slavery, in Three Negro Classics (New York: Avon, 1965), p. 29. For an excellent short biographical sketch of Washington and other important black personages, see J. A. Rogers, World's Great Men of Color, Vol. 2 (New York: Collier, 1972), pp. 383–96.

5. Washington, Up from Slavery, p. 37.

6. August Meier, Negro Protest Thought in America 1880–1915 (Ann Arbor: University of Michigan Press, 1968), p. 102.

7. Washington, Up from Slavery, p. 59.

8. Stokely Carmichael and Charles V. Hamilton, Black Power (New York: Vintage, 1967), p. 125.

9. Louis R. Harlan, Booker T. Washington: The Wizard of Tuskegee 1901–15 (New York: Oxford University Press, 1983), p. 281.

10. Ibld., pp. vii–xii.

11. Louis R. Harlan, Booker T. Washington: The Making of a Black Leader 1856–1901 (New York: Oxford University Press, 1972), p. 252.

12. James D. Anderson, The Education of Blacks in the South, 1860–1935 (Chapel Hill: University of North Carolina Press, 1988), p. 44.

13. Ibid., p. 33.

14. Ibid., p. 34.

15. Ibid., p. 35.

16. Ibid., p. 34.

17. Ibid., p. 54.

18. Ibid., p. 75.

19. Ibid., p. 59.

20. Ibid., pp. 274–75.

21. Ibid., p. 272.

22. Ibid., p. 36.

23. Ibid., p. 37.

24. Louis R. Harlan, *The Booker T. Washington Papers*, Vol. 2, 1860–89 (Urbana: University of Illinois Press, 1972), p. 70.

25. Washington, *Up from Slavery*, p. 78. The African-American sociologist Oliver Cox suggests that Washington's philosophy of education catered to the wishes of the "white ruling class" of America. Cox argues that the white ruling class would have brought Washington to his knees if he had called for a superior education for blacks. See Cox, *Caste, Class and Race* (New York: Modern Reader, 1970), see especially pp. 343–44.

26. Washington, *Up from Slavery*, p. 78.

27. Ibid., p. 77.

28. Harlan, *Booker T. Washington: Wizard of Tuskegee*, p. 436.

29. Washington, *Up from Slavery*, p. 89.

30. Ibid., p. 101.

31. Booker T. Washington, "The Virtue of Industrial Education," in *The Negro Americans: A Documentary History*, ed. Leslie H. Fishel, Jr., and Benjamin Quarles (Glenview, Ill.: Scott, Foresman, 1967), p. 364. An excellent discussion of Booker T. Washington's philosophy and the responses of his critics is given in Hugh Hawkins, *Booker T. Washington and His Critics* (Lexington, Mass.: D. C. Heath, 1962).

32. Fishel and Quarles, *Negro Americans*, p. 364. A modern version of Washington's emphasis on economic striving as the basic building block for general African-American success is pushed in the works of two African-American economists, Thomas Sowell and Walter Williams. Economic determinists like Sowell and Williams do not acknowledge the extent to which even Washington owed much of his "economic influence" to his ability to skillfully perform in the political arena of his time. See the essays in Sowell, *Compassion Versus Guilt and Other Essays* (New York: William Morrow, 1987). Also see the essays in Williams, *All It Takes Is Guts* (Washington, D.C.: Regnery, 1987).

33. Harlan, *Booker T. Washington: Making of a Black Leader*, p. 272.

34. Ibid., p. 287.

35. Fishel and Quarles, *Negro Americans*, p. 365.

36. Ibid.

37. Booker T. Washington's views never went unchallenged. For an excellent discussion of Washington's philosophy and the responses of his critics, see Hawkins, *Booker T. Washington*.

38. Washington, *Up from Slavery*, p. 192.

39. Ibid.

40. Ibid.

41. Meier, *Negro Protest Thought,* p. 105.

42. Washington, *Up from Slavery,* pp. 73–74.

43. Ibid., p. 74. Du Bois's work was instrumental in starting the reevaluation of the view that blacks played no progressive role in Reconstruction. See W.E.B. Du Bois, *Black Reconstruction in America 1860–1880* (New York: Atheneum, 1977).

44. Harlan, *Booker T. Washington: Making of a Black Leader,* p. 234.

45. Harlan, *Booker T. Washington Papers,* vol. 1, p. 403.

46. Meier, *Negro Protest Thought,* p. 112.

47. Ibid., p. 75.

48. See the selection on Plato in William Ebenstein, *Great Political Thinkers* (New York: Holt Rinehart and Winston, 1962), p. 47.

49. Washington, *Up from Slavery,* p. 126.

50. Ibid., pp. 190–91.

51. Ibid., p. 126.

52. Ibid., pp. 146–50.

53. Meier, *Negro Protest Thought,* p. 110.

54. Ibid., pp. 110–11.

55. Ibid., p. 113.

56. Ibid., p. 114.

57. Ibid.

58. Ibid.

59. Ibid., p. 115.

60. Ibid., p. 155. For a running commentary on the controversy between W.E.B. Du Bois and Booker T. Washington, see Charles Flint Kellog, *NAACP: A History.* Vol. 1, 1909–1920 (Baltimore: Johns Hopkins University Press, 1973), pp. 67–68.

61. Louis Harlan, "Booker T. Washington and the White Man's Burden," in *Black Brotherhood: Afro-Americans and Africa,* ed. Okon Edet Uya (Lexington, Mass.: D. C. Heath, 1971), p. 137. For the views of Booker T. Washington and other African-Americans on their relationship to Africa, see Harold R. Isaacs, *The New World of Negro Americans* (New York: Viking, 1963).

62. Louis R. Harlan, *The Booker T. Washington Papers.* Vol. 5, 1899–1900 (Urbana: University of Illinois Press, 1976), pp. 154–59.

63. Meier, *Negro Protest Tought,* p. 115.

64. Ibid., p. 223.

65. Harlan, *Booker T. Washington: Wizard of Tuskegee,* p. 36.

66. Ibid., p. 45.

67. Ibid., p. 148.

68. John Dollard, *Caste and Class in a Southern Town* (Garden City, N.Y.: Doubleday, 1957), p. 305.

69. Meier, *Negro Protest Thought,* p. 212.

70. Ibid., p. 210.

71. Ibid., p. 226.

72. Ibid., p. 227. For the sequel to the Brownsville incident, see "The Brownsville Incident," *Ebony* 28, no. 4 (March 1973): 31–39.

73. Harlan, *Booker T. Washington: Wizard of Tuskegee*, p. 90.

74. Ibid., p. 101.

75. Ibid., p. 378.

76. Ibid., p. 105.

77. Arnold Rampersad, *The Art and Imagination of W.E.B. Du Bois* (Cambridge, Mass.: Harvard University Press, 1976), p. 245.

78. Meier, *Negro Protest Thought*, p. 198.

79. Ibid., p. 196.

80. Ibid., p. 198.

81. W.E.B. Du Bois, *Souls of Black Folk*, in *Three Negro Classics* (New York: Avon, 1968), p. 245.

82. Ibid., p. 246.

83. Ibid., p. 241.

84. Ibid., p. 241. For the views of one who feels that Washington's emphasis on economics was justified and who sees him as a precursor of the Black Power Movement, see Harold Cruse, *Rebellion or Revolution?* (New York: William Morrow, 1969), especially pp. 156–57.

85. Du Bois, *Souls of Black Folk*, p. 246.

86. Ibid., p. 249.

87. Ibid., p. 250.

88. Fishel and Quarles, *Negro Americans*, p. 367.

89. Ibid., p. 368.

90. Ibid., p. 369.

91. Ibid.

92. Anderson, *Education of Blacks*, p. 72.

93. Rampersad, *Art and Imagination*, p. 163.

94. Ibid., p. 164.

95. Ibid., p. 168.

96. Meier, *Negro Protest Thought*, p. 203.

97. Ibid., p. 204.

98. For a documentary history of Du Bois's life, see Philip S. Foner, *W.E.B. Du Bois Speaks*, vols. 1 and 2 (New York: Pathfinder, 1970).

99. Meier, *Negro Protest Thought*, p. 206.

CHAPTER V

1. John Hope Franklin, *From Slavery to Freedom* (New York: Vintage, 1969), p. 446.

2. Ibid.

3. Ibid. As John Hope Franklin writes, among those who participated were Jane Adams, William Dean Howells, Livingstone Farr, John Dewey, John Miholand, and Oswald Garrison Villard.

4. Ibid., p. 447.

5. Louis R. Harlan, *Booker T. Washington: The Wizard of Tuskegee 1901–15* (New York: Oxford University Press, 1983), p. 436.

6. E. Franklin Frazier, "Garvey: A Mass Leader," in *Marcus Garvey and the Vision of Africa*, ed. John Henrik Clarke, with Amy Jacques Garvey (New York: Vintage, 1974), p. 237.

7. David Lowenthal and Lambros Comitas, *Consequences of Class and Color in the West Indies* (Garden City, N.Y.: Anchor, 1973), p. 6. For a further exposition of the problems of race and color in the West Indies, see David Lowenthal, "Race and Color in the West Indies," *Daedalus* 96, no. 2 (Spring 1967): 580–626.

8. Elton C. Fax, *Garvey: The Story of a Pioneer Black Nationalist* (New York: Dodd, Mead, 1970), p. 21.

9. For Garvey's tribute to Dr. Love, see Robert A. Hill, *The Marcus Garvey Papers*, vol. 1 (Berkeley: University of California Press, 1983), pp. 96–99.

10. John Hope Franklin and August Meier, *Black Leaders of the Twentieth Century* (Urbana: University of Illinois Press, 1982), p. 108.

11. Amy Jacques Garvey, ed., *Philosophy and Opinions of Marcus Garvey*, vol. 1 (New York: Atheneum, 1969), p. 126.

12. Many books have been written about Garvey, most of which will be cited in the text, but the most thorough documentation of Garvey's life is found in the superb five-volume series of Marcus Garvey papers edited by Robert A. Hill. For documentation of Garvey's early years and the founding of the UNIA, see Hill, *Marcus Garvey Papers*, vol. 1. See the chronology of Garvey's life, pp. cix–cxvii. For a West Indian immigrant's citique of Garvey, see W. A. Domingo, "Gift of the Black Tropics," in *The New Negro*, ed. Alain Locke (New York: Atheneum, 1969), especially p. 348. For a short critical assessment of the Garvey Movement, see Saunders Redding, *They Came in Chains* (New York: J. B. Lippincott, 1950), pp. 259–61. For an excellent short biography of Marcus Garvey, see Edmund David Cronin, *Black Moses: The Story of Marcus Garvey* (Madison: University of Wisconsin Press, 1968). For a biography of Marcus Garvey that focuses on his post-U.S. years, see Rupert Lewis, *Marcus Garvey: Anti-Colonial Champion* (Trenton, N.J.: Africa World Press, 1988).

13. A. J. Garvey *Philosophy and Opinions*, vol. 2, p. 128.

14. Ibid., p. 129.

15. Lawrence W. Levine, "Marcus Garvey and the Politics of Revitalization," in Franklin and Meier, *Black Leaders*, p. 117.

16. Theodore G. Vincent, *Black Power and the Garvey Movement* (Berkeley, Calif.: Ramparts Press, 1973), pp. 33–34.

17. Ibid., p. 34.

18. Ibid.

19. Franklin, *From Slavery to Freedom*, p. 489.

20. A. J. Garvey, *Philosophy and Opinions*, vol. 2, p. 357–58.

21. Franklin, *From Slavery to Freedom*, p. 491.

22. Ibid.

23. Franklin and Meier, *Black Leaders*, p. 130.

24. Judith Stein, *The World of Marcus Garvey* (Baton Rouge: Louisiana State University Press, 1986), p. 192.

25. Ibid., p. 167.

26. By far the best source for documents from which Garvey's political thought can be constructed are the first five volumes of a projected twelve-volume series of Garvey papers edited by Robert A. Hill, referred to in note 12. Numerous secondary works have been written on Garvey, and some of them, especially those by Fax, Vincent, and Cronin are outstanding. These authors are cited throughout this chapter. The best reasonably short and excellent primary sources are Amy Jacques Garvey, ed., *Philosophy and Opinions of Marcus Garvey*, cited throughout the text, and Amy Jacques Garvey, *Garvey and Garveyism* (New York: Collier, 1970). An excellent Garvey volume replete with commentary is John Henrik Clarke, with Amy Jacques Garvey, *Marcus Garvey and the Vision of Africa*, previously cited.

27. A. J. Garvey, *Philosophy and Opinions*, vol. 1, p. 89.

28. Ibid., p. 90.

29. Ibid., vol. 2, p. 32.

30. Ibid., p. 33.

31. Ibid., vol. 1, p. 22.

32. Randall K. Burkett, *Garveyism as a Religious Movement* (Metuchen, N.J.: Scarecrow Press, 1978), p. 5.

33. William Ebenstein, *Great Political Thinkers* (New York: Holt Rinehart and Winston, 1962), p. 367.

34. A. J. Garvey, *Philosophy and Opinions*, vol. 1, p. 94.

35. Ibid., vol. 2, p. 228.

36. Ibid., vol. 1, p. 96.

37. Ibid., p. 81.

38. Ibid., vol. 2, p. 118.

39. Ibid., p. 97.

40. Ibid., pp. 97–98.

41. Ibid., p. 107.

42. Ibid., vol. 1, p. 72. Hill also sees some Aristotelian influences on Marcus Garvey. For example, he considers Garvey's theory of racial separation to be based on Aristotle's view that distinctions between "'kinds of things' are not arbitrary or subjective." See Robert A. Hill, *The Marcus Garvey Papers*, vol. 6 (Berkeley: University of California Press, 1989), p. 604.

43. Ibid., p. 74.

44. Hill, *Marcus Garvey Papers*, vol 1, p. cxi.

45. A. J. Garvey, *Philosophy and Opinions*, vol. 2, p. 74.

46. Ibid.

47. Ibid., p. 75.

48. Ibid.

49. Ibid., pp. 74–75.

50. Ibid., p. 75.

51. Ibid., p. 76.

52. Ibid.

53. Ibid., p. 306.

54. Ibid., vol. 2, p. 69.

55. Ibid., p. 69. A critical analysis of Garvey's relationship with the communists is given in Harold Cruse, The Crisis of the Negro Intellectual (New York: William Morrow, 1967), especially pp. 115–80.

56. A J. Garvey, Philosophy and Opinions, vol. 2, p. 72.

57. Ibid., p. 70.

58. Ibid., p. 35.

59. Ibid., p. 62. To document the view that Garvey saw the return to Africa as taking anywhere from thirty to fifty years, see the pamphlet by Marcus Garvey, Aims and Objects of Movement for Solutions of the Negro Problem Outlined (New York: University Place Book Shop, 69 University Place, New York, New York, 10010, 1966–69), p. 7.

60. Vincent, Black Power, p. 102.

61. Ibid.

62. Ibid., p. 103.

63. Stein, World of Marcus Garvey, p. 102.

64. Vincent, Black Power, p. 103.

65. A. J. Garvey, Garvey and Garveyism, p. 50.

66. Ibid.

67. Ibid., p. 51.

68. A. J. Garvey, Philosophy and Opinions, vol. 2, p. 280.

69. Stein, World of Marcus Garvey, p. 195.

70. Hill, Marcus Garvey Papers, vol. 1, p. 515.

71. Franklin and Meier, Black Leaders, p. 134.

72. Vincent, Black Power, p. 82.

73. Ibid., p. 85.

74. Ibid., p. 86.

75. Ibid.

70. Theodoro Draper, The Rediscovery of Black Nationalism ("New York: Viking, 1970), p. 71.

77. Vincent, Black Power, p. 223.

78. Howard Brotz, The Black Jews of Harlem (New York: Schocken, 1970), p. 10.

79. Ibid., p. 11.

80. Vincent, Black Power, p. 222.

81. Brotz, Black Jews of Harlem, p. 12.

82. Vincent, Black Power, p. 228.

83. Ibid., p. 229.

84. Ibid.

CHAPTER VI

1. Joanne Grant, *Black Protest* (New York: Fawcett, 1968), p. 219.

2. Ibid.

3. Ibid., p. 220. The NAACP's international relations were decidedly pro-American. This strong Pro-Americanism is seen in the opposition of NAACP leaders like Walter White and Roy Wilkins to the often pro-Soviet stands of the famous black artist Paul Robeson, especially on racial matters. For an excellent description of this opposition see Martin Bauml Duberman, *Paul Robeson* (New York: Knopf, 1988), especially pp. 336–62.

4. Grant, *Black Protest*, p. 220.

5. Lerone Bennett, Jr., *Before the Mayflower* (Baltimore: Penguin, 1966), p. 303.

6. Grant, *Black Protest*, p. 252.

7. Ibid., p. 268.

8. Alan Pendleton Grimes, *American Political Thought* (New York: Holt Rinehart and Winston, 1967), p. 152.

9. See Grant, *Black Protest*, pp. 268–72.

10. William H. Chace and Peter Collier, eds., *Justice Denied* (New York: Harcourt Brace and World, 1970), p. 315.

11. Taylor Branch, *Parting the Waters: American in the King Years, 1954– 63* (New York: Simon and Schuster, 1988), p. 120. Branch's book is an excellent source for viewing the context within which the Civil Rights Movement developed. Branch is especially effective in drawing into the discussion those simple but effective fighters like E. D. Nixon, whose contributions tend to be overshadowed by those of national figures like Dr. Martin Luther King, Jr., and Rosa Parks. He also links the civil rights activity to other policy issues during the years 1954 to 63.

12. Ibid., p. 122.

13. Ibid., p. 121.

14. See King's outline of Moralist tactics, as discussed in Clayborne Carson's *In Struggle: SNCC and the Black Awakening of the 1960s* (Cambridge, Mass.: Harvard University Press, 1981), pp. 22–23. Another excellent history and analysis of SNCC and the involvement of the students in the Civil Rights Movement is Howard Zinn, *SNCC: The New Abolitionists* (Boston: Beacon Press, 1965). For an analysis of the various civil rights organizations, see Kenneth Clark, "The Civil Rights Movement and Organization," *Daedalus* 95, no. 1 (Winter 1966): 239–67.

15. Carson, *In Struggle*, p. 24.

16. Bennett, *Before the Mayflower*, p. 347–48.

17. Mary Frances Berry and John W. Blasingame, *Long Memory: The Black Experience in America* (New York: Oxford University Press, 1982) p. 183.

18. Ibid., p. 184.

19. Chace and Collier, *Justice Denied*, p. 315.

20. Martin Luther King, Jr., *Where Do We Go From Here: Chaos or Community?* (Boston: Beacon Press, 1968), p. 45.

21. Ibid.

22. For an excellent account of the King movement and his intellectual and spiritual odyssey within it, see David J. Garrow, *Bearing the Cross* (New York: William Morrow, 1986).

23. See Cook's introductory comments on King in Hames Walton, Jr., *The Political Philosophy of Martin Luther King, Jr.* (Westport, Conn.: Greenwood Publishing, 1971), p. xxxii.

24. Ibid., p. xxxiii.

25. Ibid.

26. Ibid.

27. Martin Luther King, Jr., *Stride Toward Freedom* (New York: Harper and Row, 1958), p. 5.

28. A very good but by no means exhaustive account of Dr. King's life and background can be seen in David Lewis, *King: A Biography* (Urbana: University of Illinois Press, 1970).

29. King, *Stride Toward Freedom*, p. 6–7.

30. Elton C. Fax, *Contemporary Black Leaders* (New York: Dodd, Mead, 1970), p. 45.

31. King, *Stride Toward Freedom*, p. 72.

32. Ibid., p. 74.

33. Ibid., p. 73.

34. Ibid., p. 22.

35. Ibid., p. 20.

36. To achieve a real feeling for the context within which Dr. King spoke these words, see Branch, *Parting the Waters*, pp. 104–205.

37. Martin Luther King, Jr., *Strength to Love* (New York: Harper and Row, 1963), p. 111.

38. Ibid., pp. 110–11.

39. Ibid., p. 111.

40. Ibid., p. 111.

41. Ibid., p. 133.

42. King, *Stride Toward Freedom*, p. 74.

43. Ibid.

44. Ibid., p. 77.

45. In his excellent narrative on the life of Dr. King, Garrow suggests that King preferred a democratic socialist system. See *Bearing the Cross*, pp. 591–92.

46. King, *Stride Toward Freedom*, p. 77.

47. Ibid., p. 78.

48. Ibid.
49. Ibid., p. 78.
50. Ibid.
51. Ibid., p. 80.
52. Ibid., p. 81.
53. Ibid., pp. 80–81.
54. Ibid., p. 81.
55. Ibid., p. 82.
56. Ibid.
57. Ibid., pp. 82–83.
58. Ibid., p. 83.
59. Ibid., p. 84.
60. Ibid.
61. Ibid.
62. Ibid., p. 85.
63. Ibid.
64. Ibid., p. 88.
65. Ibid., p. 86.
66. Ibid., p. 88.
67. King, *Strength to Love*, p. 87.
68. Ibid., p. 88.
69. Ibid.
70. Ibid.
71. Ibid.
72. Ibid., p. 89.
73. Ibid.
74. Ibid., p. 90.
75. Ibid.
76. Ibid., p. 91.
77. Ibid., p. 92.
78. Martin Luther King, Jr., *Why We Can't Wait* (New York: Signet Books, 1963), p. 34.
79. King, *Where Do We Go from Here?* p. 84.
80. Sam Cook in an introductory essay to Walton, *Political Philosophy*, p. xxxiii.
81. Julius Lester, *Revolutionary Notes* (New York: Richard W. Baron, 1969), p. 85.
82. King, *Stride Toward Freedom*, p. 139.
83. Ibid., p. 140.
84. Martin Luther King, Jr., *The Trumpet of Conscience* (New York: Harper and Row, 1967), p. 62. For perhaps the best treatment of King's plans for the "Poor People's Campaign," see Garrow, *Bearing the Cross*, pp. 575–625.
85. King, *Stride Toward Freedom*, p. 148.
86. Ibid., p. 149.
87. Ibid., p. 24.

88. Ibid., p. 25.
89. Leslie H. Fishel, Jr., and Benjamin Quarles, eds., *The Negro Americans: A Documentary History* (Glenview, Ill.: Scott, Foresman, 1967), p. 521.
90. King, *Trumpet of Conscience*, p. 71.
91. King, *Stride Toward Freedom*, p. 198.
92. Ibid., p. 199.
93. Ibid., p. 62.
94. Ibid., pp. 62–63.
95. Ibid., p. 177.
96. Ibid., p. 174.
97. King, *Why We Can't Wait*, p. 61.
98. King, *Where Do We Go from Here?* p. 20.
99. The day-to-day struggles in the Civil Rights Movement between the NAACP's more legalist approach and that of Dr. King are shown in the confrontations between Roy Wilkins and King in Branch, *Parting the Waters*. For an excellent history of the King movement and the rise of Black Power, see the essay on King in John White, *Black Leadership in America: From Booker T. Washington to Jesse Jackson* (London: Longmans, 1990), pp. 109–45.

CHAPTER VII

1. Some of the better attempts to describe and analyze Black Power are the following: Robert L. Allen, *Black Awakening in Capitalist America* (New York: Doubleday, 1969); Joyce Ladner, "What 'Black Power' Means to Negroes in Mississippi," in *Americans from Africa*, ed. Peter I. Rose (New York: Atherton Press, 1970) pp. 249–67; Stokely Carmichael, "What We Want," in Rose, *Americans from Africa*, p. 237–49; Christopher Lasch, "The Trouble with Black Power," in Rose, *Americans from Africa*, pp. 267–93; Nathan Hare, "The Case for Separatism: Black Perspective," in *Black Power and Student Rebellion*, ed. James McEvoy and Abraham Miller (Belmont, Calif.: Wadsworth, 1969) pp. 233–35; Roy Wilkins, "The Case Against Separatism Black Jim Crow," in McEvoy and Miller, *Black Power and Student Rebellion*, pp. 235–37; Melvin H. Posey, "Toward a More Meaningful Revolution: Ideology in Transition," in McEvoy and Miller, *Black Power and Student Rebellion*, pp. 253–77; Harold Cruse, *The Crisis of the Negro Intellectual* (New York: William Morrow, 1967) pp. 544–67; Stokely Carmichael, "Black Poor," in *The Voices of Black Rhetoric*, ed. Arthur L. Smith and Stephen Robb (Boston: Allyn and Bacon, 1971) pp. 264–83; John Henrik Clarke, "Black Power and Black History," in *What Black Educators Are Saying*, ed. Nathan Wright, Jr. (New York: Hawthorne Books, 1970) pp. 217–27; Nathan Wright, Jr., "The Crisis Which Bred Black Power," in *The Black Power Revolt*, ed. Floyd B. Barbour (Boston: Porter Sargent, 1968) pp. 124–25; LeRoi Jones, "The Need for a Cultural Base to Civil Rights and Black Power Movements," in Barbour, *Black Power Revolt*, pp. 119–26; Maulana Ron Karenga "Maulana Ron Ka-

renga," in Barbour, *Black Power Revolt*, pp. 162–70; Larry Neal, "New Space: The Growth of Black Consciousness in the Sixties," in *The Black Seventies*, ed. Floyd B. Barbour (Boston: Porter Sargent, 1970), pp. 9–31; James Boggs, "The Revolutionary Struggle for Black Power," in Barbour, *Black Seventies*, pp. 33–48; H. Rap Brown "A Letter from H. Rap Brown," in Barbour, *Black Seventies*, pp. 311–13; LeRoi Jones, "What Does Non-Violence Mean?" in *Crisis: A Contemporary Reader*, ed. Peter Collier (New York: Harcourt Brace and World, 1969), pp. 69–85; Nathan Hare, "How White Power Whitewashes Black Power," in Barbour, *Black Power Revolt*, pp. 182–88; Theodore Cross, *The Black Power Imperative* (New York: Faulkner Books, 1986).

2. For an excellent discussion of the problem of definition, including the philosopher Ludwig Wittgenstein's concept of "family resemblances" as a legitimate form of definition, see Gajo Petrovic, *Marx in the Mid-Twentieth Century* (New York: Anchor, 1967), pp. 198–217.

3. Cross expresses this view in *Black Power Imperative*, p. 613.

4. Charles V. Hamilton, "An Advocate of Black Power Defines It," in *The Rhetoric of Black Power*, ed. Robert Scott and Wayne Brockriede (New York: Harper and Row, 1969), p. 179.

5. Ibid., p. 178.

6. Ibid.

7. Ibid., pp. 178–79.

8. See Clayborne Carson, *In Struggle: SNCC and the Black Awakening of the 1960s* (Cambridge, Mass.: Harvard University Press, 1981), especially pp. 287–304.

9. Other less successful attempts to categorize the Black Power Movement and put it in a historical context are the following: Ronald Walters, "Afro-American Nationalism," *Black World* 22, no. 12 (October 1973): 9–28; Obi Antarah, "A Blueprint for Black Liberation," *Black World* 22, no. 12 (October 1973): 60–68; Cross, *Black Power Imperative*.

10. John Conyers, "Politics and the Black Revolution," *Ebony* 24, no. 10 (August 1969): 162.

11. Ibid., 165.

12. Ibid., 163.

13. "Black Lawmakers in Congress," *Ebony* 36, no. 4 (February 1971): 117.

14. Philip S. Foner, *The Black Panthers Speak* (Philadelphia: J. B. Lippincott, 1970), p. 70.

15. Carl Joachim Friedrich, *Man and His Government* (New York: McGraw-Hill, 1963), p. 553.

16. Nathan Wright, Jr., *Black Power and Urban Unrest* (New York: Hawthorne Books, 1967), pp. 8–9.

17. Shirley Chisholm, *Unbought and Unbossed* (Boston: Houghton Mifflin, 1970), p. 157.

18. Ibid., p. 159.

19. Stokely Carmichael and Charles V. Hamilton, *Black Power* (New York: Vintage, 1967), p. 51.

20. Friedrich, *Man and His Government*, p. 145.

21. Huey Newton, "The Black Panthers," *Ebony* 24, no. 10 (August 1969): 107.

22. Ibid., 108.

23. James Boggs, *Racism and the Class Struggle* (New York: Monthly Review Press, 1970), p. 37.

24. Barbour, *Black Power Revolt*, pp. 124–25.

25. Robert Sherill, "We Also Want Four Hundred Billion Dollars Back Pay," *Esquire* 71, no. 1 (January 1969): 148.

26. Stokely Carmichael, "Stokely Carmichael Explains Black Power to a White Audience in White Water, Wisconsin," in Scott and Brockriede *Rhetoric of Black Power*, p. 99.

27. James H. Cone, *Black Power and Black Theology* (New York: Seabury Press, 1969), p. 6.

28. James Boggs, "Black Revolutionary Power," *Ebony* 25, no. 10 (August 1970): 152.

29. Huey P. Newton, "Black Capitalism Reanalyzed," *Black Panther*, Saturday, 5 June 1971, p. 9.

30. Friedrich, *Man and His Government*, p. 160.

31. Ibid., pp. 160–61.

32. Ibid., p. 161.

33. Ibid., p. 165.

34. Martin Luther King, Jr., *Where Do We Go from Here: Chaos or Community?* (Boston: Beacon Press, 1968), p. 48.

35. For a good description of the U.S. Communist Party's view of black self-determination, see Mark Naison, *Communists in Harlem* (New York: Grove Press, 1984), pp. 3–30.

36. Harry R. Davis and Robert C. Good, *Reinhold Niebuhr on Politics* (New York: Scribner's, 1960) p. 64.

37. Ibid.

38. Ibid.

39. Chisholm, *Unbought and Unbossed*, p. 149.

40. Ibid., p. 150.

41. Julius Lester, *Look Out, Whitey!* (New York: Dial Press, 1968), p. 42.

42. Elijah Muhammad, *Message to the Black Man in America*, no. 2 (Chicago. Muhammad's Mosque of Islam, 1965), p. 33.

43. "Black Politics: New Way to Overcome," *Newsweek* 77 (7 June 1971): 33.

44. Ibid.

45. Ibid.

46. David J. Garrow, *Bearing the Cross* (New York: William Morrow, 1986) p. 478.

47. King, *Where Do We Go from Here?* p. 31.

48. Ibid., p. 32.

49. For an excellent overview of the change from Civil Rights to Black

Power, see James Forman, *The Making of Black Revolutionaries* (New York: Macmillan, 1972); Forman, *Sammy Younge, Jr.* (New York: Grove Press, 1968); Lerone Bennett, Jr., *The Negro Mood* (New York: Ballantine, 1964); Claude Sitton, "Negroes Queue in Mississippi in Symbol of Frustration in Voter Registration Drive," in *Black Protest in the Sixties*, ed. August Meier and Elliott Rudwick (Chicago: Quadrangle Books, 1970), pp. 53–61.

50. King, *Where Do We Go from Here?* p. 33.

51. Ibid., p. 34.

52. For an early analysis of individual versus institutional racism, see Carmichael and Hamilton, *Black Power*, pp. 2–32.

53. King, *Where Do We Go from Here?* pp. 34–35.

54. Ibid., p. 35.

55. Ibid., p. 36.

56. Ibid., p. 37.

57. Ibid., p. 38.

58. Ibid., p. 41.

59. Ibid., p. 43.

60. Ibid., p. 44.

61. Ibid.

62. Ibid., p. 46.

63. Ibid., p. 47.

64. Ibid., p. 48.

65. Charles Fager, *White Reflections on Black Power* (Grand Rapids, Mich.: William B. Eerdman, 1967), pp. 41–57.

66. King, *Where Do We Go from Here?* p. 48.

67. Ibid., p. 66.

68. Ibid., p. 49.

69. Ibid., p. 50.

70. Ibid., p. 51.

71. Ibid., p. 54.

72. Ibid., p. 55.

73. Ibid.

74. Ibid., p. 57.

75. Ibid.

76. Ibid., p. 58.

77. Ibid., p. 59.

78. Ibid., p. 64.

79. Ibid.

CHAPTER VIII

1. For a review of black protest Counter-Communalist style, see Phil Hutchings, "What Program for Black Liberation Movement?" *Guardian* 26, no. 36 (19 June 1974): 8, 19. For a short recent review of the black Left and the

general leftist movement of the 1960s, see Robert L. Allen, *Reluctant Reformers* (Washington, D.C.: Howard University Press, 1983), pp. 313–42. A stirring portrait of an African-American woman who began as a reformist and became a Counter-Communalist is given in Assata Shakur, *Assata Shakur: An Autobiography* (Westport, Conn.: Lawrence Hill, 1987), p. 226.

2. Bert Cochran, "In the Grip of the Egalitarian Passion," *Nation* 214, no. 26 (20 June 1972): 822.

3. Tim Findley, "Huey Newton Twenty-five Floors from the Street," *Rolling Stone* 14 (3 August 1972): 31.

4. Huey P. Newton, *Revolutionary Suicide* (New York: Harcourt Brace Jovanovich, 1973), pp. 11–35.

5. Findley, "Huey Newton," 31.

6. Newton, *Revolutionary Suicide*, p. 63.

7. Ibid., p. 111.

8. Findley, "Huey Newton," 32.

9. For the Black Panther program, see Huey P. Newton, *To Die for the People* (New York: Vintage, 1972), pp. 3–13. The Black Panther ten-point program called for the following:

(1) We want freedom. We want power to determine the destiny of our black community.
(2) We want full employment for our people.
(3) We want an end to the robbery by the capitalists of our Black Community.
(4) We want decent housing fit for shelter of human beings.
(5) We want education for our people that exposes the true nature of this decadent American society. We want education that teaches us our true history and our role in present-day society.
(6) We want all black men exempt from military service.
(7) We want an immediate end of police brutality and murder of black people.
(8) We want freedom for all black men held in federal, state, county and city prisons and jails.
(9) We want all back people, when brought to trial, to be tried in court by a jury of their peer group or people from their black communities as defined by the Constitution of the United States.
(10) We want land, bread, housing, education, clothing, justice and peace.

10. "Black Panther Co-founder Slain," *USA Today*, 23 August 1989, p. 2A.

11. Ibid. For another excellent description of the circumstances of Newton's death, see "Huey Newton, Head of Black Panthers, Found Shot to Death," *New York Times*, Wednesday, 23 August 1989, sec. A.

12. V. I. Lenin, *Materialism and Empirio-Criticism* (New York: International Publishers, 1970), p. 126. Lenin in this essay also criticizes the followers of the idealist Bishop Berkeley, who argues in his *Principles* that sensible things are "collections or combinations of 'sensations or ideas' and . . . draws the conclusion that they cannot exist otherwise than in a mind perceiving them." See Frederick Copleston, *A History of Philosophy*, vol. 5, pt. 2 (New York: Image Books, 1964), p. 28.

13. Ibid., p. 190.

14. Mao Tse-tung, *Selected Readings* (Peking: Foreign Language Press, 1971), pp. 90–91.

15. Amilcar Cabral, *Unity and Struggle* (New York: Monthly Review Press, 1979), p. 142.

16. Newton, *To Die for the People*, p. 23.

17. George H. Sabine, *A History of Political Theory* (Hillsdale, Ill.: Dryden Press, 1973), p. 585. In his essay on a correct method, Newton does say that in all phenomena there is a unity of opposites as the thesis struggles against the antithesis, and a higher synthesis of both results from the struggle and will be replicated in a new phenomena. Also like Mao, Newton argues that two forces may be "contrary" yet not "in contradiction." But unlike Mao, Newton does not describe clearly the conditions under which these differences occur, nor does he demonstrate, like Mao, how that which is contrary at point "a" may become contradictory at point "b" and vice versa!

18. Newton, *To Die for the People*, p. 23.

19. Sabine, *History of Political Theory*, pp. 686–87.

20. Several books and articles deal with the history of the Black Panther Party and aspects of its ideology: Gene Marine, *The Black Panthers* (New York: Signet, 1969); Lee Lockwood, *Conversations with Eldridge Cleaver* (New York: Delta Book, 1970); Don Schance, *The Panther Paradox* (New York: Paperback Library, 1971); Reginald Major, *A Panther Is a Black Cat* (New York: William Morrow, 1971); Theodore Draper, *The Rediscovery of Black Nationalism* (New York: Viking, 1970); Eldridge Cleaver, *Soul on Ice* (New York: McGraw-Hill, 1968); George Feaver, "Black Power," in *Prophetic Politics*, ed. Maurice Cranston (New York: Simon and Schuster, 1972); Earl Anthony, *I Pick Up the Gun* (New York: Dial Press, 1970).

21. James Boggs, "Beyond Nationalism" *Monthly Review* (26 January 1974): 37.

22. Robert L. Allen, *Black Awakening in Capitalist America* (New York: Doubleday, 1969), p. 237.

23. James Forman, *The Making of Black Revolutionaries* (New York: Macmillan, 1972), p. 551.

24. Julius Lester, *Look Out, Whitey!* (New York: Dial Press, 1968), p. 14.

25. James H. Cone, *Black Power and Black Theology* (New York: Seabury Press, 1969), p. 37.

26. Newton, *To Die for the People*, p. 220.

27. Newton, *Revolutionary Suicide*, p. 4.

28. Ibid., p. 5.

29. Ibid.

30. Newton, *To Die for the People*, pp. 217–18.

31. Ibid., pp. 221–22.

32. Ibid., p. 64.

33. Ibid., p. 65.

34. Ibid., p. 67.

35. Ibid., p. 31.

36. Ibid.

37. Ibid., p. 32.

38. Ibid., p. 33.

39. Ibid., p. 37.

40. Sabine, History of Political Theory, p. 763.

41. Floyd B. Barbour, ed., The Black Seventies (Boston: Porter Sargent, 1970), pp. 42–45.

42. Lester, Look Out, Whitey! p. 132.

43. Ibid.

44. Cone, Black Power and Black Theology, p. 144.

45. See Allen, Black Awakening.

46. James Forman, "Control, Conflict and Change," in Black Manifesto, ed. Robert S. Lecky and H. Eliot Wright (New York: Sheed and Ward, 1969), p. 49.

47. Newton, To Die for the People, p. 156.

48. Ibid., pp. 157–58.

49. Ibid., p. 158.

50. Ibid., p. 157.

51. Ibid., p. 160.

52. Ibid., p. 159.

53. Ibid., p. 161.

54. Ibid., p. 15.

55. Ibid., p. 17.

56. Ibid., p. 106.

57. Ibid., p. 108.

58. Findley, "Huey Newton," p. 34.

59. Newton, To Die for the People, p. 198.

60. Philip S. Foner, The Black Panthers Speak (Philadelphia: J. B. Lippincott, 1970), p. 45.

61. Ibid., p. 54.

62. Ibid.

63. Ibid., p. 55.

64. Ibid. For an interesting observation from a member of the "white Left" on the Black Panther Party see Dorothy Healey and Maurice Isserman, Dorothy Healey Remembers: A Life in the American Communist Party (New York: Oxford University Press, 1990), especially pp. 210–12.

65. James Boggs, quoted in Barbour, Black Seventies, p. 46. A similar opinion is expressed by Boggs in Boggs, "Uprooting Racism and Racists in the United States," The Black Scholar 2, no. 2 (October 1970): 2–10.

66. Barbour, Black Seventies, p. 46.

67. Ibid., p. 106.

68. Ibid., pp. 182–83.

69. Ibid., p. 183.

70. Ibid., pp. 120–21.

71. Ibid., p. 121.

72. Julius Lester, *Revolutionary Notes* (New York: Richard W. Baron, 1969), p. 187.

73. Ibid., p. 196.

74. Lester, *Look Out, Whitey!* p. 142.

75. Allen, *Black Awakening*, p. 234.

76. Ibid., p. 236.

77. Ibid., p. 238.

78. See Robert L. Allen, "An Historical Synthesis: Black Liberation and World Revolution," *Black Scholar* 3, no. 6 (February 1972): 7–23.

79. Allen, *Black Awakening*, p. 235.

80. Ibid., p. 236.

81. Forman, *Making of Black Revolutionaries*, p. 516.

82. Ibid.

83. Cone, *Black Power and Black Theology*, p. 55.

CHAPTER IX

1. Charles Hamilton, "An Advocate of Black Power Defines It," in *The Rhetoric of Black Power*, ed. Robert Scott and Wayne Brockriede (New York: Harper and Row, 1969), p. 181.

2. Two excellent studies of the political thought and tactics of the Reverend Jesse Jackson are Adolph L. Reed, Jr., *The Jesse Jackson Phenomenon* (New Haven, Conn.: Yale University Press, 1986.); Sheila D. Collins, *The Rainbow Coalition* (New York: Monthly Review Press, 1986).

3. Other books and articles used to develop the Pluralist case but not cited directly in the text are Lerone Bennett, Jr., *Black Power USA* (Baltimore: Penguin, 1967); Floyd McKissick, *Three-fifths of a Man* (London: Macmillan, 1969); William E. Nelson, Jr., *Black Politics in Gary: Problems and Prospects* (Washington, D.C.: Joint Center for Political Studies, 1972); Edward Greer, "The First Year of Black Power in Gary, Indiana," in *Black Liberation Politics: A Reader*, ed. Edward Greer (Boston: Allyn and Bacon, 1971), pp. 208–33; Charles Denby, "Black Caucuses in the Union," in Greer, *Black Liberation Politics*, pp. 370–79; I. F. Stone, "Why They Cry Black Power," in *In a Time of Torment*, ed. I. F. Stone (New York: Vintage, 1968), pp. 166–68; James H. Stephen, Jr., "The State Delegates to the National Black Convention," *Jet* 42, no. 1 (30 March 1972): 8–10; Simeon Booker, "Black Political Convention Is Successful Despite Splits and Tactical Differences," *Jet* 42, no. 1 (30 March, 1972): 12–18; Warren Brown, "Black Convention Solves Problems Without Clubs, Bullets or Blood," *Jet* 42, no. 1 (30 March 1972): 24–30; William L. Clay, "Emerging New Black Politics," *Black World* 21, no. 12 (October 1972): 32–39; Dempsey Travis, "Barriers to Black Power in the American Economy," *Black Scholar* 3, no. 2 (October 1971): 21–25; Talmadge Andersen, "Black Economic Liberation Under Capitalism," *Black Scholar* 2, no. 2 (October

1970): 11–14; Paul King, "The Role of Black Business: Delirium or Imperium?" Black Scholar 3, no. 6 (February 1972): 49–56; King, "The Role of Black Business: Delirium or Imperium? Part II," Black Scholar 3, no. 7–8 (March 1972): 27–35; "The Troubled American," Newsweek 74, no. 14 (6 October 1969): 29–40; Imamu Amiri Baraka, "Black and Angry," Newsweek 80 (10 July 1972): 35–36; Alex Poinsett, "Unity Without Uniformity," Ebony 27, no. 8 (June 1972): 45–54; Herrington Bryce, "Putting Black Economic Progress in Perspective," Ebony 28, no. 10 (August 1973): 59–62.

4. Shirley Chisholm, Unbought and Unbossed (Boston: Houghton Mifflin, 1970), p. 4.

5. Ibid., p. 14.

6. Ibid., p. 37.

7. Reba Carruth and Vivian Jenkins Nelsen, "Shirley Chisholm: Woman of Complexity, Conscience, and Compassion," in Women Leaders in Contemporary U. S. Politics, ed. Frank P. LeVeness and Jane P. Sweeney (Boulder, Colo.: Lynne Rienner, 1987), p. 12.

8. Chisholm, Unbought and Unbossed, p. 171.

9. Shirley Chisholm, The Good Fight (New York: Harper and Row, 1973), p. 97.

10. Ibid., pp. 97–98.

11. Chisholm, Unbought and Unbossed, p. 146.

12. Chisholm, Good Fight, p. 37.

13. Ibid., pp. 88–89.

14. Ibid., p. 89.

15. Charles V. Hamilton, "Riots, Revolts and Relevant Responses," in Justice Denied, ed. William H. Chace and Peter Collier (New York: Harcourt Brace and World, 1967), p. 514.

16. Charles Hamilton "An Advocate of Black Power Defines It," in Scott and Brockriede, Rhetoric of Black Power, p. 189.

17. Stokely Carmichael, Stokely Speaks, (New York: Vintage, 1971), p. 21.

18. Ibid., p. 12.

19. Nathan Wright, Jr., Black Power and Urban Unrest (New York: Hawthorne Books, 1967), p. 7.

20. Chisholm, Unbought and Unbossed, p. 82.

21. Ibid., p. 83.

22. Ibid., pp. 87–88.

23. Ibid., p. 118.

24. Ibid., p. 108.

25. Ibid., pp. 108–9.

26. For an excellent article on the subsequent "Watergate morality," see Arthur M. Schlesinger, Jr., "What If We Don't Impeach Him?" Harper's 248, no. 1488 (May 1974): 17.

27. Chisholm, Unbought and Unbossed, p. 103.

28. Ibid., p. 104.

29. Ibid., pp. 103–4.

30. Ibid., pp. 105–6.

31. James Q. Wilson, *American Government* (Lexington, Mass.: D. C. Heath, 1987), p. 188.

32. Chisholm, *Good Fight*, p. 46.

33. For a short but excellent discussion of the financing of U.S. political campaigns, see Wilson, *American Government*, p. 164–69.

34. The authors, Josiah Lee Auspitz and Clifford W. Brown, Jr., in an excellent article ("What's Wrong with Politics," *Harper's* 248, no. 1488 [May 1974]: especially p. 61) echo Chisholm's sentiments regarding the need to make the political process more democratic. However, they argue that the answer to the Watergate scandal, which confirmed many of Chisholm's views on the crisis of the American political process, is to spend more money, not less, on recruiting new aspirants to political office. Furthermore, they recommend expanding, not limiting, the number of political appointees to bureaucratic posts; not overregulating campaigns, but simplifying the procedures for entering them; not bewailing the corruption of state legislatures, but spending time and effort to enable competent people to serve in them, and so on. Finally, they insist that all the aforementioned mean little if the American public continues to be flippant about its civic responsibilities.

35. Chisholm, *Good Fight*, p. 6.

36. Mary Frances Berry and John W. Blasingame, *Long Memory: The Black Experience in America* (New York: Oxford University Press, 1982), pp. 187–88.

37. Chisholm, *Good Fight*, p. 9.

38. Ibid., p. 10.

39. For a discussion of the 1982 rule changes, see Collins, *Rainbow Coalition*, pp. 254–69.

40. Carmichael, *Stokely Speaks*, p. 15.

41. Ibid., p. 22.

42. Ibid., p. 23.

43. Chisholm, *Good Fight*, pp. 140–41.

44. Ibid., p. 142.

45. Ibid.

46. Ibid.

47. Chisholm, *Unbought and Unbossed*, p. 137.

48. Ibid., pp. 142–43.

49. Ibid., p. 143.

50. Ibid., p. 144.

51. W. Arthur Lewis, "The Road to the Top Is Through Higher Education—Not Black Studies," in *Prejudice and Race Relations* ed. Raymond W. Mack (Chicago: Quadrangle Books, 1970), p. 243.

52. Chuck Stone, "Black Politics," *Black Scholar* 1, no. 1 (December 1969): 10.

53. Hamilton, "Advocate of Black Power," in Scott and Brockriede, *Rhetoric of Black Power*, p. 182.

54. Ibid.

55. Ibid., p. 187.

56. Ibid., p. 182.

57. Carmichael, *Stokely Speaks*, p. 27.

58. Chisholm, *Unbought and Unbossed*, p. 128.

59. Richard Hatcher, "The Black City in Crisis," *Black Scholar* 1, no. 6 (April 1970): 60.

60. Chisholm, *Good Fight*, p. 157.

61. Hamilton, "Advocate of Black Power," in Scott and Brockriede, *Rhetoric of Black Power*, p. 158.

62. Wright, *Black Power and Urban Unrest*, p. 90–91.

63. Chisholm, *Good Fight*, p. 152.

64. Meier and Rudwick, *Black Protest in the 1960s*, p. 158.

CHAPTER X

1. Other books and articles useful in the development of this chapter were Malcolm X, with Alex Haley, *The Autobiography of Malcolm X* (New York: Grove Press, 1964); Albert Cleage, *Black Christian Nationalism* (New York: William Morrow, 1972); Cleage, *The Black Messiah* (New York: Sheed and Ward, 1968); LeRoi Jones, *Blues People* (New York: William Morrow, 1963); Theodore Draper, *The Rediscovery of Black Nationalism* (New York: Viking, 1970); Eugene D. Genovese, "The Legacy of Slavery and the Roots of Black Nationalism," in *Black Liberation Politics: A Reader*, ed. Edward Greer (Boston: Allyn and Bacon, 1971) pp. 43–65; Herbert Aptheker, "Comment on the Above Essay by Genovesse," in Greer, *Black Liberation Politics*, pp. 65–71; W. Haywood Burns, "The Black Muslims in America: A Reinterpretation," in Greer, *Black Liberation Politics*, pp. 72–85; Gary T. Marx, "Religion: Opiate or Inspiration of Civil Rights Militancy Among Negroes?" in Greer, *Black Liberation Politics*, pp. 86–102; S. E. Anderson, "Revolutionary Black Nationalism and the Pan-African Idea," in *The Black Seventies*, ed. Floyd B. Barbour (Boston: Porter Sargent, 1970), pp. 99–126; Maulana Ron Karenga, "Maulana Ron Karenga," in *The Black Power Revolt*, ed. Floyd B. Barbour (Boston: Porter Sargent, 1968), pp. 162–71; Ronald Walters, "Afro-American Nationalism" *Black World* 22, no. 12 (October 1973). 9–28, Rodney Carlisle, "Black Nationalism: An Integral Tradition," *Black World* 22, no. 4 (February 1973): 4–10; Julius Lester, "The Necessity for Separation," *Ebony*, 24, no. 10 (August 1970): 166–69; Gertrude Samuels, "Two Ways: Black Muslim and the NAACP," in *Black Protest in the Sixties*, ed. August Meier and Elliott Rudwick (Chicago: Quadrangle Books, 1970), pp. 37–45.

2. Elijah Muhammad, *Message to the Black Man in America*, no. 2 (Chicago: Muhammad's Mosque of Islam, 1965), p. 178.

3. Ibid., p. xii.

4. Ibid., p. 179.

5. Ibid.

6. E. U. Essien-Udom, *Black Nationalism* (New York: Dell, 1964), p. 67.

7. Ibid.

8. C. Eric Lincoln, *The Black Muslims in America* (Boston: Beacon Press, 1963), pp. 16–17.

9. Wallace D. Muhammad, quoted in Mary Frances Berry and John W. Blasingame, *Long Memory: The Black Experience in America* (New York: Oxford University Press, 1982), p. 112. For an excellent case study of the educational theory of an orthodox Muslim offshoot of the Nation of Islam, see Michael D. Schaffer, "Muslim Education Aims to Put Youth on Mainstream Course," *Philadelphia Inquirer*, Tuesday, 30 May 1989, p. 1B.

10. Muhammad, *Message*, p. 116.

11. Ibid., p. 120.

12. For a severe criticism of King's philosophy of brotherhood, see Muhammad's commentary "The True Solution," which criticized King's Nobel Peace Prize speech. Ibid., pp. 240–42.

13. Ibid., p. 18.

14. Ibid., p. 31.

15. Ibid., pp. 31–32.

16. Ibid., p. 275.

17. Draper, *Rediscovery of Black Nationalism*, p. 80.

18. LeRoi Jones, *Home: Social Essays* (New York: William Morrow, 1956), p. 83.

19. Imari Abubakari Obadele I, "The Struggle Is for Land," *Black Scholar* 3, no. 6 (February 1972): 24.

20. LeRoi Jones (Imamu Amiri Baraka), "The Need for a Cultural Base for Civil Rights and Black Power Movements," in *The Black Power Revolt*, ed. Floyd B. Barbour (Boston: Porter Sargent, 1968), p. 126.

21. Muhammad, *Message*, p. 317.

22. Imamu Amiri Baraka (LeRoi Jones), "The Pan-African Party and the Black Nation," *Black Scholar* 2, no. 7 (March 1971): 26.

23. Obadele I, "Struggle Is for Land," 25.

24. Baraka, "Pan-African Party," 26.

25. Muhammad, *Message*, p. 47.

26. Obadele I, "Struggle Is for Land," 24.

27. Howard Brotz, *The Black Jews of Harlem* (New York: Schocken, 1970), p. 12.

28. Theodore G. Vincent, *Black Power and the Garvey Movement* (Berkeley, Calif.: Ramparts Press, 1973), p. 222.

29. Maurice Cranston, *Freedom* (New York: Basic Books, 1954), p. 17.

30. Ibid.

31. St. Augustine, *The City of God* (New York: Image Books, 1958), p. 248.

32. Muhammad, *Message*, p. 54.

33. Jones, *Home*, p. 245.

34. Robert S. Browne, "The Case for Black Separatism," *Ramparts* 6, no. 5

(December 1967): 51. Browne was professor of economics at Fairleigh Dickinson University and an influential personality at the "first" Black Power Conference in 1967 held in Newark, New Jersey.

35. Muhammad, *Message*, p. 303.

36. Ibid., p. 304.

37. Ibid. For a detailed description of the Black Muslim internal organization, see Essien-Udom, *Black Nationalism*, pp. 143–82.

38. Yusufu Sonebeyatta (Joseph F. Brooks), "Ujamma for Land and Power," *Black Scholar* 3, no. 2 (October 1971): 15.

39. Ibid., 14.

40. Muhammad, *Message*, p. 125.

41. Ibid., p. 202.

42. Ibid., p. 29.

43. Ibid., p. 242.

44. Jones, *Home*, p. 246.

45. Muhammad, *Message*, p. 138.

46. Ibid., p. 172.

47. Ibid., p. 173.

48. Baraka, "Pan-African Party," 24.

49. For a report on Newark, New Jersey, of the 1960s and Baraka's role there, see David K. Shipler, "The White Niggers of Newark," *Harper's* 245, no. 1467 (August 1972): 77–83.

50. Baraka, "Pan-African Party," 25.

51. Ibid., 30.

52. Obadele I, "Struggle Is for Land," 32.

53. Ibid., 31.

54. Ibid., 34.

55. Ibid., 32.

56. Ibid., 36.

CHAPTER XI

1. For two excellent articles that illustrate how most black goals parallel those of whites, see Richard Lacayo, "Between Two Worlds," *Time* 133, no. 11 (March 1989): 58–68. See Also Bill Nicholas, "Some Fear Young Take Past for Granted," *USA Today*, Thursday, 29 June 1989, p. 7A.

2. For a short survey of the Stoic philosophy, see William Ebenstein, *Great Political Thinkers* (New York: Holt Reinhart and Winston, 1962) pp. 136–67. Also, for an excellent critical discussion of Stoicism, see St. Augustine, *The City of God* (New York: Image Books, 1958), especially pp. 108–19 and 175–76.

3. Malcolm X, with Alex Haley, *The Autobiography of Malcolm X* (New York: Grove Press, 1964), p. 151.

4. Ibid., p. 301. When President Kennedy was killed, Malcolm stated that he saw it as a case of the "chickens com[ing] home to roost," and he scolded blacks for mourning. Elijah Muhammad told Malcolm that it was a bad statement because "the whole country is in mourning," and such a statement could make it hard on Muslims in general.

5. Ibid., p. 340.

6. Ibid., p. 433.

7. Ibid., p. 340.

8. Ossie Davis, "Our Shining Black Prince," in *Malcolm X: The Man and His Times*, ed. John Henrik Clarke (New York: Macmillan, 1969), p. xii.

9. C. Eric Lincoln, "The Meaning of Malcolm X," in Clarke, *Malcolm X*, p. 7.

10. Mburumba Kerina, "The Apostle of Defiance: An African View," in Clarke, *Malcolm X*, p. 119.

11. James Boggs, "The Influence of Malcolm X on the Political Consciousness of Black Americans," in Clarke, Malcolm X, pp. 51–52.

12. Malcolm X, *Autobiography of Malcolm X*, p. 315. A new set of Malcolm X's last speeches, which reiterate the themes of black pride and the Islamic universalism that he adopted in his last years, has recently been published. See Bruce Perry, *Malcolm X: The Last Speeches* (New York: Pathfinder, 1989), especially pp. 174–75.

13. George Breitman, *The Last Year of Malcolm X* (New York: Merit Publishers, 1967), p. 109.

14. For Martin Luther King, Jr., as an "organic intellectual," see Cornel West, *Prophetic Fragments* (Trenton, N.J.: Africa World Press, 1988), p. 3.

15. Clarke, *Malcolm X*, p. 303.

16. Ibid., p. 306.

17. Ernest Barker, *Greek Political Theory* (New York: University Paperbacks, 1961), p. 8.

18. Ibid., pp. 7–8.

19. Murray Bookchin, "Toward a Liberatory Technology," in *The Case for Participatory Democracy*, ed. G. George Benello and Dimitrius Roussapoulous (New York: Viking, 1971), p. 138.

20. Ibid., p. 139.

21. Edwin S. Redkey, *Black Exodus* (New Haven, Conn.: Yale University Press, 1969), p. 300.

22. Bayard Rustin, "The Myths of the Revolution," *Ebony* 24, no. 10 (August 1969): 96.

23. Malcolm X, *Autobiography of Malcolm X*, p. 371.

Bibliography

Adelaja, Kola. "Sources in African Political Thought—Part 1." *Presence Africaine* 70 (2d Quarter 1969): 7–26.

"African-American or Black: What's in a Name?" *Ebony* 44, no. 9 (July 1989): 76–80.

Allen, Robert L. *Black Awakening in Capitalist America.* New York: Doubleday, 1969.

———. "An Historical Synthesis: Black Liberation and World Revolution." *Black Scholar* 3, no. 6 (February 1972): 7–23.

———. *Reluctant Reformers.* Washington D.C.: Howard University Press, 1983.

Andersen, Talmadge. "Black Economic Liberation Under Capitalism." *Black Scholar,* 2, no. 2 (October 1970): 11–14.

Anderson, James D. *The Education of Blacks in the South, 1860–1935.* Chapel Hill: University of North Carolina Press, 1988.

Anderson, S. E. "Revolutionary Black Nationalism and the Pan-African Idea." In *The Black Seventies,* ed. Floyd B. Barbour, pp. 99–126. Boston: Porter Sargent, 1968.

Antarah, Obi. "A Blueprint for Black Liberation." *Black World* 22, no. 12 (October 1973): 60–68.

Anthony, Earl. *I Pick Up the Gun.* New York: Dial Press, 1970.

Aptheker, Herbert. "Comment on Above the Essay by Genovese." In *Black Liberation Politics: A Reader,* ed. Edward Greer, pp. 65–71. Boston: Allyn and Bacon, 1971.

Aristotle. *Politics.* Trans. Benjamin Jowett. New York: Modern Library, 1943.

Augustine, Saint. *The City of God.* New York: Image Books, 1958.

Auspitz, Josiah Lee, and Clifford W. Brown, Jr. "What's Wrong with Politics." *Harper's* 248, no. 1488 (May 1974): 55–61.

Baraka, Imamu Amiri (LeRoi Jones). "Black and Angry." *Newsweek* 80 (10 July 1972): 35–36.

———. "The Pan-African Party and the Black Nation." *Black Scholar* 2, no. 7 (March 1971): 24–32.

Barbour, Floyd B. *The Black Seventies.* Boston: Porter Sargent, 1970.

———, ed. *The Black Power Revolt.* Boston: Porter Sargent, 1968.

Barker, Ernest. *Greek Political Theory.* New York: University Paperbacks, 1961.

Benello, George G., and Dimitrius Roussapoulous. *The Case for Participatory Democracy.* New York: Viking, 1971.

Bennett, Lerone, Jr. *Before the Mayflower.* Baltimore: Penguin, 1966.
———. *Black Power USA.* Baltimore: Penguin, 1967.
———. *The Negro Mood.* New York: Ballantine, 1964.
Berkeley, George. *A Treatise Concerning the Principles of Human Knowledge.* Chicago: Open Court, 1928.
Berry, Mary Frances, and John W. Blasingame. *Long Memory: The Black Experience in America.* New York: Oxford University Press, 1982.
Bittle, William, and Gilbert Geis. "Alfred Charles Sam and an African Return: A Case Study in Negro Despair." In *Black Brotherhood: Afro-Americans and Africa,* ed. Okon Edet Uya (Lexington Mass.: D. C. Heath, 1971), pp. 113–27.
"Black Lawmakers in Congress. *Ebony* 36, no. 4 (February 1971): 115–22.
"Black Panther Co-founder Slain." *USA Today,* 23 August 1989, p. 2A.
"Black Politics: New Way to Overcome." *Newsweek* 77, 7 June 1971: 30–39.
"Black Power: A Discussion." *Partisan Review* 25, no. 2 (Spring 1968): 195–232.
Blyden, Edward. "The Call of Providence to the Descendants of Africa in America." In *Black Brotherhood: Afro-Americans and Africa,* ed. Okon Edet Uya, pp. 83–95. Lexington, Mass.: D. C. Heath, 1971.
Boggs, James. "Beyond Nationalism." *Monthly Review* 26 (January 1974): 34–48.
———. "Black Revolutionary Power." *Ebony* 125, no. 10 (August 1970): 152–56.
———. "The Influence of Malcolm X on the Political Consciousness of Black Americans." In *Malcolm X: The Man and His Times,* ed. John Henrik Clarke, pp. 50–55. New York: Macmillan, 1969.
———. *Racism and the Class Struggle.* New York: Monthly Review Press, 1970.
———. "The Revolutionary Struggle for Black Power." In *The Black Seventies,* ed. Floyd B. Barbour, pp. 33–48. Boston: Porter Sargent, 1970.
———. "Uprooting Racism and Racists in the United States." *Black Scholar* 2, no. 2 (October 1970): 2–10.
Bookchin, Murray. "Toward a Liberatory Technology." In *The Case for Participatory Democracy,* ed. George G. Benello and Dimitrius Roussapoulous, pp. 95–139. New York: Viking, 1971.
Dooker, Simeon. "Black Political Convention Is Successful Despite Splits and Tactical Differences." *Jet* 42, no. 1 (30 March 1972): 12–18.
Branch, Taylor. *Parting the Waters: America in the King Years, 1954–63.* New York: Simon and Schuster, 1988.
Breitman, George. *The Last Year of Malcolm X.* New York: Merit Publishers, 1967.
Brotz, Howard. *The Black Jews of Harlem.* New York: Schocken, 1970.
Brown, H. Rap. "A Letter from H. Rap Brown." In *The Black Seventies,* ed. Floyd B. Barbour, pp. 311–13. Boston: Porter Sargent, 1970.

Brown, Warren. "Black Convention Solves Problems Without Clubs, Bullets or Blood." *Jet* 42, no. 1 (30 March 1972): 24–30.

Browne, Robert S. "The Case for Black Separatism." *Ramparts* 6, no. 5 (December 1967): 46–51.

"The Brownsville Incident." *Ebony* 28, no. 4 (March 1973): 31–39.

Bryce, Herrington. "Putting Black Economic Progress in Perspective." *Ebony* 28, no. 10 (August 1973): 59–62.

Burkett, Randall K. *Garveyism as a Religious Movement*. Metuchen, N.J.: Scarecrow Press, 1978.

Burns, W. Haywood. "The Black Muslims in America: A Reinterpretation." In *Black Liberation Politics: A Reader*, ed. Edward Greer, pp. 72–85. Boston: Allyn and Bacon, 1971.

Cabral, Amilcar. *Unity and Struggle*. New York: Monthly Review Press, 1979.

Carlisle, Rodney. "Black Nationalism: An Integral Tradition." *Black World* 22, no. 4 (February 1973): 4–10.

Carmichael, Stokely. "Black Poor." In *The Voices of Black Rhetoric*, ed. Arthur L. Smith and Stephen Robb, pp. 264–83. Boston: Allyn and Bacon, 1971.

———. "Stokely Carmichael Explains Black Power to a White Audience in White Water, Wisconsin." In *The Rhetoric of Black Power*, ed. Robert Scott and Wayne Brockriede, pp. 96–112. New York: Harper and Row, 1969.

———. *Stokely Speaks*. New York: Vintage, 1971.

———. "What We Want." In *Americans from Africa*, ed. Peter I. Rose, pp. 237–49. New York: Atherton Press, 1970.

Carmichael, Stokely, and Charles V. Hamilton. *Black Power*. New York: Vintage, 1967.

Carruth, Reba, and Vivian Jenkins Nelsen. "Shirley Chisholm: Woman of Complexity, Conscience, and Compassion." In *Women Leaders in Contemporary U. S. Politics*, ed. Frank P. LeVeness and Jane P. Sweeney, pp. 9–21. Boulder, Colo.: Lynne Rienner, 1987.

Carson, Clayborne. *In Struggle: SNCC and the Black Awakening of the 1960s*. Cambridge, Mass.: Harvard University Press, 1981.

Chace, William H., and Peter Collier, eds. *Justice Denied*. New York: Harcourt Brace and World, 1970.

Chisholm, Shirley. *The Good Fight*. New York: Harper and Row, 1973.

———. *Unbought and Unbossed*. Boston: Houghton Mifflin, 1970.

Clark, Kenneth. "The Civil Rights Movement and Organization." *Daedalus* 95, no. 1 (Winter 1966): 239–67.

Clarke, John Henrik. "Black Power and Black History." In *What Black Educators Are Saying*, ed. Nathan Wright, Jr., pp. 217–27. New York: Hawthorne Books, 1970.

———. *Malcolm X: The Man and His Times*. New York: Macmillan, 1969.

Clarke, John Henrik, with Amy Jacques Garvey. *Marcus Garvey and the Vision of Africa*. New York: Vintage, 1974.

Clay, William L. "Emerging New Black Politics." *Black World* 21, no. 12 (October 1972): 32–39.

Cleage, Albert. *Black Christian Nationalism*. New York: William Morrow, 1972.

———. *The Black Messiah*. New York: Sheed and Ward, 1968.

Cleaver, Eldridge. *Soul on Ice*. New York: McGraw-Hill, 1968.

Cochran, Bert. "In the Grip of the Egalitarian Passion." *Nation* 214, no. 26 (20 June 1972): 822–24.

Coker, Francis W. *Recent Political Thought*. New York: Appleton Century, 1934.

Coles, Robert, Ivanhoe Donaldsen, Paul Feldman, Charles V. Hamilton, Abbie Hoffman, Tom Kahn, William Melvin Kelley, Norman Mailer, Jack Newfield, Fred Powledge, Stephen Thernstrom, and Nathan Wright, Jr. "Black Power: A Discussion." *Partisan Review* 35, no. 2 (Spring 1968): 195–232.

Collier, Peter, ed. *Crisis: A Contemporary Reader*. New York: Harcourt Brace and World, 1969.

Collins, Shiela D. *The Rainbow Coalition*. New York: Monthly Review Press, 1986.

Cone, James H. *Black Power and Black Theology*. New York: Seabury Press, 1969.

Conyers, John. "Politics and the Black Revolution." *Ebony* 24, no. 10 (August 1969): 162–66.

Copleston, Frederick. *A History of Philosophy*, vol. 5, pt. 2. New York: Image Books, 1964.

Cox, Oliver. *Caste, Class and Race*. New York: Modern Reader, 1970.

Cranston, Maurice. *Freedom*. New York: Basic Books, 1954.

———. *Prophetic Politics*. New York: Simon and Schuster, 1972.

Cronin, Edmund David. *Black Moses: The Story of Marcus Garvey*. Madison: University of Wisconsin Press, 1968.

Cross, Theodore. *The Black Power Imperative*. New York: Faulkner Books, 1986.

Crummell, Alexander. "The Relations and Duties of Free Colored Men in America to Africa." In *Black Brotherhood: Afro Americans and Africa*, ed. Okon Edet Uya, pp. 63–71. Lexington, Mass.: D. C. Heath, 1971.

Cruse, Harold. *The Crisis of the Negro Intellectual*. New York: William Morrow, 1967.

———. *Rebellion or Revolution?* New York: William Morrow, 1969.

Curtin, Philip D. *The Atlantic Slave Trade*. Madison: University of Wisconsin Press, 1969.

Darwin, Charles Robert. *The Origin of Species*. New York: D. Appleton, 1937.

Davis, Harry R., and Robert C. Good. *Reinhold Niebuhr on Politics*. New York: Scribner's, 1960.

Davis, Ossie. "Our Shining Black Prince." In *Malcolm X: The Man and His Times*, ed. John Henrik Clarke, pp. xi–xii. New York: Macmillan, 1969.

Dean, David M. *Defender of the Race: James Theodore Holly, Black Nationalist Bishop*. Boston: Lambeth Press, 1979.

Delany, Martin R. "A Project for an Expedition of Adventure to the Eastern Coast of Africa." In *Black Brotherhood: Afro-Americans and Africa*, ed. Okon Edet Uya, pp. 71–82. Lexington, Mass.: D. C. Heath, 1971.

Denby, Charles. "Black Caucuses in the Union." In *Black Liberation Politics: A Reader*, ed. Edward Greer, pp. 370–79. Boston: Allyn and Bacon, 1971.

DeParle, Jason. "An Architect of the Reagan Vision Plunges into Inquiry on Race and I.Q." *New York Times*, Friday, 30 November 1990, sec. A.

Dollard, John. *Caste and Class in a Southern Town*. Garden City, N.Y.: Doubleday, 1957.

Domingo, W. A. "Gift of the Black Tropics." In *The New Negro*, ed. Alain Locke, pp. 341–49. New York: Atheneum, 1969.

Douglass, Frederick. *The Life and Times of Frederick Douglass*. New York: Collier, 1962.

———. *My Bondage and My Freedom*. New York: Dover, 1969.

———. *Narrative of the Life of Frederick Douglass*, ed. Benjamin Quarles. Cambridge, Mass.: Belknap, 1960.

Draper, Theodore. *The Rediscovery of Black Nationalism*. New York: Viking, 1970.

Duberman, Martin Bauml. "Black Power in America." *Partisan Review* 35, no. 1 (Winter 1968): 33–48.

———. *Paul Robeson*. New York: Knopf, 1988.

Du Bois, W. E. B. *Black Reconstruction in America 1860–1880*. New York: Atheneum, 1977.

———. *Dusk of Dawn*. New York: Library of America, 1986.

———. *John Brown*. New York: International Publishers, 1962.

———. *The Philadelphia Negro*. New York: B. Blom, 1967.

———. *Souls of Black Folk*, in *Three Negro Classics*. New York: Avon, 1968.

———. *The Suppression of the African Slave Trade*. New York: Library of America, 1986.

Ebenstein, William. *Great Political Thinkers*. New York: Holt Rinehart and Winston, 1962.

Elkins, Stanley M. *Slavery*. New York: Universal Library, 1963.

Essien-Udom, E. U. *Black Nationalism*. New York: Dell, 1964.

Fager, Charles. *White Reflections on Black Power*. Grand Rapids, Mich.: William B. Eerdman, 1967.

Fanon, Frantz. *The Wretched of the Earth*. New York: Grove Press, 1968.

Fax, Elton C. *Contemporary Black Leaders*. New York: Dodd, Mead, 1970.

———. *Garvey: The Story of a Pioneer Black Nationalist*. New York: Dodd, Mead, 1972.

Feaver, George. "Black Power." In *Prophetic Politics*, ed. Maurice Cranston, pp. 139–55. New York: Simon and Schuster, 1972.

Findley, Tim. "Huey Newton Twenty-five Floors from the Street." *Rolling Stone* 14 (3 August 1972): 30–35.

Fishel, Leslie H., Jr., and Benjamin Quarles, eds. *The Negro Americans: A Documentary History*. Glenview, Ill.: Scott, Foresman, 1967.

Fogel, Robert William, and Stanley L. Engerman. *Time on the Cross*. Boston: Little, Brown, 1974.

Foner, Eric. "Blacks and the U.S. Constitution 1789–1989." *New Left Review* 183 (September–October 1990): 63–75.

Foner, Philip S. *The Black Panthers Speak*. Philadelphia: J. B. Lippincott, 1970.

———. *W.E.B. Du Bois Speaks*, vols. 1 and 2. New York: Pathfinder, 1970.

Forman, James. "Control, Conflict and Change." In *Black Manifesto*, ed. Robert S. Lecky and H. Eliot Wright, pp. 34–52. New York: Sheed and Ward, 1969.

———. *The Making of Black Revolutionaries*. New York: Macmillan, 1972.

———. *Sammy Younge, Jr.* New York: Grove Press, 1968.

Foster, William Z. *The Negro People in American History*. New York: International Publishers, 1970.

Franklin, John Hope. *From Slavery to Freedom*. New York: Vintage, 1969.

Franklin, John Hope, and August Meier. *Black Leaders of the Twentieth Century*. Urbana: University of Illinois Press, 1982.

Frazier, E. Franklin. "Garvey: A Mass Leader." In *Marcus Garvey and the Vision of Africa*, ed. John Henrik Clarke, with Amy Jacques Garvey, pp. 236–42. New York: Vintage, 1974.

———. *The Negro Church in America*. New York: Schocken, 1964.

Friedrich, Carl Joachim. *Man and His Government*. New York: McGraw-Hill, 1963.

Garrow, David J. *Bearing the Cross*. New York: William Morrow, 1986.

Garvey, Amy Jacques. *Garvey and Garveyism*. New York: Collier, 1970.

———, ed. *Philosophy and Opinions of Marcus Garvey*, vols. 1 and 2. New York: Atheneum, 1969.

Garvey, Marcus. *Aims and Objects of Movement for Solutions of the Negro Problem Outlined*. New York: University Place Book Shop, 69 University Place, New York, New York, 10010, 1966–69.

Geiss, Immanuel. *The Pan-African Movement*. New York: Africana, 1974.

Genovese, Eugene D. "The Legacy of Slavery and the Roots of Black Nationalism." In *Black Liberation Politics: A Reader*, ed. Edward Greer, pp. 65–71. Boston: Allyn and Bacon, 1971.

———. *The Political Economy of Slavery*, 2d ed. Middletown, Conn.: Wesleyan University Press, 1989.

Grant, Joanne. *Black Protest*. New York: Fawcett, 1968.

Greenwood, Frank S. "Frederick Douglass and U.S. Imperialism." *Monthly Review* 2411 (April 1973): 41–51.

Greer, Edward. "The First Year of Black Power in Gary, Indiana." In *Black Liberation Politics: A Reader*, ed. Edward Greer, pp. 208–33. Boston: Allyn and Bacon, 1971.

———, ed. *Black Liberation Politics: A Reader*. Boston: Allyn and Bacon, 1971.

Grier, William H., and Price M. Cobbs. *Black Rage*. New York: Bantam, 1968.

Grimes, Alan Pendleton. *American Political Thought*. New York: Holt Rinehart and Winston, 1967.

Hall, Walter Phelps, Robert Greenhalgh Albion, and Jennie Barnes Pope. *A History of England and the Empire-Commonwealth*. Boston: Ginn, 1969.

Hamilton, Charles V. "An Advocate of Black Power Defines It." In *The Rhetoric of Black Power*, ed. Robert Scott and Wayne Brockriede, pp. 178–207. New York: Harper and Row, 1969.

———. "Riots, Revolts and Relevant Responses." In *Justice Denied*, ed. William Chace and Peter Collier, pp. 511–18. New York: Harcourt Brace and World, 1967.

Hare, Nathan. "The Case for Separatism: Black Perspective." In *Black Power and Student Rebellion*, ed. James McEvoy and Abraham Miller, pp. 233–35. Belmont, Calif.: Wadsworth, 1969.

———. "How White Power Whitewashes Black Power." In *The Black Power Revolt*, ed. Floyd B. Barbour, pp. 182–88. Boston: Porter Sargent, 1968.

Harlan, Louis R. *Booker T. Washington: The Making of a Black Leader 1856–1901*. New York: Oxford University Press, 1972.

———. *Booker T. Washington: The Wizard of Tuskegee 1901–15*. New York: Oxford University Press, 1983.

———. "Booker T. Washington and the White Man's Burden." In *Black Brotherhood: Afro-Americans and Africa*, ed. Okon Edet Uya, pp. 130–53. Lexington Mass.: D. C. Heath, 1971.

———. *The Booker T. Washington Papers*, vol. 1, *The Autobiographical Writings*. Urbana: University of Illinois Press, 1972.

———. *The Booker T. Washington Papers*, vol. 2, 1860–89. Urbana: University of Illinois Press, 1972.

———. *The Booker T. Washington Papers*, vol. 5, 1899–1900. Urbana: University of Illinois Press, 1976.

Harris, Fred R., and Roger W. Wilkins. *Quiet Riots*. New York: Pantheon, 1988.

Hatcher, Richard. "The Black City in Crisis." *Black Scholar*, no. 6 (April 1976): 54–62.

Hawkins, Hugh. *Booker T. Washington and His Critics*. Lexington, Mass.: D. C. Heath, 1962.

Healey, Dorothy, and Maurice Isserman. *Dorothy Healy Remembers: A Life in the American Communist Party*. New York: Oxford University Press, 1990.

Hegel, G.W.F. *Phenomenology of Mind*. Oxford: Clarendon Press, 1894.

———. *Philosophy of History*. Trans. J. Sibree. London: G. Bell, 1902.

————. *Philosophy of Right.* Oxford: Oxford University Press, 1973.

Helper, Hilton Rowan. *The Impending Crisis: How to Meet It.* Cambridge, Mass.: Belknap Press, 1968.

Herrnstein, Richard. "I.Q." *Atlantic* 228, no. 3 (September 1971): 43–65.

Herskovits, Melville. *The Myth of the Negro Past.* Boston: Beacon Press, 1958.

Hill, Robert A. *The Marcus Garvey Papers,* vol. 1. Berkeley: University of California Press, 1983.

————. *The Marcus Garvey Papers,* vol. 6. Berkeley: University of California Press, 1989.

Hoetink, Harry. *The Two Variants in Caribbean Race Relations.* London: Oxford University Press, 1967.

"Huey Newton, Head of Black Panthers, Found Shot to Death." *New York Times,* Wednesday, 23 August 1989, sec. A.

Hutchings, Phil. "What Program for Black Liberation Movement?" *Guardian* 26, no. 36 (19 June 1974): 8, 19.

Isaacs, Harold R. *The New World of Negro Americans.* New York: Viking, 1963.

Jensen, Arthur. "How Much Can We Boost IQ and Scholastic Achievement?" *Harvard Educational Review* 39 (Winter 1969): 1–124.

Jones, LeRoi (Imamu Amiri Baraka). *Blues People.* New York: William Morrow, 1963.

————. *Home: Social Essays.* New York: William Morrow, 1956.

————. "The Need for a Cultural Base for Civil Rights and Black Power Movements." In *The Black Power Revolt,* ed. Floyd B. Barbour, pp 119–26. Boston: Porter Sargent, 1968.

————. "What Does Non-Violence Mean?" In *Crisis: A Contemporary Reader,* ed. Peter Collier, pp. 69–85. New York: Harcourt Brace and World, 1969.

Karenga, Maulana Ron. "Maulana Ron Karenga." In *The Black Power Revolt,* ed. Floyd B. Barbour, pp. 162–71. Boston: Porter Sargent, 1968.

Kellog, Charles Flint. *NAACP: A History,* vol. 1, 1909–1920. Baltimore: Johns Hopkins University Press, 1973.

Kerina, Mburumba. "The Apostle of Defiance: An African View." In *Malcolm X: The Man and His Times,* ed. John Henrik Clarke, pp. 114–19. New York: Macmillan, 1969.

King, Martin Luther, Jr. *Strength to Love.* New York: Harper and Row, 1963.

————. *Stride Toward Freedom.* New York: Harper and Row, 1958.

————. *The Trumpet of Conscience.* New York: Harper and Row, 1967.

————. *Where Do We Go from Here: Chaos or Community?* Boston: Beacon Press, 1968.

————. *Why We Can't Wait.* New York: Signet Books, 1963.

King, Paul. "The Role of Black Business: Delirium or Imperium?" *Black Scholar* 3, no. 6 (February 1972): 49–56.

————. "The Role of Black Business: Delirium or Imperium? Part II." *Black Scholar* 3, no. 7–8 (March 1972): 27–35.

King, Wayne. "Bad Times on Bayou." *New York Times Mazagine* 138, no. 47, 898 (11 June 1989): 56–68.

Knowles, Louis L., and Kenneth Prewitt. *Institutional Racism in America.* Englewood Cliffs, N.J.: Prentice Hall, 1969.

Kriegel, Leonard. "Academic Freedom and Racial Theories." *New York Times,* Thursday, 3 May 1990, sec. A.

Lacayo, Richard. "Between Two Worlds." 33, no. 11 *Time* (March 1989): 58–68.

Ladner, Joyce. "What 'Black Power' Means to Negroes in Mississippi." In *Americans from Africa,* ed. Peter I. Rose, pp. 249–67. New York: Atherton Press, 1970.

Lasch, Christopher. *The Agony of the American Left.* New York: Knopf, 1969.

————. "The Trouble with Black Power." In *Americans from Africa,* ed. Peter I. Rose, pp. 267–93. New York: Atherton Press, 1970.

Lecky, Robert S., and Eliot Wright. *Black Manifesto.* New York: Sheed and Ward, 1969.

Lenin, V. I. *Materialism and Empirio-Criticism.* New York: International Publishers, 1970.

Lester, Julius. *Look out, Whitey!* New York: Dial Press, 1968.

————. "The Necessity for Separation." *Ebony* 24, no. 10 (August 1970): 166–69.

————. *Revolutionary Notes.* New York: Richard W. Baron, 1969.

LeVeness, Frank P., and Jane P. Sweeney. *Women Leaders in Contemporary U.S. Politics.* Boulder, Colo.: Lynne Rienner, 1987.

Levine, Lawrence W. "Marcus Garvey and the Politics of Revitalization." In *Black Leaders of the Twentieth Century,* ed. John Hope Franklin and August Meier, pp. 105–39. Urbana: University of Illinois Press, 1982.

Levy, Martin R., and Michael S. Kramer. *The Ethnic Factor: How American Minorities Decide Elections.* New York: Simon and Schuster, 1973.

Lewis, David. *King: A Biography.* Urbana: University of Illinois Press, 1970.

Lewis, Gordon K. *Main Currents of Caribbean Thought.* Baltimore: Johns Hopkins University Press, 1983.

Lewis, Rupert. *Marcus Garvey: Anti-Colonial Champion.* Trenton, N.J.: Africa World Press, 1988.

Lewis, W. Arthur. "The Road to the Top Is Through Higher Education—Not Black Studies." In *Prejudice and Race Relations,* ed. Raymond W. Mack, pp. 242–54. Chicago: Quadrangle Books, 1970.

Lincoln, Eric C. *The Black Muslims in America.* Boston: Beacon Press, 1963.

————. "The Meaning of Malcolm X." In *Malcolm X: The Man and His Times,* ed. John Henrik Clarke, pp. 7–12. New York: Macmillan, 1969.

Locke, Alain. *The New Negro.* New York: Atheneum, 1969.

Locke, John. *An Essay Concerning Human Understanding*. Oxford: Clarendon Press, 1975.

Lockwood, Lee. *Conversations with Eldridge Cleaver*. New York: Delta Book, 1970.

Lowenthal, David. "Race and Color in the West Indies." *Daedalus* 96, no. 2 (Spring 1967): 580–626.

Lowenthal, David, and Lambros Comitas. *Consequences of Class and Color in the West Indies*. Garden City, N.Y.: Anchor, 1973.

Lynch, Hollis R. *Edward Wilmot Blyden: Pan-Negro Patriot, 1832–1912*. New York: Oxford University Press, 1967.

———. "Pan-Negro Nationalism in the New World Before 1862." In *Black Brotherhood: Afro-Americans and Africa*, ed. Okon Edet Uya, pp. 41–62. Lexington, Mass.: D.C. Heath, 1971.

McAllister, Bill. "The Plight of Young Black Men in America." *Washington Post National Weekly Edition* 17, no. 15 (12–18 February 1990): 6–7.

McEvoy, James, and Abraham Miller. *Black Power and Student Rebellion*. Belmont, Calif.: Wadsworth, 1969.

Mack, Raymond W., ed. *Prejudice and Race Relations*. Chicago: Quadrangle Books, 1970.

McKissick, Floyd. *Three-fifths of a Man*. London: Macmillan, 1969.

McPherson, James M. *The Struggle for Equality*. Princeton, N.J.: Princeton University Press, 1969.

Major, Reginald. *A Panther Is a Black Cat*. New York: William Morrow, 1971.

Malcolm X, with Alex Haley. *The Autobiography of Malcolm X*. New York: Grove Press, 1964.

Mao Tse-tung. *Selected Readings*. Peking: Foreign Language Press, 1971.

Marine, Gene. *The Black Panthers*. New York: Signet, 1969.

Martin, Waldo E., Jr. *The Mind of Frederick Douglass*. Chapel Hill: University of North Carolina Press, 1984.

Marx, Gary T. "Religion: Opiate or Inspiration of Civil Rights Militancy Among Negroes?" In *Black Liberation Politics: A Reader*, ed. Edward Greer, pp. 86–102. Boston: Allyn and Bacon, 1971.

Marx, Karl. *Das Kapital*. Translated from the 4th German edition, ed. by Eden and Cedar Paul. Introduction by G.D.H. Cole. London: J. M. Dent, 1933.

Marx, Karl, and Friedrich Engels. *Communist Manifesto*. New York: International Publishers, 1989.

Mehlinger, Louis. "The Attitude of the Free Negro Toward African Colonization." In *Black Brotherhood: Afro-Americans and Africa*, ed. Okon Edet Uya, pp. 24–40. Lexington Mass.: D.C. Heath, 1971.

Meier, August. *Negro Protest Thought in America 1880–1915*. Ann Arbor: University of Michigan Press, 1968.

Meier, August, and Elliot Rudwick. *Black Protest in the Sixties*. Chicago: Quadrangle Books, 1970.

Moore, Barrington, Jr. *Social Origins of Dictatorship and Democracy*. Boston: Beacon Press, 1966.

Muhammad, Elijah. *Message to the Black Man in America*, no. 2. Chicago: Muhammad's Mosque of Islam, 1965.

Murray, Charles. *Losing Ground: American Social Policy 1950–80*. New York: Basic Books, 1984.

Myrdal, Gunnar. *An American Dilemma*. New York: McGraw-Hill, 1964.

Naison, Mark. *Communists in Harlem*. New York: Grove Press, 1984.

Neal, Larry. "Any Day Now: Black Art and Black Liberation." *Ebony* 24, no. 10 (August 1969): 54–64.

———. "New Space: The Growth of Black Consciousness in the Sixties." In *The Black Seventies*, ed. Floyd B. Barbour, pp. 9–31. Boston: Porter Sargent, 1970.

Nelson, William E., Jr. *Black Politics in Gary: Problems and Prospects*. Washington, D.C.: Joint Center for Political Studies, 1972.

Newton, Huey P. "Black Capitalism Reanalyzed." *Black Panther*. Saturday, 5 June 1971, p. 9.

———. "The Black Panthers," *Ebony* 24, no. 10 (August 1969): 106–12.

———. *To Die for the People*. New York: Vintage, 1972.

———. *Revolutionary Suicide*. New York: Harcourt Brace Jovanovich, 1973.

Nichols, Bill. "Some Fear Young Take Past for Granted." *USA Today*, Thursday, 29 June 1989, p. 7A.

Niebuhr, Reinhold. *Moral Man and Immoral Society*. New York: Scribner's, 1932.

Nietzsche, Friedrich Wilhelm. *A Genealogy of Morals*. Trans. William A. Haussman Press, John Gray. New York: Macmillan, 1907.

Obadele I, Imari Abubakari. "The Struggle Is for Land." *Black Scholar* 3, no. 6 (February 1972): 24–32.

Ofari, Earl. *The Myth of Black Capitalism*. New York: Monthly Review Press, 1970.

Orwell, George. *1984*. San Diego: Harcourt Brace Jovanovich, 1977.

Parrington, Vernon. *Main Currents in American Thought*. New York: Harcourt Brace and World, 1954.

Perry, Bruce. *Malcolm X: The Last Speeches*. New York: Pathfinder, 1989.

Petrovic, Gajo. *Marx in the Mid-Twentieth Century*. New York: Anchor, 1967.

Pinkney, Alphonso. *The Myth of Black Progress*. New York: Cambridge University Press, 1984.

Plato. *Laws*. Trans. R. G. Bury. Cambridge, Mass.: Harvard University Press, 1926.

———. *Sophist and Statesman*, ed. Raymond Klibansky and Elizabeth Anscombe. New York: Barnes and Noble, 1971.

Poinsett, Alex. "Unity Without Uniformity." *Ebony* 27, no. 8 (June 1972): 45–54.

Ponton, M. M. *The Life and Times of Henry M. Turner*. Reprint. New York: Negro Universities, 1970.

Posey, Melvin. "Toward a More Meaningful Revolution: Ideology in Transition." In *Black Power and Student Rebellion*, ed. James McEvoy and Abraham Miller, pp. 253–77. Belmont, Calif.: Wadsworth, 1969.

Rampersad, Arnold. *The Art and Imagination of W.E.B. Du Bois*. Cambridge, Mass.: Harvard University Press, 1976.

Rauschenbach, Walter. *Christianity and Social Crisis*. New York: George H. Doran, 1907.

Redding, Saunders. *They Came in Chains*. New York: J. B. Lippincott, 1950.

Redkey, Edwin S. "Bishop Turner's African Dream." In *Black Brotherhood: Afro-Americans and Africa*, ed. Okon Edet Uya, pp. 96–112. Lexington, Mass.: D.C. Heath, 1971.

———. *Black Exodus*. New Haven, Conn.: Yale University Press, 1969.

Reed, Adolph L., Jr. *The Jesse Jackson Phenomenon*. New Haven, Conn.: Yale University Press, 1986.

Rogers, J. A. *World's Great Men of Color*, vol. 2. New York: Collier, 1972.

Rose, Peter I., ed. *Americans from Africa*. New York: Atherton Press, 1970.

Rustin, Bayard. "The Myths of the Revolution." *Ebony* 24, no. 10 (August 1969): 96–104.

Sabine, George H. *A History of Political Theory*. Hillsdale, Ill.: Dryden Press, 1973.

Samuels, Gertrude. "Two Ways: Black Muslim and the NAACP." In *Black Protest in the Sixties*, ed. August Meier and Elliott Rudwick, pp. 37–45. Chicago: Quadrangle Books, 1970.

Schaffer, Michael D. "Muslim Education Aims to Put Youth on Mainstream Course." *Philadelphia Inquirer*, Tuesday, 30 May 1989, p. 1B.

Schance, Don. *The Panther Paradox*. New York: Paperback Library, 1971.

Schlesinger, Arthur M., Jr. "What If We Don't Impeach Him?" *Harper's* 248, no. 1488 (May 1974): 12–18.

Scott, Robert, and Wayne Brockriede. *The Rhetoric of Black Power*. New York: Harper and Row, 1969.

Shakur, Assata. *Assata Shakur: An Autobiography*. Westport, Conn.: Lawrence Hill, 1987.

Sherill, Robert. "We Also Want Four Hundred Billion Dollars Back Pay." *Esquire* 71, no. 1 (January 1969): 72–75, 146–48.

Shipler, David K. "The White Niggers of Newark." *Harper's* 245, no. 1467 (August 1972): 77–83

Sibley, Mulford Q. *Political Ideas and Ideologies*. New York: Harper and Row, 1970.

Sitton, Claude. "Negroes Queue in Mississippi in Symbol of Frustration in Voter Registration Drive." In *Black Protest in the Sixties*, ed. August Meier and Elliott Rudwick, pp. 53–61. Chicago: Quadrangle Books, 1970.

Smith, Arthur L., and Stephen Robb. *The Voices of Black Rhetoric*. Boston: Allyn and Bacon, 1971.

Sonebeyatta, Yusufu (Joseph F. Brooks). "Ujamma for Land and Power." *Black Scholar* 3, no. 2 (October 1971): 13–20.

Sowell, Thomas. *Compassion Versus Guilt and Other Essays*. New York: William Morrow, 1987.

Stein, Judith. *The World of Marcus Garvey*. Baton Rouge: Louisiana State University Press, 1986.

Stephen, James H., Jr. "The State Delegates to the National Black Convention." *Jet* 42, no. 1 (30 March 1972): 8–10.

Stone, Chuck. "Black Politics." *Black Scholar* 1, no. 1 (December 1969): 8–13.

Stone, I. F. *In a Time of Torment*. New York: Vintage, 1968.

———. "Why They Cry Black Power." In *In a Time of Torment*, ed. I. F. Stone, pp. 166–68. New York: Vintage, 1968.

Stowe, Harriet Elizabeth Beecher. *Uncle Tom's Cabin*. Columbus, Ohio: C. E. Merril, 1969.

Sunshine, Catherine A. *The Caribbean*. Washington, D.C.: Ecumenical Program on Central America and the Caribbean, 1470 Irving Street, NW, Washington, D.C. 20010, 1985 edition and 1988 edition.

Tellenbach, Gerd. *Church, State and Christian Society at the Time of the Investiture Contest*. Oxford: Basil Blackwell, 1959.

Thelwell, Michael. "What Is to Be Done? A Review Article on *The Crisis of the Negro Intellectual* by Harold Cruse." *Partisan Review* 35, no. 4 (Fall 1969): 619–22.

Thomas Aquinas, Saint. *Summa Theologica*. Cambridge, England: Blackfriars; New York: McGraw-Hill, 1964.

Thoreau, Henry David. *Walden and Civil Disobedience*. New York: Norton, 1966.

Travis, Dempsey. "Barriers to Black Power in the American Economy." *Black Scholar* 3, no. 2 (October 1971): 21–25.

"The Troubled American." *Newsweek* 74, no. 14 (6 October 1969): 29–40.

Uya, Okon Edet. *Black Brotherhood: Afro-Americans and Africa*. Lexington, Mass.: D. C. Heath, 1971.

Venessle, Frank, and Jane P. Sweeney. *Women Leaders in Contemporary U.S. Politics*. Boulder, Colo.: Lynne Rienner, 1987.

Vincent, Theodore G. *Black Power and the Garvey Movement*. Berkeley, Calif.: Ramparts Press, 1973.

Walters, Ronald. "Afro-American Nationalism." *Black World* 22, no. 12 (October 1973): 9–28.

Walton, Hanes, Jr. *The Political Philosophy of Martin Luther King, Jr.* Westport, Conn.: Greenwood Publishing, 1971.

Washington, Booker T. *The Future of the American Negro*. Boston: Small, Maynard, 1899.

———. *My Larger Education*. Garden City, N.Y.: Doubleday, Page, 1911.

———. *The Story of the Negro*. New York: Doubleday, Page, 1909.

———. *Up from Slavery*, in *Three Negro Classics*. New York: Avon, 1965.

———. "The Virtue of Industrial Education." In *The Negro Americans: A Documentary History*, ed. Leslie H. Fishel, Jr., and Benjamin Quarles, pp. 364–66. Glenview, Ill.: Scott, Foresman, 1967.

Wattenberg, Ben J., and Richard M. Scammon. *This USA: An Unexpected Family Portrait.* New York: Doubleday, 1965.

West, Cornel. *Prophetic Fragments.* Trenton, N.J.: Africa World Press, 1988.

White, John. *Black Leadership in America: From Booker T. Washington to Jesse Jackson.* London: Longmans, 1990.

Wicker, Tom. *Report of the National Advisory Commission on Civil Disorders.* New York: Bantam, 1968.

Wilkins, Roy. "The Case Against Separatism Black Jim Crow." In *Black Power and Student Rebellion,* ed. James McEvoy and Abraham Miller, pp. 235–37. Belmont, Calif.: Wadsworth, 1969.

Williams, Walter. *All It Takes Is Guts.* Washington, D.C.: Regnery, 1987.

Wilson, James Q. *American Government.* Lexington, Mass.: D. C. Heath, 1987.

Wilson, William Julius. *The Declining Significance of Race: Blacks and Changing American Institutions.* Chicago: University of Chicago Press, 1978.

Wright, Nathan, Jr. *Black Power and Urban Unrest.* New York: Hawthorne Books, 1967.

———. "The Crisis Which Bred Black Power." In *The Black Power Revolt,* ed. Floyd B. Barbour, pp. 124–25. Boston: Porter Sargent, 1968.

———. *What Black Educators Are Saying.* New York: Hawthorne Books, 1970.

Zinn, Howard. *SNCC: The New Abolitionists.* Boston: Beacon Press, 1965.

Index